AF870315

Constitutionalism and Transitional Justice in South Africa

Human Rights in Context

Research on human rights, or social and political issues closely related to human rights, is nowadays carried out in many academic departments, from law to anthropology, from sociology to philosophy. Yet, there is surprisingly little communication amongst scholars working in these different disciplines, and research that takes more than one perspective into account is seldom encouraged. This series bridges the divide between the social sciences and the law in human rights scholarship.

Volume 1
BETWEEN BOMBS AND GOOD INTENTIONS
The Red Cross and the Italo-Ethiopian War, 1935–1936
Rainer Baudendistel

Volume 2
ADVANCING REFUGEE PROTECTION IN SOUTH AFRICA
Edited by Jeff Handmaker, Lee Anne de la Hunt and Jonathan Klaaren

Volume 3
BEYOND PRISON
The Fight to Reform Prison Systems around the World
Ahmed Othmani

Volume 4
SOCIAL TORTURE
The Case of Northern Uganda, 1986-2006
Chris Dolan

Volume 5
CONSTITUTIONALISM AND TRANSITIONAL JUSTICE IN SOUTH AFRICA
Andrea Lollini

CONSTITUTIONALISM AND TRANSITIONAL JUSTICE IN SOUTH AFRICA

Andrea Lollini

Translated by
Alexandra T. Marot Pollard

Berghahn Books
New York • Oxford

Published in 2011 by

Berghahn Books

www.berghahnbooks.com

©2011 Andrea Lollini
©English translation: Alexandra T. Marot Pollard 2011

Originally published as *Costituzionalismo e giustizia di transizione: il ruolo costituente della Commissione sudafricana verità e riconciliazione*
© 2005, Società editrice il Mulino, Bologna.

The translation of this work has been funded by SEPS
SEGRETARIATO EUROPEO PER LE PUBBLICAZIONI SCIENTIFICHE

SEPS
SEGRETARIATO EUROPEO PER LE PUBBLICAZIONI SCIENTIFICHE

Via Val d'Aposa 7 – 40123 Bologna – Italy
seps@seps.it – www.seps.it

All rights reserved. Except for the quotation of short passages for the purposes of criticism and review, no part of this book may be reproduced in any form or by any means, electronic or mechanical, including photocopying, recording, or any information storage and retrieval system now known or to be invented, without written permission of the publisher.

Library of Congress Cataloging-in-Publication Data

Lollini, Andrea.
[Costituzionalismo e giustizia di transizione. English]
Constitutionalism and transitional justice in South Africa / Andrea Lollini ; translated by Alexandra Tatiana Pollard.
p. cm. — (Human rights in context ; v. 5)
Includes bibliographical references and index.
ISBN 978-1-84545-764-8 (hardback : alk. paper)
1. Constitutional history—South Africa. 2. Transitional justice—South Africa. 3. Post-apartheid era—South Africa. I. Pollard, Alexandra Tatiana. II. Title.
KTL2101.L65 2010
342.6802'9—dc22

2010019547

British Library Cataloguing in Publication Data
A catalogue record for this book is available from the British Library

Printed in the United States on acid-free paper.

ISBN: 978-1-84545-764-8 (hardback)

Contents

Foreword

Roberto Toniatti*

The study of the constituent function and the process of drafting and enacting a new constitution is a constant area of interest for legal scholars. This field is all the more interesting when it leads to gleaning general information from the analysis of a specific historic event, mainly through the comparative method; and when that historic event is intertwined with or, better yet, coincides with a radical constitutional transition (which, in this case, is meant to be a reform in the direction of liberal constitutionalism and a repudiation of the previous apartheid regime); and when that transition takes place in an area where different legal cultures coexist – corresponding with the different cultural identities of a pluralist society – as is the case in South Africa.

The genesis of the current South African Constitution evolved in a complex context, which requires analysis from a number of investigative points of view. One of the methodological strengths of Andrea Lollini's book is his careful reconstruction of all the main components of the South African constitution-making experience (which Romano Orrù brilliantly described as a 'constitution making process (in terms of form and substance) divided into a number of moments and in a plurality of actors').[1] In fact, he makes a basic distinction between the transition's political events and its formal legal dimension. On the one hand, concrete political events refer to the constitution-making process in the widest sense of the term, the actors involved, the political negotiation's documents that in a juridical perspective become normative facts of constitutive importance; on the other hand, the transition's formal legal dimension can be divided into a number of acts with constitutive significance, including the Interim Constitution, the thirty-four Constitutional Principles (a super-constitutional parameter of judicial review overseeing the definitive Constitution in addition to being a formalization of the political constitution) and the decision of the Constitutional Court, with regard to its 'certification' of the Constitution's compliance with the Constitutional Principles, such certification being an additional formal factor – indeed, quite an innovative factor from a comparative perspective – in fulfilling the constituent function.

Andrea Lollini's book examines and pays due attention to political and pre-juridical elements without abandoning the appropriate investigative tools and categories employed by legal scholarship. Regarding this methodological framework, what does deserve to be stressed is that, by following the method defined by Giuseppe de Vergottini in *Le transizioni costituzionali*, Lollini anchors his analysis by using the category of normative facts (such as decisions and even unilateral political statements by all the actors having the power to be involved in the negotiations, multilateral acts, formal acts that can be attributed to the government and parliament of the constitutional system under apartheid on its way to (self-) extinction but that are simultaneously also normative facts of the constitution-making procedure, etc.). Though these facts had no normative relevance on their own, they each represented a decisive step in the gradual legitimation of the whole process, of the very formal constitution-making procedure and of its actors.

The outcome of such a comprehensive methodological approach is that we can observe a series of relationships that coincide with one another: the relationship between constituent facts and acts, between the constitution-making process and its formal procedure, between the political constitution (a substantive extra-legal factor for the legitimacy of the supreme source of law) and the formal Constitution. Yet another result is a theoretical distinction between constituent power and constituent function.

Constituent power is dispersed power, the de facto situation, rooted in the self-assertion and also in the mutual recognition of social institutions as being actors who provide concrete evidence of their ability to negotiate a transition (political adversaries – indeed, the former enemies and protagonists of a violent conflict – who become partners in the constituent pact) using a format experimented with in Europe from the Spanish Moncloa Pact of the 1970s to the Round Table Talks in Eastern Europe of the 1990s. The constituent function, on the other hand, manifests itself in a formal juridical sense as a unitary and concentrated power. Although in the case of South Africa the exercise of this unitary and concentrated constituent function was politically and chronologically segmented, it is nevertheless recognizable as a whole when viewed as representing the steps leading up to the enactment of the fundamental source of law. One of the most original – and in some ways paradoxical and contradictory – aspects of the genesis of post-apartheid South Africa emerges with more clarity in Lollini's book: constituent power was mainly the domain of the multilateral political negotiation, yet the constituent function's fulfilment hinged on the Constitutional Court's certification of the Constitution's legitimacy, creating an unusual situation in which a constituted body formally participated in performing the constituent function and thereby foreshadowing the most important role that the South African Constitutional Court would later assume – which it undoubtedly deserves. With methodological precision, Lollini enriches his juridical and constitutional analysis with the well-balanced inclusion of the historical and political events that set the stage for and accompanied the formal exercising of the constitutive function in South Africa.

A significant part of this book focuses on the role of supplementary constitution-making tools such as the Truth and Reconciliation Commission. Here they are inserted in a framework where there is a dialectical relationship between history and law, between fragmentation of the social body and a determined political will to build a unified political body (as can be seen, for instance, the recognition of 'non-racialism and non-sexism' as fundamental values, as mentioned in Section 1 of the South African Constitution), between contingent claims and underlying ideological postulates of post-apartheid constitutionalism.

In describing the post-apartheid constituent phase, Lollini defines it as having the same function as a 'peace treaty'. His analysis evaluates and describes the legal nature and the constituent scope of the constitutionalization of transitional justice, as well as the basic choice guiding it: constructing the political body's unity by also including both sides involved in perpetrating acts of violence under apartheid, even at the institutional cost of temporarily suspending a strictly penal or criminal approach and the use of punishment. Indeed, in order to do so, personal criminal liability had to be established with a voluntary confession made by the perpetrators of crimes with political objectives.

Abstaining from punishing the guilty and the voluntary self-incriminating testimony involved are actually a kind of dramatic, symbolic and solemn consecration of individual and collective acceptance of the new order. It is as though, for most citizens, the signing of the political and social contract (in the form of the Constitution) takes place through the mechanisms of representative democracy, while for others – the perpetrators of violence – the personal fulfilment of an explicit public obligation was required. Another element of the process was the use of what Lollini describes as a 'pact of remembrance', which projects the constitutional order's turbulent genesis into the future (as can be read in the powerful words of the preamble: 'We, the people of South Africa, Recognise the injustices of the past; Honour those who suffered for justice and freedom in our land; Respect those who have worked to build and develop our country; and Believe that South Africa belongs to all who live in it, united in our diversity'). In this context we can see an effort to take over (or almost destroy) potentially hostile points of view by using a militant constitutionalism that is almost dominating and illiberal in tone, yet which echoes community dispute resolution methods of traditional African law, which take place in the presence of the whole village because personal responsibility always has meaning on a collective level.

However, in the context of institutional and axiological modernization (the primacy of the Bill of Rights over native law, which is also an expressly recognized source of law), traditional African culture seems to resurface and reclaim its place with the use of the *ubuntu* (humanity, community, inclusion, forgiveness) concept, mentioned in the Interim Constitution as one of the fundamental concepts of unity through reconciliation:

> This Constitution provides a historic bridge between the past of a deeply divided society characterized by strife, conflict, untold suffering and injustice, and a future founded on the recognition of human rights, democracy and peaceful co-existence and development opportunities for all South Africans, irrespective of colour, race, class, belief or sex. The pursuit of national unity, the well-being of all South African citizens and peace require reconciliation between the people of South Africa and the reconstruction of society. The adoption of this Constitution lays the secure foundation for the people of South Africa to transcend the divisions and strife of the past, which generated gross violations of human rights, the transgression of humanitarian principles in violent conflicts and a legacy of hatred, fear, guilt and revenge. These can now be addressed on the basis that there is a need for understanding but not for vengeance, a need for reparation but not for retaliation, a need for ubuntu but not for victimization.

Once again, South Africa's constituent experience indicates a dialectical relationship between history and law, tradition and modernization, cultural values and the transitional government, and the establishment of the new constitutional order.

Andrea Lollini's work is marked by the underlying unity of a well-considered reconstruction of the historical events of the post-apartheid constitution-making experience and the treatment of its particular form of transitional justice – all of which are fortified by ample theoretical and comparative references.

As for reconstructing historical events, this book provides important input for understanding the constituent phenomenon as the full expression of sovereignty, free to choose not only the content (which, in this case, inevitably shows signs of the influence of the international climate and the spirit of the age) but also how to exercise its authority. As such, this is a sovereignty that must account for the past experience of the people – especially because of its painful and dramatic history – in order to build a common future.

As for the the experience of transitional justice, Lollini's scholarly work is a contribution aimed at elevating the value of new forms of justice – more specifically, 'reconstructive justice', the basic function of which, according to Antoine Garapon (considering that 'reconstructive justice looks towards the future, while retributive justice is oriented only towards the past'), lies in 're-creating the conditions for reconstruction', in 'rendering a new co-existence possible, relaunching institutions', in the 'production of a collective truth, the benefits of which can be enjoyed by the entire political community', in the 'restoration of a common way of living by spreading democratic culture'.[2] Andrea Lollini's intellectual contribution therefore offers important and interesting points of departure on a plurality of issues and disciplines that are rooted in established academic culture but that may also anticipate the outcome of future research.

*Professor of Comparative Constitutional Law University of Trento.

Notes

1. English translation of the original Italian citation from R. Orrù. 1998. La Costituzione di tutti, Turin: Giappichelli, 94. The original reads: '*processo costituente frazionato (in termini formali e sostanziali) in più momenti e tra più soggetti.*'
2. English translation from the Italian edition of Garapon's book. A. Garapon. 2005. *Crimini che non si possono né punire né perdonare. L'emergere di una giustizia internazionale,* Bologna: Il Mulino. The original text reads: '*la giustizia ricostruttiva guarda verso l'avvenire, mentre il giudizio retributivo è interamente rivolto al passato*' (250), '*ricreare le condizioni per la ricostruzione*' (253), '*rendere possibile una nuova coesistenza, rilanciare le istituzioni*' (246), '*produzione di una verità collettiva i cui benefici saranno goduti dalla comunità politica per intero*' and '*restaurazione del vivere comune attraverso la diffusione di una cultura democratica*' (240).

List of Abbreviations

AC	Amnesty Committee
ANC	African National Congress
APLA	Azanian People's Liberation Army
art.	Article
AZAPO	Azanian People's Organisation
CODESA	Convention for a Democratic South Africa
CP	Constitutional Principles
EL	Evidence Leader
FA	Freedom Alliance
FF	Freedom Front
GNU	Government of National Unity
HRVC	Human Rights Violations Committee
ICC	International Criminal Court
IFP	Inkatha Freedom Party
JSC	Judicial Service Commission
KZN	KwaZulu-Natal
MPNP	Multiparty Negotiating Process
NCOP	National Council of Provinces
NDB	National Data Base
NDPP	National Director of Public Prosecution
NP	National Party
PAC	Pan Africanist Congress
PanSALB	Pan South African Language Board
PCLU	Priority Crimes Litigation Unit
RRC	Reparation and Rehabilitation Committee
s.	Section(s)
SACP	South African Communist Party
SADF	South African Defence Force
StC	Steering Committee

SWAPO	South West Africa People's Organization
TAC	Treatment Action Campaign
TEC	Transitional Executive Council
TRC	Truth and Reconciliation Commission
VC	Volkstaat Council

Introduction

Preliminary Remarks

Over the last fifteen years, the South African post-apartheid *Transitional Amnesty Process* – implemented by the Truth and Reconciliation Commission (TRC) – has been extensively analysed by scholars and commentators from around the world and from almost every discipline of human sciences. Lawyers, historians, anthropologists, sociologists and political scientists have tried to understand, describe and comment on the 'shocking' South African political decision to give amnesty to all who fully disclosed their politically motivated crimes committed during the apartheid era.

Several delicate issues arising from the TRC experience have gradually been debated, such as the legal functioning of the procedures and the controversial implementation of some of the TRC Statute provisions, the veracity of the type of 'truth' revealed by the Commission, the real impact on the notion of 'reconciliation' and the impact of amnesties on apartheid victims. In the background lurked a question about the moral and political acceptability of the transitional amnesty scheme, which was perceived as a trade-off system of justice. Many surveys discussing the TRC's social and political outcomes have tried to measure the results and the coherence of implementing the entire process in terms of the number of amnesties granted, which applications succeeded and why amnesty was granted. The arguments of TRC supporters and sceptics converge on one point: the South African experience was a highly innovative and, at the same time, disorienting experiment.

The research published in this volume began as a doctoral thesis at the *Ecoles des Hautes Etudes en Sciences Sociales* in Paris focusing on the function of the transitional amnesty process, and it seeks to explore a different path.

From this perspective, it is often claimed that the TRC's mandate – helping to establish the 'truth' about the past and participating in the 'reconciliation' process – was crafted in order to facilitate the post-apartheid nation building process. According to the categories of continental European constitutionalism, the process of nation building is one of the fundamental preconditions of the constitution-making process. Continental European scholars, due to a different usage of the adjectives *constituent* and *constitutive*, define the constitution-making process as a *constituent process.*[1] According to this reasoning, it may be said that the TRC (and in particular the transitional amnesty process) was established in order to perform a *constituent function*. Hence, the main question becomes why was this pivotal function also assigned to a body like the TRC and how was this function carried out? This book tries to answer this question by investigating the basic problem facing South Africa at the end of the apartheid regime: how to bring about the unity of the new post-apartheid political body (the Rainbow Nation).

On the one hand, with South Africa's historical heritage and the asymmetries and divisions between the social groups living there, this feat seemed to be an almost utopian challenge. On the other hand, establishing a new *corps politique unitaire* was necessary because it was the most profound rejection of the apartheid ideology, which was based on the institutionalization of fragmentation, separation and exclusion.

In this context, we can imagine the importance of the historic and 'revolutionary' political decision to build the unity of a new political body that included all segments of South African society despite past conflicts and injustice. This fundamental constituent act[2] was the main objective of the nation-building process and the precondition of the constitution-making process. An effective constitution occurs in conjunction with a political body containing centripetal forces that harmonize the differences within it. In order to achieve this very difficult goal (one of the cornerstones on which the new democratic constitutional structure was to be built), a number of mechanisms had to be activated. The main hypothesis guiding this book is that the issue of the political body's unity is the key to a deep understanding of the very innovative post-apartheid constitution-making and transitional amnesty processes.

For these reasons, the theoretical approach of this book analyses the constitution-making process (to which Part 1 of this volume is dedicated) and the transitional amnesty process (to which Part 2 is dedicated) side by side, while simultaneously investigating how they are interconnected. This approach shows that both processes contain mechanisms encouraging the constitution of the unity of the political body while ensuring future solidity and stability. Indeed, the innovative step-by-step procedure of the constitution-making process and the procedure of public confessions, which was the basis of the amnesty process, were mechanisms activating a similar dynamic: inclusion. If the fragmented constitution-making process was meant to gradually lead all the political actors into the process of writing down a new constitutional order, the 'natural' attributes of the confession statement sought an analogous goal: to include the perpetrators of political violence under apartheid in the new nation after they accepted the ritual of publicly disclosing their actions. With historical analysis, these general attributes of the confession can be seen in all contexts that have employed this form of spoken act. It is interesting to note that confession has been historically used in circumstances where there is an underlying problem of constituting or preserving the unity of a determined social structure.

The guiding idea of the research published in this volume (the function focused approach) is to bring the transitional amnesty process into the domain of the concept of constitutionalism while demonstrating all the innovative aspects that the post-segregationist experience contributed.

Post-apartheid Constitutionalism: Continuity and Discontinuity with Tradition

Many contemporary constitution-making processes sprang from crises in authoritarian states and illiberal regimes that were responsible for large scale violations of fundamental rights. During the last two decades of the twentieth century, in different geopolitical areas (Latin America, Africa, Eastern Europe and Asia), many countries initiated the difficult journey of democratization with outcomes that are as yet unclear.[3] The resulting constitutionalism had to deal with the problem of justice for the crimes committed by military oligarchies or by bodies of the criminal state, though mostly in an implicit manner. These constitutional transitions, often under conditions agreed upon by the new political players and the protagonists of the previous regime, had to activate forms of transitional justice squeezed between two opposing forces: the need to preserve the successful transfer of political power from the old authoritarian system to the new 'democratic' political players (which basically meant abandoning the use of penal action against those who had committed political crimes under the old constitutional system) and the opposing need of both alleviating the built-up tension of the victims for retribution and not refraining from the use of law (in a judicial perspective) as a means for delegitimizing the old oppressors.

The rapid development of international criminal justice is another variable that makes the structure of these legal and political dynamics more complex, and yet it is also true that transitional justice has only been carried out on an individual state level. The case of post-apartheid South Africa is undoubtedly the experience that has defined the relationship between justice and the process of building a new democratic constitutional system in a more innovative (and controversial) way. The guiding idea of this book is that the post-apartheid constitution-making process produced a highly innovative constitutional model. In adapting to the political particularities of the transition to a democracy, post-segregationist constitutionalism used techniques for codifying fundamental rules that appear to introduce new elements in comparison with the liberal-democratic constitutionalism that had gained ground in the second half of the twentieth century. This particular constitutional phenomenon is suspended between the inclusion of elements that traditionally characterize modern constitutionalism and the working out of innovative substantive and procedural solutions.[4] The new state, through the construction of an intelligent political mythology, transformed the near-impossibility of exercising punitive action against crimes of the past in an event that could work in favour of the construction of the constitutional system. At the heart of this transformation is the constitutionalization of a model of transitional justice based on the exchange of confession for amnesty. This model is not a tool for justice (for paying the price of the crime), but a complex mechanism enacted in order to establish the unity of the political body and, paradoxically, to demonstrate the power of the new post-apartheid 'sovereignty'. Self-restraining (for a limited period of time) its power to punish but simultaneously ordering 'capitulation' before the new constitutional order (through a public confession statement), the new democratic state preferred to show its strength through pardoning and seeking a path to re-include those who had committed political violence (including national liberation movements) in the new political body.

Continuity

The concept of constitutionalism traditionally means a legal, political and cultural movement based on the principles and values (formalized in writing) that a certain community considers fundamental. In order to protect individual rights against the latitude of institutional power, the characteristics of state organization, the form of government and especially the limits of the public authorities have to be put down in legal texts of the highest order. The very notion of constitutionalism, however, has changed throughout the years, evolving according to different theoretical, philosophical, juridical and political approaches.[5] However, the central political and juridical issue has always been how to limit public power. This can be seen in a variety of the historical configurations of constitutionalism, from the Anglo-Saxon notion of constitutionalism (based on liberal contractualism)[6], the Jacobin version (based on democratic radicalism), the strictly legal and positivist constitutionalism of the German *Rechtsstaat* of the nineteenth century (with its theories of state self-limitations, the radical positivist conception of law and the strict separation of state and civil society in accordance with the doctrine of freedom of economic enterprise)[7] up to the constitutionalism that gained ground in the second half of the twentieth century. This last form established the social dimension of the state and the widespread acceptance of systems of judicial review. In other words, as legal doctrine has often demonstrated, the main problem that constitutionalism (in its various legal, philosophical and political forms) has always sought to resolve is how to control the natural tendency of power to expand chaotically. As a theory that collects strategies for protecting fundamental individual freedoms, constitutionalism has provided legal and philosophical notions that have led to reflection on the meaning of the word 'constitution', on the notion of state (in its different meanings as social state, constitutional state or rule of law) and on sovereignty.

The analysis of the elements of modern constitutionalism in post-apartheid constitutionalism cannot ignore the theories that began to establish themselves at the end of the Second World War. The profound evolution in constitutional theories, demonstrated by the meeting of the 'old' list of fundamental individual rights with the 'new' social rights, is the foundation and the starting point of the constitutionalism of the new South Africa. On the one hand, the constitutions conceived in the second half of the twentieth century gave importance to the constitutionalization of social rights as part of the fundamental rights making up the new social state, following the model of the Weimar Constitution;[8] on the other hand, they embraced and developed the idea of constitutional justice as a pillar of the constitutional state. In this context, post-apartheid South African constitutionalism includes a highly evolved Bill of Rights that eliminates the kinds of discrimination characterizing apartheid in its political form. By providing an extremely solid social state order (at least on paper) and a model of strong protection of fundamental rights (through a well-defined system of judicial review and with the aid of numerous supervising constitutional bodies) and by proposing a form of government that focuses on the problematic issue of the presence of different ethnic, linguistic and racial groups, South African constitutionalism places itself in an evolving dialogue with the liberal-democratic constitutional tradition of the twentieth century.[9] More specifically, the South African Interim Constitution of 1993 as well as the definitive Constitution approved by the Constitutional Assembly, aside from creating a modern Bill of Rights based on the Canadian model, instituted a number of supervising constitutional bodies under the heading 'State Institutions Supporting Constitutional Democracy':[10] the Public Prosecutor (s. 182–83), the Human Rights Commission (s. 184), the Commission for the Promotion and Protection of the Rights of Cultural, Religious and Linguistic Communities (s. 185–86), the Commission for Gender Equality (s. 187), the Auditor-General (s. 188–89), the Electoral Commission (s. 190–91) and the Broadcasting Authority (s. 192).

Instituted with the Land Claims Act 22 of 1994, the Land Claims Court is another important body in the task of breaking with the previous order and pursuing constitutional objectives for the gradual redistribution of access to economic resources. The constitutional foundation for the law and the judicial body instituted by it is s. 25(7) of the Bill of Rights of the 1996 Constitution. This provision governs the individual and collective right of persons or communities dispossessed of property due to racially discriminatory laws and policies after 19 June 1913 to restitution of the property or an equal redress, and it is the Land Claims Court that is the body designated for the enforcement of this provision.[11]

These constitutional bodies are supported by the introduction of judicial review with different procedures of recourse (among which is the possibility for direct recourse based on s. 167–72),[12] and the Constitutional Court becomes the new authoritative reference point for justice. In this framework, post-apartheid constitutionalism appears to inherit a legal-constitutional and philosophical-political form rooted in the idea that public powers can be limited through bodies to which citizens may appeal for potential violations of fundamental rights, a situation that in turn could create a conflicting relationship between citizen and state. On the one hand, this shows an attempt to give the citizen an active role in building and maintaining a democratic system; on the other hand, it reveals the deep wounds in a society that harbours mistrust towards a state that was criminal in the past.[13]

Discontinuity: the Peculiarities of Post-apartheid Constitutionalism

The peculiarities of the constitutionalism of the new South Africa are many and should be analysed considering both the political setup of the constitutional transition and the specific needs deriving from the structure of the South African political body. In other words, the peculiarities and innovations of post-segregationist constitutionalism were shaped by the problematic characteristics of the historical, political and social context of dismantling apartheid and the simultaneous creation of the new democratic system. Basically, these peculiarities can be summarized as follows: some of them concern what we can define as techniques for constructing the unity of the political body. In reality, these are peculiarities connected to the process of constructing (in line with a specific political plan) the preliminary legal and political conditions for drafting the new Constitution. In this sense, post-segregationist constitutionalism sought to substitute the political form of apartheid, which had fuelled the fragmentation of the political body for decades,[14] with a system that was capable of standing up to the centrifugal forces (due to ethno-racial particularism) that tended towards the country's disintegration.[15] This was accomplished using diverse techniques, procedures and ways of constructing the unity of the political body. The following pages will analyse: a) the creation of unity by making the new democratic rules acceptable to all segments of the South African political body; b) building unity around the political myth of the Rainbow Nation as a symbol of the new political citizenship; c) the construction of unity through constitutional negotiations held by representatives of opposing political forces during the conflict between the national liberation movements and the forces of the segregationist regime[16] – these talks determined the various stages of the constitution-making process and led to the creation of a dialogue between 'enemies' aiming to gradually reduce the distance separating them with the common goal of signing the new democratic constitutional covenant; and

d) the creation of unity through an intricate constitution-making procedure, which developed in a series of phases according to formalized rules approved by the Constitutional Court. These features amount to a practice producing a constitutional text that – even if used in other constitution-making experiences – was of a hitherto-unknown level of complexity.

Other characteristics of post-apartheid constitutionalism regard the creation of what I define as supplementary constitution-making tools. These are constitutional bodies authorized to carry out specific constitution-making tasks such as reinforcing the process of constructing the unity of the political body. The most important body among these is the South African Truth and Reconciliation Commission (TRC), whose analysis makes up a great part of this work. The hypothesis made here is that a detailed analysis of the experience of the TRC reveals its constitution-making role.[17] In fact, according to specific constitutional norms innovatively regulating the issue of 'transitional justice' for crimes committed during apartheid, the TRC was authorised to grant amnesty to those who were willing to publicly 'confess' crimes committed for political reasons between 1960 and 1997, in the spirit of pacifying the country and opposing any form of revenge as endorsed by the Constitution. In other words, the TRC was the body where an exchange (confession – amnesty) took place in accordance with the Constitution. This exchange was a part of the democratic constitutional covenant and the source of a series of peculiarities of post-apartheid constitutionalism such as: a) constitutional suspension of a strictly criminal approach to political crimes in the past; b) the process of constructing the unity of the new South African political body by including the 'enemy' and therefore creating a kind of constitutional ban on purging; and c) the use of confession as a tool serving the constitution-making process. Hence, *testis contra se* (testifying against oneself), a practice used in the proceedings before the Amnesty Committee of the TRC, will be analysed as a dialogue technique used to construct the unity of the political body.

There are two fundamental themes of research that ensure a proper analysis of the constitutional model created in response to the collapse of segregationist ideology: on the one hand, the study of the constitution-making process that enabled the confrontation of different constitutional ideas of the various political players who had conflicting ideas on government, state institutions, fundamental law principles and socio-political relationships; on the other hand, the analysis of the constitutionalization of an innovative form of transitional justice.[18]

In this context, the political reasoning of the entire political and constitutional transition was to move away from apartheid, and the underlying political action consisted in rejecting an extreme differentialist and segregationist rationale. There was a need to symbolically break from the past and, simultaneously, there was also a need to build a constitutional system that adopted new rights and guarantees for the individual in the face of public authorities. Therefore, it was necessary to define the ways in which the new democratic state would act.

This constitutionalized system of transitional justice set out to confine the actions of the new state towards the past, limiting its use of punitive action. This limited form of judicial action towards the past coincided with the removal of a fundamental feature of sovereignty from the state, that is, the power to judge and to punish. It also allowed the new democratic system to differentiate itself from its predecessor by emphasizing a new democratic identity. In the creation phase of the new democratic South Africa, a shift was made from sovereignty as authority expressed through the power to judge and punish to a form of sovereignty whose power resided in the choice to limit its ability to punish and purge. Between the power to punish and the power to pardon – the two attributes of sovereignty identified by Bodin – the new South Africa chose the latter by using confession (which, as we shall see, produces a much more ethical state). We therefore find ourselves dealing with a differentiation on two levels: the new South Africa distinguishes itself from its predecessor and, simultaneously, from other states involved in a constitution-making process triggered by the fall of authoritarian regimes but that chose to deal with the past by trial and punishment.

The Establishment of the Post-apartheid Constitutional System

According to categories of continental European constitutionalism, the multifaceted formation of a constitution has been associated with specific models. In this context, European scholars have drawn a first distinction between external and internal formal constitution-making processes. Within this subdivision, the South African phenomenon falls under the latter process because it took place without influence from foreign countries or international political actors (as was the case, for example, in Germany and Japan after the Second World War).

Implemented with special terms regarding the right to and method of exercising constituent power, the South African constitution-making process was both temporary (the approval of a provisional text) and consensual (the agreement between the old regime's bodies and the de facto political actors of the transition). These two qualities determined the complex evolution of the initiative, preparatory and deliberative phases.[19] As we shall see, the procedure used in South Africa added other complex features in comparison with those produced in other semi-fragmented constitution-making processes, such as in Portugal, in Spain, in the shift from socialist models that took place after the end of the Cold War era in Hungary, Poland and the former Czechoslovakia, or in the negotiated transitions from military oligarchies in Latin America.[20]

During the post-apartheid South African transition, a number of facts/events took place one after another that together defined the framework of the entire constitution-making process. Simultaneously, a series of strictly constitutional acts determined the framework of the constitution-making procedure.

In this book, a distinction is made between facts/events and acts. Both categories relate to the constitution that was being drafted. However, facts/events were de facto situations that indirectly but substantially impacted and influenced the drafting of the constitution. The term 'act' does not refer to the general legal meaning of statutes or laws made by a legislative body; instead it refers to all those 'moments' in which political decisions or agreements regarding the new constitution were formally set down in written documents. They are an ensemble of fragments that were agreed upon step-by-step and were used to build up the new constitutional system. These constituent acts gradually framed both the Interim Constitution and, later, the definitive Constitution.

The distinction between facts/events and acts with a constituent value is not meaningless or hollow. Indeed, this differentiation is the basis of the distinction between the concept of constitution-making process and constitution-making procedure.[21] According to this distinction, the constitution-making process is a broad concept because it covers historical and political facts and events of constitutional relevance, whereas the concept of a constitution-making procedure is narrower, referring only to those specific decisions or agreements translated in written texts with which the constitution is gradually drafted and adopted.[22]

The process of writing the new democratic constitution of South Africa shows degrees of complexity that have no precedent and cannot be studied by separating historical and political events from strictly legal events. Constituent facts and acts are intimately connected and mutually support each other. The constitution-making procedure and the constituent acts were shaped by facts of a political, military, cultural and social nature. Due to the necessity of constructing the unity of the political body, the constituent acts had to be as consensual as possible and include the various players of the transition. These actors gradually determined the legal content of the transitional constituent acts and the procedure for adopting subsequent acts up until the adoption of the definitive Constitution. The constitution-making process and procedure evolved in the following phases: 1) the negotiation phase (in which constituent facts dominate); 2) the multiparty forums (in which the constituent acts begin to take the place of the facts); 3) the last phase of adopting the Constitution (dominated by constituent acts).

Over the course of the second phase, very important constituent acts – individual, interim and definitive – were adopted, such as the approval of the Interim Constitution of 1993 and the 34 Constitutional Principles (CPs) that the definitive Constitution had to comply with, the institution of the Constitutional Court, which had the task of certifying the compliance of the definitive text with the CPs, and the creation of the Truth and Reconciliation Commission.

The Constitutional Assembly, which was formally given the task of adopting the definitive Constitution, was summoned only after the first fully multiracial election in 1994 under the 1993 Interim Constitution and other temporary and definitive constituent acts that had been previously adopted. When the Assembly began to work, the procedure had already reached a high degree of formalization because many basic elements of the definitive Constitution had already been determined. If we add to this the fact that a body already existed for controlling the evolution of the procedure and its final outcome (the Constitutional Court), it seems to be evident that the classic notion of process is insufficient for explaining the constitution-making phenomenon in South Africa. In fact, since a sort of 'supra-Constitution' was already negotiated and drafted (the 34 CPs) along with a body (the Constitutional Court) that could verify the compliance of the definitive text with the constituent acts previously adopted (the 34 CPs), we can see that the Constitutional Assembly worked within a limited space. In other terms, it seems that the Constitutional Assembly's constituent power was partially limited or guided. The Constitutional Assembly was surely carrying out a pivotal step of the constitution-making process, but its creative action was not unlimited; it was performing a fundamental task but within a pre-established procedure.

Notes

1. In this book I will often use the adjectives 'constituent' and 'constitutive' as they are employed in continental European legal theory. Paying tribute to the historical differentiation between 'constituent and constituted powers' made by Sieyès, the meaning of 'constituent' and 'constitutive' is creating, shaping, constituting a new constitutional order. The adjectives 'constituent' and 'constitutive', when used to refer to several nouns such as power, act, pact, instances, assembly, remembrance and confession, recognize that these elements either played a role or performed a function in setting down the new constitutional order. In English, these concepts of continental European constitutionalism are used and discussed in M. Loughlin and N. Walker (eds). 2007. *The Paradox of Constitutionalism: Constituent Power and Constitutional Form*. Oxford: Oxford University Press.
2. By the expression 'constituent or constitutive act' I refer to a 'moment' that encompasses both the break from the rationale, principles and values of the previous constitutional order and the founding of the basic substantive principles of the new order.
3. G. de Vergottini. 1998. *Le transizioni costituzionali*. Bologna: Il Mulino; L. Mezzetti. 2000. *Le democrazie incerte. Transizioni costituzionali e consolidamento della democrazia in Europa orientale, Africa, America Latina, Asia*. Turin: Giappichelli; L. Mezzetti. 2003. *Teoria e prassi delle transizioni costituzionali e del consolidamento democratico*. Padua: CEDAM.
4. See R. Orrù. 1999. 'Transizione e avvio del consolidamento democratico in Sudafrica: la complessa attuazione della Costituzione del 1996', *Rivista di diritto pubblico comparato ed europeo* 3: 903–28.
5. The term 'constitutionalism', which began to be used in the nineteenth century, has always focused on the problem of defining a system of checks and balances capable

of limiting public power. Generally speaking, the notion of constitutionalism goes hand in hand with principles like the authority of the law, the separation of powers and the creation of representative institutions that can protect individual and collective rights of the people, who, although governed, are the true sovereigns: see A. Lloyd Howell. 1997. 'Le Constitutionnalisme', in J. Burns Handerson (ed.), *Histoire de la pensée politique moderne*. Paris: Presses Universitaires de France, pp. 230–69. For some scholars, constitutionalism as an act formalizing a system of limiting public powers can be distinguished in two forms: ancient and modern. The former dates back to Cicero's definition of the Roman Republic and the latter to eighteenth century revolutions; see H.C. McIlwain. 1947. *Constitutionalism: Ancient and Modern*. New York: Cornell University Press. What changes is the notion of a constitution. Other scholars, however, consider only the modern form of constitutionalism as valid; see G. Sartori. 1990. *Elementi di teoria politica*. Bologna: Il Mulino, p. 12; M. Troper. 1994. 'Le concept de constitutionnalisme et la théorie moderne du droit', in *Pour une théorie juridique de l'état*. Paris: Presses Universitaires de France, pp. 203–21. Interestingly, the concept of constitution is what determines the difference between those who claim that an ancient form of constitutionalism exists and those who recognize only its modern form. For example, McIlwain considers 'constitution' a normative term designating a group of rules limiting political power, whose origin may include tradition or divine right. On the other hand, Troper and positivist doctrine regard constitutions and constitutionalism as only modern because constitutions are texts consciously written by people beginning in a specific historical moment. A constitution's essential characteristics are fundamental rights, the authority of constituent power, hierarchy and stability. According to this approach, the constitution is a *technique de liberté inedite* that appeared only in the eighteenth century; see M. Troper. 1992. 'Le concept d'État de droit', in *Droits* 15: 51–63; Sartori, *Elementi di teoria politica*, p. 23; M. Matteucci. 2003. 'Costituzionalismo', in N. Bobbio, M. Matteucci and G. Pasquino (eds), *Dizionario di politica*. Turin: Utet. A reconstruction of the historical and legal origins and evolution of the ideas of constitution and constitutionalism can be found in M. Dogliani. 1994. *Introduzione al diritto costituzionale*. Bologna: Il Mulino; A. Barbera. 1997. 'Le basi filosofiche del costituzionalismo', in A. Barbera (ed.), *Le basi filosofiche del costituzionalismo*. Bari: Laterza, pp. 3–42; G. Rebuffa. 1990. *Costituzioni e costituzionalismi*. Turin: Giappichelli; A. Larry (ed.). 1998. *Constitutionalism. Philosophical Foundations*. Cambridge: Cambridge University Press; L. Campagna. 1998. *Gli opposti sentieri del costituzionalismo*. Bologna: Il Mulino. See also G. de Vergottini. 2004. *Diritto costituzionale comparato*, 6th ed., Padua: CEDAM, pp. 142–63; G. Volpe. 2000. *Il Costituzionalismo del novecento*. Bari: Laterza; G. Morbidelli. 2001. *Lezioni di diritto pubblico comparato. Costituzioni e Costituzionalismo*. Bologna: Monduzzi. Constitutionalism referred to here in relation to the South African constitution-making process consists in the production of constitutional texts that codify a modern system of public power limitation and establish protection from the abuses and risks of authoritarian regression, which are part of South Africa's past. This point is stressed by R. Orrù. 1998. *La Costituzione di tutti. Il Sudafrica dalla segregazione razziale alla democrazia della Rainbow Nation*. Turin: Giappichelli, p. 181; and by H. Klug. 2000. *Constituting Democracy. Law, Globalism and South Africa's Political Reconstruction*. Cambridge: Cambridge University Press, p. 2.

6. See J.R. Pennock and J.W. Chapman (eds). 1979. *Constitutionalism*. New York: New York University Press.
7. Von Mohl and Stahl were the first theorists of this juridical approach to organizing public powers; the theory was then developed in the nineteenth century by the German public law experts Gerber, Jhering, Laband and Jellineck. According to theories grounding the *Rechtsstaat* in law, the state acts exclusively through the law;

since the state is sovereign, it sets its own rules for limiting its range of action. As such, it implies a type of self-limitation through norms that it self-produces. The state is a source of law, defining its tasks, its attributes and powers without other institutions qualified to verify whether the rules set down are properly applied; see G. Gozzi. 1999. *Democrazia e Diritti. Germania: dallo Stato di diritto alla democrazia costituzionale*. Bari: Laterza; G. Gozzi. 2002. 'Stato di diritto e diritti soggettivi nella storia costituzionale tedesca', in P. Costa and D. Zolo (eds), *Lo Stato di diritto. Storia, teoria, critica*. Milan: Feltrinelli, pp. 260–83; and C. Galli. 1996. *Genealogia della politica. Carl Schmitt e la crisi del pensiero politico moderno*. Bologna: Il Mulino, pp. 283–93. This doctrine deeply influenced the public law of the French Third Republic: see G. Burdeau, F. Hamon and M. Troper. 1995. *Droit Constitutionnel*. Paris: Librairie Générale de Droit et de Jurisprudence; and P. Pactet. 1998. *Institutions Politiques et droit constitutionnel*. Paris: Armand Colin. An analysis of the relationship between the German *Allgemeine Staatslehre* and the legal doctrine of the *IIIe République* can be found in J. Chevallier. 1999. *L'État de droit*. Paris: Montchrestien; P.M. Gaudemet. 1989. 'Paul Laband et la doctrine française de droit public', *Revue de Droit Public* 4: 957 *et seq*.

8. See the theory of H. Heller. 1971. *Gesammelte Schriften, II: Recht, Staat, Macht*. Leiden: Sijthoff. His model of constitutionalism aspired to give full constitutional recognition to the state's social dimension (solidarity and redistribution of economic resources to the least affluent groups of the population); the state should reduce the inequalities within the social structure. The constitutionalism that inspired social state theories established a new constitutional order so as to rebuild the political unity of the European states torn apart by totalitarianism and fascist authoritarianism. Important criticism of this model can be found in E. Forsthoff. 1964. *Rechtsstaat im Wandel*. Stuttgart: Kohlhammer; E. Forsthoff. 1968. *Rechtsstaatlichkeit und Sozialstaatlichkeit. Aufsätze und Essay*. Darmstadt: Wissenschaftliche Buch Gesellschaft.
9. The type of liberal democratic constitutionalism referred to here is made up of many variables that first developed in a British context and later in a North American context. Scholars usually consider it in opposition to the radical democratic constitutionalism that developed after the French Revolution. The main difference between the two concepts is how public powers are checked: C. Friedrich. 1968. 'Constitutions and Constitutionalism', in David L. Sills (ed.), *International Encyclopedia of the Social Sciences*. New York: Macmillan and Free Press, vol. 3, pp. 318–26. The Jacobin model of radical democratic constitutionalism emphasizes the direct control exerted by the *corps social*, which can put pressure on the state's power. With a rather different conception of the judiciary's role and exercise of judiciary power, the different versions of liberal democratic constitutionalism developed the checks and balances system in order to keep sovereignty under control. Here there is quite a different conception of the 'law': based on a system of controlling public power in which the judge has a fundamental role, the law is customarily subject to judicial review. The historical roots of this distinction can be found in the medieval division between *gubernaculum* and *jurisdictio*. According to this doctrine, certain governmental acts of the monarchs were subject (*sub-legem*) to fundamental ethical and moral principles that the government had to comply with. This concept of constitutionalism therefore evolved from the idea that state power is inherently limited: J.G.A. Pocock. 1987. *The Ancient Constitution and the Feudal Law. English Historical Thought in the Seventeenth Century*. Cambridge: Cambridge University Press; McIlwain, *Constitutionalism: Ancient and Modern*; McIlwain. 1939. *Constitutionalism and the Changing World*. Cambridge: Cambridge University Press. The state must recognize and protect fundamental rights (paying tribute to the ideas of Locke, Burke and Hume is very important). The North American version of liberal democratic constitutionalism introduces some radical developments like the

written constitution, enlarging fundamental rights on the basis of freedom and property, the federal model, the presidential system (based on the separation between executive and legislative powers) and especially judicial review. Judicial review was later introduced in Europe in the twentieth century with the development of mechanisms for checking constitutionality (see J. Ely. 1980. *Democracy and Distrust: A Theory of Judicial Review*. Cambridge (Mass.): Harvard University Press). North American liberal democratic constitutionalism thereafter developed a strong inclination towards using judicial review procedures and means for checking the public powers (see B. Ackerman. 1991. *We the People, I: Foundations*. Cambridge (Mass.): Harvard University Press; B. Ackerman. 1998. *We the People II: Transformations*. Cambridge (Mass.): Harvard University Press; S.M. Griffin. 1996. *American Constitutionalism*. Princeton: Princeton University Press. In Italy, see G. Bognetti. 1998. *Lo spirito del costituzionalismo americano*. Turin: Giappichelli, vol. 1; G. Bognetti. 2000. *Lo spirito del costituzionalismo americano*. Turin: Giappichelli, vol. 2.

10. See Chapter IX, *Constitution of the Republic of South Africa, Act* 108/1996 (1996 Constitution).
11. See S. Nadesen. 1997. 'Restitution, Reconstruction, Reconciliation and Redistribution: Land Reform Balancing the Interests of the Dispossessed, the Homeless and Development', *Stellenbosh Law Review*, 360–77.
12. See R. Pretorius. 1994. 'Enforcement Mechanisms in the 1993 Constitution', *South African Public Law* 9: 265–77; I. Routenbach and E. Malherbe. 1999. *Constitutional Law*, 3rd ed. Durban: Butterworths; J. Sarkin. 2000b. 'An Evaluation of the Role of the Independent Complaints Directorate for the Police, the Inspecting Judge for Prisons, the Legal Aid Board, the Human Rights Commission, the Commission on Gender Equality, the Auditor General, the Public Protector and the Truth and Reconciliation Commission in Developing a Human Rights Culture in South Africa', *South African Public Law* 15: 385–425. An analysis of how the judicial review bodies functioned in applying the constitutional principle of multilingualism can be found in A. Lollini. 2004b. 'L'isola e l'arcipelago: la Francia ed il Sudafrica post-apartheid come modelli antitetici di tutela costituzionale di lingue minoritarie e regionali', in A. Lollini (ed.), *Pluralismo linguistico e costituzioni. Un'analisi comparata*. Bolzano: Alpha-Beta, pp. 25–84.
13. See M. Chaskalson and D. Davis. 1997. 'Constitutionalism, the Rule of Law and the First Certification Judgment', *South African Journal on Human Rights* 13(3): 430–35; D. van Wyk, J. Dugard, B. de Villiers and D. Davis. 1994. *Right and Constitutionalism: The New South Africa Legal Order*. Cape Town: Juta, pp. 200 *et seq*; P. Olivier. 1995. 'Constitutionality and Society in South Africa: What Sort of Democracy', in G. Conac, F. Dreyfus and J. Montero (eds), *L'Afrique du Sud en Transition. Réconciliation et coopération en Afrique Australe*. Paris: Economica, pp. 88–109; D. Marais. 1993. *South Africa: Constitutional Development. A Multi-disciplinary Approach*, 2nd ed. Pretoria: Southern Book Publishers.
14. The Republic of South Africa was instituted with law of 24 April 1961, promulgated by the Governor-General of the Union of South Africa (see note 41 in Chapter 1) and approved by the Queen of England and the Union's Parliament. Ever since the beginning of the twentieth century, a racist political ideology known as apartheid was practised in South Africa. Under H.F. Verwoerd (1958–66) this ideology had reached an advanced phase of implementation, and it was definitively consolidated under B.J. Voster (1966–78). The spread of Afrikaner nationalism was fundamental to the rise of republicanism; in fact, this movement helped radicalize the discriminatory policies towards the native population, policies that were in place before the National Party took political control. The evolution of these policies gradually created the apartheid system through a series of laws making distinctions about the practice of political and civil liberties (political citizenship) and the enjoyment of

economic and social rights. Up until 1980, South Africa was formally a parliamentary republic, but excluded the majority of the population from political and social citizenship. In 1983 a constitutional reform took place under P.W. Botha. It was a timid attempt to renew the constitutional system that began to show signs of being inadequate (see L.J. Boulle. 1984a. *Constitutional Reform and the Apartheid State: Legitimacy, Consociationalism, and Control in South Africa.* New York: St. Martin's Press; L.J. Boulle. 1984b. *South Africa and the Consociational Option. A Constitutional Analysis*, Johannesburg: Juta). Obviously there was no interest in radically reforming the foundation of the segregationist constitutionalism. The Parliament was changed into a tri-cameral body; one house was made up of representatives elected by the Indian population (House of Delegates, 45 members), one house for those elected by the coloured population (House of Representatives, 85 members), and one house for those elected by the white population (House of Assembly, 178 members). Each of the three houses had an executive body (Ministers' Council) accountable to the Assembly and responsible for issues concerning their particular ethno-racial group (Own Affairs). National issues (General Affairs) required the approval from all three houses. The President (through the President's Council) decided which of the two categories was part of the law in discussion. The House of Assembly had more authority because it could decide on the national interests by potentially vetoing the decisions made by the other houses. The black majority was completely excluded from political participation. The 1983 Constitution did nothing more than recognize the Indian and coloured population as partners in exercising political power based on the exclusion of largest demographic segment of the country. On the South African tricameral parliament in Italian, see P. Biscaretti di Ruffía. 1986. 'La Costituzione Tricamerale del 1983: una ricetta insufficiente per una conflittuale società plurinazionale', *Rivista trimestrate di diritto pubblico*, 665 *et seq*; L. Pegoraro and A. Reposo. 1986. 'Repubblica del Sudafrica', *Quaderni Costituzionali*, 197 *et seq*; R. Orrù, *La Costituzione di tutti*, pp. 52–55.

15. See L. Du Plessis. 2002. 'Legal and Constitutional Means Designed to Facilitate the Integration of Diverse Cultures in South Africa: a Provisional Assessment', *Stellenbosh Law Review* 3: 367–86.
16. Although the political arena was made up of rather distinct units (like an intricate mosaic of paramilitary groups and political movements), the main 'war of liberation' actors who participated in the constitutional negotiations were the African National Congress (ANC), the South African Communist Party (SACP), the Pan Africanist Congress (PAC), the Azanian People's Organisation (AZAPO) and the Inkatha Freedom Party (IFP); the IFP derived much of its support from the Zulu people. Sitting at the other end of the negotiation table was the National Party (NP), the predominantly Afrikaner political party that had institutionalized racial segregation and governed the country since 1948. See L. Thompson. 1990. *A History of South Africa.* New Haven: Yale University Press; T.R.H. Davenport. 1991. *South Africa: A Modern History.* London: MacMillan; W. Beinart. 1994. *Twentieth-Century South Africa.* Oxford, New York: Oxford University Press; R. Abel. 1995. *Politics by Other Means: Law in the Struggle against Apartheid.* New York: Routledge; T.R.H. Davenport. 2000. *The Birth of a New South Africa.* Toronto, Buffalo, London, University of Toronto Press; R. Davenport and C. Saunders. 2000. *South Africa. A Modern History.* London: MacMillan.
17. Some scholars connect the TRC experience directly with the constitution-making process and post-apartheid constitutionalism; see J. Klaaren. 1998. 'The Truth and Reconciliation Commission, the South African Judiciary, and Constitutionalism', *African Studies* 57: 203 *et seq*; Sarkin, 'An Evaluation of the Role of the Independent Complaints Directorate'; S. Stacey. 1999. 'A New South Africa: The South Africa Truth and Reconciliation Commission's Vexed Nation-building Project', *TRC:*

Commissioning the Past Conference, Johannesburg, 14 June 1999. Johannesburg: University of Witwatersrand. The idea that the TRC was a tool for reconstructing the political body can also be found in South African newspaper debates; see 'The Bringing of Truth', *Mail & Guardian*, 21 March 2003. Amnesty Committee members express a similar idea in *TRC Final Report*. 2003. London: MacMillan, vol. 6, Section I, Chapter 5, 91, §38. A study that partially agrees with the arguments made here can be found in A.M. Gross. 2004. 'The Constitution, Reconciliation, and Transitional Justice: Lessons from South Africa and Israel', *Stanford Journal of International Law* 40: 47–99.

18. See P. van Zyl. 1999. 'Dilemma of Transitional Justice: the Case of South Africa's Truth and Reconciliation Commission', *Journal of International Affairs* 52: 649 *et seq*.
19. See G. de Vergottini, *Diritto costituzionale comparato*, 164 *et seq*; G. de Vergottini, *Le transizioni costituzionali*; A. Pace. 1997. *Potere Costituente, rigidità costituzionale, autovincoli legislativi*. Padua: CEDAM, pp. 97 *et seq*.
20. See G. de Vergottini. 1977. *Le origini della seconda repubblica portoghese. 1974-1976*. Milan: Giuffrè; G. de Vergottini (ed.). 1978. *Una costituzione democratica per la Spagna*. Milan: Franco Angeli; S. Bartole. 1993. *Riforme costituzionali nell'Europa centro-orientale, Da satelliti comunisti a democrazie sovrane*. Bologna: Il Mulino; S. Bartole and P. Grilli di Cortona (eds). 1998. *Transizioni e consolidamento democratico nell'Europa centro-orientale*. Turin: Giappichelli; de Vergottini (ed.). 1997. *Costituzione ed emergenza in America Latina*. Turin: Giappichelli; G. Rolla. 2001. 'Luci ed ombre dell'esperienza delle transizioni pactdas', *Diritto pubblico comparato ed europeo* 3: 1084–96; M. Carducci. 1999. *Il costituzionalismo "parallelo" delle nuove democrazie. Africa e America Latina*. Milan: Giuffré; L. Mezzetti, *Le democrazie incerte*; and L. Mezzetti, *Teoria e prassi*.
21. On this point, see A. Lollini and F. Palermo. 2009. 'Comparative Law and the "Proceduralization" of Constitution-building Processes', in J. Raue and P. Sutter (eds), *Facets and Practices of State-building*. Leiden: Brill/Martinus Nijhoff, pp. 301–26. In Italian legal scholarship, the distinction between constituent facts and constituent acts is discussed by de Vergottini, *Diritto costituzionale comparato*, p. 186.
22. Here again I pay tribute to legal theory concepts used in continental European thought. These categories and concepts are slightly more precise than those proposed by scholastic traditions of other legal cultures (like the Anglo-American one). In Italy, for example, authoritative scholars divide constitution-making procedures into legal procedures of constitutional amendment according to express laws (*procedimenti giuridici*) and de facto procedures that do not respect a formalized constitutional amendment procedure (*procedimenti di fatto*); see P. Biscaretti di Ruffía. 1988. *Introduzione al Diritto costituzionale comparato*, 6th ed. Milan: Giuffrè, pp. 638 *et seq*. According to this theory, de facto procedures can be anti-juridical (*antigiuridici*) or a-juridical (*agiuridici*). Some contemporary constitution-making procedures that did not respect the formalized constitutional amendment procedure have anti-juridical or a-juridical characteristics. These procedures are generally legally recognized *a posteriori*. De facto establishment of a new constitutional system has been studied by S. Romano. 1950. 'L'instaurazione di fatto di un ordinamento costituzionale e la sua legittimità (1901)', *Scritti Minori*, Milan: Giuffrè, vol. 1, pp. 110 *et seq*; and C. Mortati. 1972. 'La Costituente (1945)', in *Raccolta di scritti*, Milan: Giuffré, vol. 1, pp. 26 *et seq*. This classic scholarly opinion was criticized by Pace, *Potere costituente*, pp. 97 et seq. These scholarly opinions conflict on the concept of constituent power. Romano claims that de facto establishment takes place mostly through anti-juridical means (in contrast with the system in force), but also through a-juridical means (with procedures outside the law in force). Using a

procedure of constitutional amendment excludes de facto establishment because, in Romano's opinion, exercising constituent power in this way falls within a constituted power. Mortati and Pace criticize Romano's claim, especially its contradictory nature. Pace shares Romano's idea that new orders can be established in an a-juridical manner (e.g., after a military defeat, the winning powers dictate a new constitutional text); however, using a procedure of constitutional amendment according to law never leads to the creation of a new constitution and therefore neither does it lead to exercising constituent power. As a result, according to Pace, a new order means a radical break from and abandonment of the old regime's rules (pp. 105 *et seq*). Sometimes the use of constitutional amendment procedures is simply a formality; in this case, if the results give rise to a renewal of the order, then the constitutional amendment procedures were either forced or violated. This leads Pace to reflect on constituent power, the only power that can actually establish a new order. It is a purely de facto power (which cannot be limited by the law) just as constitution-making processes are only de facto. This approach greatly changes the distinction between constituent facts and acts. Establishing a new order is a political journey in which constituent power can be seen in action. According to Pace, the constituent power stimulates constituent facts which, in turn, pave the way for the new order's foundation. Theoretically, the constituent power operates undisturbed until the final outcome, that is, the new constitution, and it is unresponsive to acts calling for formalization or juridical self-limitation. Nevertheless, as we shall see, the South African constituent experience cannot be easily broken down into these categories, demonstrating the need for fresh reflection. The notion of constitution-making procedure used in this study does not always refer to merely any procedure of constitutional amendment provided by the previous segregationist constitutional order. Using the categories suggested by Romano and Pace, the post-apartheid system was established through a-juridical facts occurring in a constitutional void as opposed to through facts violating the norms of the system in force. As we shall see, forces outside of the law acted and governed the events. If we agree with Alessandro Pace that the constitution-making power is a de facto power that cannot be limited by the law (Pace, *Potere costituente*, pp. 122 *et seq*), the empirical study of the post-apartheid constitutional phenomenon shows us that it found a way of limiting itself, of watering down its power and its intensity in juridical acts, which had an increasingly normative nature. These were steps that were taken in order to respond to the particular needs of the political, social and cultural context.

PART I

THE CONSTITUTION-MAKING PROCESS AND PROCEDURE

1

Constituent Facts

Apartheid's Legacy and Constructing the New Political Body's Unity

During South Africa's transition to a democracy, the country had to face the problem of establishing its post-segregationist political form; the most difficult challenge was to construct the new political body's unity. The post-apartheid political body was divided by deep-rooted racist ideologies and held back by conflicting and divisive forces. From a legal and political standpoint, creating a unified base (the people, the nation, a homogeneous and stable social unit) has been a fundamental step in forming a modern state.[1] Political philosophy and law theory concepts of contractualism have tried to explain this fundamental feature of the modern state.[2] This same political and legal need with the same problematic nature can also be seen in strictly theological or religious contexts. In the great monotheistic religions, the Jewish people, the Christian *ecclesia* and the Islamic *ummah* all represent ways of creating the political body's unity (the believers) on which to build the institution or structures for the community's self-regulation.[3]

During decolonization in Africa, constructing political unity as a basis for new states proved to be a very complex problem, which has not yet been satisfactorily resolved. The lack of national homogeneity, the presence of different ethnolinguistic and religious groups, economic discrepancies and backwardness, internal conflicts and separatist tendencies have all contributed to making unstable social and political structures that can be easily manipulated internally and externally. Pronounced nationalism, centralization of power and repression of personal and collective freedom have almost always been a part of the political action of various governing elites, even as a means to compensate for the incurable lack of homogeneity.[4]

In South Africa, the process of constructing the political body's unity featured significant political and symbolic elements, such as the radical break from apartheid as a political form. One of apartheid's main features was a forced division and differentiation of the political body. In fact, apartheid's institutionalized racial discrimination was founded on the principle of inequality and a social hierarchy based on racial categories – in order to regulate *ad escludendum* access to socioeconomic and political citizenship. For this reason, unity of the people through a new and equal South African citizenship symbolized a radical break from the segregationist state.[5] The polarization of South African society developed not only along racial lines between the native and European populations (between blacks and whites), but also within these two groups. The Dutch and British populations have a history of violent conflicts, and their respective ethnic, linguistic and nationalistic claims were a feature of South Africa's political evolution. Similarly, the black population is a complex and heterogeneous entity; ethnic, linguistic and cultural differences are not simply confined to the historically hostile opposition between the Xhosa and Zulu peoples, but also include other groups that today have citizenship under the new constitutional order.[6] In addition, there is an Indian social segment that settled in South Africa over the course of the nineteenth and twentieth centuries (which gradually received property rights) as well as ethnoracial groups created by miscegenation. Last but not least, South Africa continued to receive immigration waves from Europe.

Post-apartheid South Africa, just like all African states, had to face challenges that seemed insurmountable. For this reason, its political and constitutional transition has been defined as 'miraculous', sometimes to the point of exaggeration.[7] The forces able to produce group fragmentation and conflicts seemed to outweigh unifying forces. This imbalance between fragmentation and cohesion explains the need to use formal legal procedures and symbolic political methods in order to make the unity of the new South African people possible.

During the negotiated transition, an effort was made to neutralize rigid points of view and the most extreme differences.[8] More specifically, this effort consisted in merging – at times in a forced way – the ethnopolitical differences in a shared vision of the new democratic constitution and its principles. Any attempt to spark differences between the various political actors or to create new social or political divisions had to be blocked. This choice of political action, mostly promoted by the African National Congress (ANC), was gradually accused of being nationalist and in favour of a centralized state with strong directive influence.

The reason for using the expression 'constructing' when describing the political body requires some explanation. It refers to the juridical and political will of some of the political elite (black and white) that led the transition. In other words, considering the multifaceted composition of South African society, the creation of the political body's unity in reality was the result of a rational process of social and constitutional engineering. This objective of this process was to lay the groundwork for the peaceful coexistence of different social groups. This unwavering political will corresponded to a clear vision of the post-apartheid state's new form and the democratic constitution, and it set in motion a very complex juridical, political and social process. Its results still require evaluation. As opposed to its predecessor, the new post-apartheid people were unified through a new sense of nationalism built around the political symbol of the Rainbow Nation. The need for unity led to the creation of an ambiguous political process involving the common ideals of the struggle for freedom, such as equality and democracy, which were to be spread top-down by the political elite. When in power, the political elite sometimes turned their back on the principles of solidarity.[9]

Unity as Collective Acceptance of Post-apartheid Constitutional Principles

The concept of the political body's unity is not used here for the sake of reflecting on contractualism or neo-contractualism. In other words, the analysis of the genesis of the post-apartheid state is not to be placed within the scheme of differing notions of political body's unity such as Hobbes's 'radical-absolutist' notion of unity-representation,[10] Locke's 'liberal' concept of unity and 'contract', Rousseau's idea of general will and the criticism of Sièyes, Kant, Fichte, Feuerbach and Hegel.[11] Even though the classic concepts of contractualist political philosophy, such as contract, unity of the political body, representation and sovereignty, are still a fundamental starting point, the concept of unity of the political body employed here has a distinctively legal and constitutional nature. It is based on unified consent regarding the principles embodied in the new post-apartheid constitution. Thus, the concept of unity used in this study incorporates: 1) the idea of unity through controlling the centrifugal forces of social division and territorial disintegration – the claim of common citizenship was the main response to this issue; 2) the idea of unity in terms of creating the acceptance of a new constitution founded on shared values (basically formal and substantive equality) that were a radical break from apartheid's legal system and political form. For this reason, it is fundamental to reflect on the procedural techniques and methods enacted by the transition's dominant political forces in order to generate consent on the new constitution's contents. Indeed, the principles codified by the new constitution had to satisfy, convince and be accepted by everyone.

According to the analysis proposed here, unity arises in the form of identification, acceptance and sharing of new democratic values subsequently formalized in the text of the democratic constitution. As a result, we can view constructing the political body's unity as a process of gradually increasing the acceptability of the new basic rules (legal rules) establishing the post-apartheid state.[12] However, for the constitution-making process in question, not only was it necessary to obtain collective acceptance of the final product (the constitution), but the decision-making methods and procedures for the constitution's adoption also had to be acceptable. As a result, the real problem here consists of analysing the strategies, methods and procedures for constructing acceptance of the constitution as a group of basic rules, as well as the procedures for attaining its adoption without creating divisions or strain.[13]

The Dogma of National Unity, Common Citizenship and the Political Myth of the Rainbow Nation

As stated before, the political form of the segregationist regime was based on division and discrimination, whereas constructing the unity of the political body and the state was the underlying idea of the post-apartheid political form. The ANC would become the main promoter of this political form, and its political and constitutional ideas were already apparent by the end of the 1980s with its publication *Constitutional Guidelines*.[14] Represented by the political symbol of the Rainbow Nation, the concept of unity is the underlying idea of the break from the segregationist system both on a political and legal level. Ever since the Freedom Charter, the concept of unity has been one of the most important political messages transmitted by the ANC. In fact, during the second half of the twentieth century, some of the universalist characteristics of the ANC's pan-Africanist ideology merged with important legal principles as part of the fight against institutionalized discrimination.[15] One of its central features was based on the idea that the ethnoracial, linguistic, cultural and religious groups coexisting in South Africa could be incorporated into a single state identity. They all would belong to this identity through a common citizenship (today symbolized by the Rainbow Nation), created, in turn, by the recognition of individual and collective rights. The ANC's political and social vision was trapped for a long time between Afrikaner nationalism (and its demand for a *Volksstaat Afrikaner*) and Zulu ethnonationalism (and its demand for an independent *Zulu Land* in the KwaZulu Natal Province).[16] The difference between the universalist idea promoted by the ANC and the relativist idea promoted by the National Party (NP) and the Inkatha Freedom Party (IFP) took on a legal format during the constitution-making process when a choice had to be made as to whether to create a centralized or a federal state (supported at length by the NP's and IFP's ethnonationalism).[17] In reality, requesting a federal state was a request for a juridical formalization of refusing to form the unity of the political body. A territorial subdivision not based on decentralized local bodies (the provinces) but based on areas with increasing degrees of sovereignty had the ultimate aim of creating, more or less artificially, ethnically uniform enclaves and continuing radical relativism.[18] Although through compromise it accepted some relativist changes, the ANC's universalist vision eventually triumphed at the end of the constitution-making process. On a political and symbolic level, the myth of the Rainbow Nation described this attempt to create unity out of a society containing deep differences.[19]

Two opposing ideas of constructing the political body (the people), citizenship and state clashed right from the early phases preceding the constitutional transition: the idea of an ethnic nation and the idea of a civic nation.[20] These ideas had radically different criteria for defining an individual's belonging to a group (the nation); the choice between ethnicizing and 'secularizing' (in the sense of ethnically 'neutral') the public sphere was a core issue of the constitution-making process. Basically, the new state could have been designed as a public space where groups interacted (group belonging determined at birth) or as a public space for actions of individuals, who nevertheless maintained their group belonging, recognized and protected by the state through the constitutionalization of collective rights. Each of these was open to criticism and risks. On the one hand, there was the risk that groups could generate centrifugal forces that would eventually weaken the unity of the political body; on the other hand, a forced universalization could arbitrarily deny collective entities individual rights of belonging (based on identity, language, religion and culture). These visions of the political body pay tribute to distinct philosophical and juridical conceptions of constructing the political body, the most apparent of which are the realist theory and the normativist theory for defining the political body, both areas of bitter dispute.

An evaluation of the consequences of these processes at play during the genesis of post-apartheid South Africa must consider the risks related to creating political myths.[21] As has been widely studied, political myths are capable of triggering processes that invent or manipulate the concepts of people and ethnicity.[22]

The construction of the Rainbow Nation sprang from the need to symbolically define the post-apartheid political body and required clear legal and constitutional structures, which would become a characteristic of post-apartheid constitutionalism. There were numerous intricate constitutional rules and supervising constitutional bodies that endeavoured to make the Rainbow Nation a legal reality. Even though the political idea of a Rainbow Nation was founded on the notion of a universalist, common citizenship, it is nevertheless mitigated by a strong interest in protecting group rights. The post-apartheid constitutional plan tends to find a balance between universalist and relativist elements for creating unity so as not to repress particularist impulses.

Section 3 of the 1996 Constitution states in the first subsection: 'There is a common South African citizenship.' The second and third subsections provide equal rights, privileges and benefits for all as well as duties and responsibilities. As such, citizenship is juridically formalized as a double bond binding individuals to a political body: entitlement to constitutional rights connected to citizenship, which, in turn, corresponds to duties and responsibilities on the part of the citizen.

Constitutional rules balancing a universalist political citizenship with group recognition are sanctioned by the Bill of Rights of the 1996 Constitution.[23] The third subsection of s. 9, which deals with equality, provides new and broader parameters for prohibiting discrimination. Aside from the classic categories protected from discrimination such as race, sex, language, culture and religion, s. 9 also constitutionalizes pregnancy, marital status, ethnic or social origin, sexual orientation, age and disability as categories that cannot be discriminated against.

Sections 30 and 31, respectively titled 'Language and Culture' and 'Cultural, Religious and Linguistic Communities', help to establish the relationship between individuals, nations and intermediate groups. Section 30 recognizes and protects the right to belong to communities aside from the national community. This recognition translates into the right to use the language and to participate in the cultural life of a particular community. Exercising this right, however, must not clash with the Constitution.

Section 31, in some ways a repetition of the preceding section, expressly authorizes that individuals belonging to a cultural, religious or linguistic community may not be denied the collective right to practise their religion, use their own language or form religious, cultural and linguistic associations, as long as this is consistent with the Constitution.

As provided by the Constitution, the rights protecting communities or subgroups within the Rainbow Nation are not absolute. First of all, these rights must be exercised in accordance with the Constitution. Second, these rights are subject to balancing and limitation expressly provided by s. 36. Section 37(5) contains a special table listing 'Non-Derogable Rights', which do not include collective rights. All of this shows how the right to act as individuals belonging to a sub-community receives constitutional protection, even if this is hierarchically subordinate to other principles. The prohibition to act in contrast with the Constitution and particularly the Bill of Rights officially recognizes the prevalence of a unitary constitutional order based on a universalist definition of citizenship. However, this same order includes and regulates many forms of relativism and particularism without ever derogating from the universalist nature of the Bill of Rights.[24]

In this context, the attempt to create unity out of the ethnolinguistic diversity of the South African political body can be seen in the new state's active commitment to recognizing and protecting the plurality of languages spoken in South Africa and cultures organized in specific communities. The state recognizes eleven official languages as part of its commitment to promoting and protecting multilingualism as a fundamental feature of a multiethnic post-apartheid constitutionalism.[25] In fact, s. 6 of the 1996 Constitution provides that the following are the official languages of the new republic: 'Sepedi, Sesotho, Setswana, SiSwati, Tshivenda, Xitsonga, Afrikaans, English, isiNdebele, isiXhosa and isiZulu.' The second subsection of s. 6 orders that the new state recognize the discrimination that the indigenous languages have historically been subject to and that it must 'take practical and positive measures' to recognize and protect languages whose use and status have traditionally been marginalized.

According to the third subsection of s. 6, state, provincial and municipal institutions have to take steps to officially protect multilingualism (making use of at least two of the official languages in the public sphere) based on the ethnolinguistic composition of their territory. The Constitution[26] grants these local bodies the ability to use legislative measures in order to 'regulate and monitor their use of official languages. Without detracting from the provisions of subsection (2), all official languages must enjoy parity of esteem and must be treated equitably'. To make these constitutional principles effective, s. 6(5) provides for the creation of a special body for multilingual policies regarding the official languages and other languages that are to be recognized and protected, despite the fact that they are not official state languages.[27] In fact, this subsection states that the Pan South African Language Board (PanSALB), established by national legislation, must promote the development and use of all the official languages.

The PanSALB was formed during the transition from the 1993 Interim Constitution (which already included in s. 3 the norm later adopted in s. 6 of the 1996 Constitution) to the definitive 1996 Constitution. With Law 59/1995, the PanSALB became active during the constitution-making process.[28] Such a vast multilingual policy is still difficult to implement today (even if, for example, the Western Cape Province included in its provincial constitution the obligation of institutions to use the area's three main languages: Xhosa, Afrikaans and English). Nevertheless, these constitutional measures use an openly symbolic register. Indeed, just like the political symbol of the Rainbow Nation, multilingual and other policies for including the different ethnocultural communities in the new citizenship demonstrate the attempt to activate dynamics using constitutional engineering and legal constructions that would eventually lead to the unity of the political body.

As part of the same sphere of protection, the post-apartheid Constitution provided for the creation of another constitutional body for the protection of various communities: the Commission for the Promotion and Protection of the Rights of Cultural, Religious and Linguistic Communities (s. 185 and 186).[29]

The Volkstaat Council (VC) is an additional constitutional body that was created over the course of the constitution-making process. It was founded on the basis of s. 184A and B(1)(a)(b) of the Interim Constitution, and the Volkstaat Council Act 30/1994 governs its functions. Subsequently, s. 20(5) of Schedule 6 of the 1996 Constitution incorporated this body, granting it the status of a constitutional institution. The Repeal of Volkstaat Council Act 30/2001 recently defined further the body's tasks and functions.

The organization was made up of twenty Parliament-elected members and had the purpose of exploring the creation of an ethnically homogeneous

(Afrikaner) sub-national entity within the territory of the new South African Republic. Even though it seems contradictory to the underlying principles of the new constitutional order, the reasoning behind the VC was to co-opt large segments of the political body otherwise capable of engaging in seditious and disruptive activities. The basic objective was to gradually construct the political body's unity by accepting the existence of political positions antithetical to the universalist vision promoted by the ANC. Formally, the VC had no binding decision-making power, but merely the ability to offer consultation and carry out research. During the constitution-making phase, the VC was able to submit opinions and reports to the Constitutional Assembly and to the Commission on Provincial Government, whereas after the adoption of the definitive Constitution, it continued to be a consultative body, working in particular with provincial and local institutions. Its purpose was to measure the viability of creating ethnically uniform Afrikaner enclaves (within the Gauteng, North West and Mpumalanga provinces) with broad autonomy (according to the constitutional principle of self-determination).

Active in 1995, the VC started an advocacy campaign towards transitional institutions and members of the new multiracial Parliament in order to create this type of state. A series of reports written by the VC containing research results were published annually. In reality, the VC's political and symbolic function seems to outweigh its legal and constitutional function. Its creation can in fact be traced back to a strategy for including all ethnic, linguistic and group components within the new, united political body. This strategy created political spaces for dialogue between extremely different interests (such as the nationalist, secessionist and differentialist impulses of the Afrikaner population).

Constructing the political body's unified identity in such a way as to protect the affiliations between individuals and sub-national entities (groups and communities) required the creation of institutions that could strengthen the constitution-making process. These institutions were created when the Constitutional Assembly was still in control of this process. They were established in order to create the preconditions for drafting the new democratic Constitution. In other words, they had to act in such a way as to encourage the creation of a social fabric willing to accept and recognize itself in the Constitution.[30]

Unity through the Technique of (Pre-)Constitution-making Negotiations: a Clash between Different Theories

How the new constitution was drafted is a distinctive feature of South African post-apartheid constitutionalism. The pre-constitution-making negotiations coincided with numerous constituent facts and were the phase in which the transition's protagonists were able to reach a compromise about their different visions of state and government.[31]

Drafting the new constitution was the result of a long series of steps.[32] Not only was there the problem of writing down a new constitution, but there were also issues regarding the fixing of rules for accepting political decisions and their legal-constitutional formalization. As a result, preconditions had to be established so that constituent power could be effectively exercised. Establishing these preconditions led to a juridification or proceduralization of the exercise of constituent power.[33] The South African experience appears to deviate from the classic idea of a constitution written in a single moment through the work of representatives who meet in a body based on the powers granted to them by a unitary political body that is already perfectly formed. In the case of South Africa, it seems that the process of writing the constitution was complex and based on a succession of constituent facts and acts. The latter were adopted by different institutions that all exercised constituent power to varying degrees and in different ways. The decisions made by these bodies produced constitutional material which gradually settled into the post-apartheid constitutional order.

Fully decoding the transition's events requires more than just an analysis of its legal and formal qualities. The transition should also be read in its historical and political context. The transition took place through negotiations according to methods that had already been experimented with in other twentieth-century regime transitions. Studying constituent facts allows us to understand the constituent acts, demonstrating the ability of constitutional models to adapt to the social and cultural context.

In South Africa, political power was gradually transferred to the black population through negotiations between and co-participation of the government led by the NP (supporters of apartheid) and the national liberation movements.[34] The regime was in crisis due to political and economic failure, a lack of international legitimacy, distorted geopolitical relations once the opposition of blocs disappeared and constant pressure from liberation movements. Nevertheless, regime followers fought to have an active role in establishing the new order by threatening a non-peaceful transition. As a result, the new order also took form constitutionally because the creators and supporters of the segregationist system participated, and without their contribution the democratic transition probably would not have ended in a peaceful way.[35]

Over the course of the negotiations, the threat of internal violence, the desire for revenge and ethnoracial hatred (which in some ways recalls the *state of nature*)[36] often determined the political decisions of the negotiator. Nelson Mandela himself recognized the difficult political situation in 1991, stating that: 'Despite our own heroic efforts, we have not defeated the regime. Consequently, we see negotiations as a continuation of the struggle leading to our central objective: the transfer of power to the people.'[37]

The fight against apartheid began to take on a substantially different shape with the beginning of the negotiations. Politics began to slowly replace weapons (even if political violence continued to claim thousands of victims until the mid 1990s);[38] the language of constitutional law became the syntax and shared language for articulating a new kind of communication.[39] A rigid constitution whose contents could be discussed and negotiated was a form of last defence for the Afrikaner oligarchy. In fact, the crisis of the apartheid system was already evident by the end of the 1980s, and the only way to control the crushing demographic force of the black population was by instituting a new constitutional order. If writing a new constitution was the culminating moment of the battle for civil and political rights for the liberation movements, for the white oligarchy it constituted a form of protection for the future. In this context, constitutionalism – as an instrument for legally formalizing political mediation in a written constitution – became a meeting ground between opposing interests.

During the twentieth century, South Africa had experienced significant constitutional events. From the foundation of the South African Union in 1910 to the formation of the Republic of South Africa in 1961, up to the last major constitutional reform in 1983 (with the creation of the Tricameral Parliament),[40] the 'battle over the Constitution' had already begun to expose the problematic relations between the Afrikaner and British populations and, later, between the white oligarchy and the black majority.[41]

As such, the distinguishing feature of post-apartheid constitutionalism is a constituent compromise between opposing constitutional conceptions reached through negotiations. Choices had to be made about whether to create a unitary or federal state, a majoritarian government or one based on power-sharing,[42] writing a constitution through a multiparty convention with a fixed number of delegates for every accredited political organization or through the constituent power exercised by an elected constitutional assembly in which the black majority would have an overwhelming demographic power due to race-based voting.

There are other substantial historical and legal variables involved in the constitution-making process to consider. These variables weighed on the negotiations, re-creating traditional polarizations between the different communities of the South African political body. The South African legal system contains elements that clearly show its hybrid nature, being a system that historically integrated two different legal cultures: Romano-Germanic elements (due to Dutch colonization of the Cape Province, starting in the seventeenth century) and elements of British common law (as a result of British colonization).[43] This double influence inevitably affected South Africa's constitutional order. Its contradictions appeared frequently throughout the process of writing the new constitution and took a political form that was often difficult to interpret. For example, the creation of the Constitutional Court (and the introduction of centralized judicial review) encountered serious scepticism in judicial and legal milieus heavily influenced by the British legal tradition.[44]

African National Congress's Universalist Constitutionalism

'One person, one vote in a unitary state' was the ANC's slogan for its idea of constitutionalism;[45] the constitutional model that the ANC historically demanded was for a unitary state under majority rule,[46] the pooling and control of resources, and the effective exercise of executive power (without the overlapping, contradictions or repetitions of a federated state). Its main objective was to gradually reduce economic disparities and to create a social state that would ensure the enjoyment by all citizens of economic and social rights in addition to civil and political rights. From an economic perspective, the ANC especially criticized the exorbitant costs of a federal model, claiming that the limited resources available had to be allocated to redistribution policies benefiting the black population (which is today still very far from being completed). However, the issue underlying the ANC's preference for a unitary and centralized constitutional model related to the desire to contain ethnoracial centrifugal forces that could have been fuelled by a federal model with territorial enclaves based on ethnicity.[47] Furthermore, the ANC associated the federal model with the racist and discriminatory policies that created the African Homelands[48] from which the inhabitants could not move freely. Throughout the negotiations, the ANC gradually accepted the idea of a decentralized model which would enable the creation of local bodies (provinces and municipalities) with executive and legislative powers (based on the distribution of competences provided by Schedule 5(a)(b) of the 1993 Constitution, and s. 44 and 104 of 1996 Constitution) but without allowing the term 'federalism' to be mentioned in the drafts of the Constitution.[49] Basically, the ANC's constitutionalists feared that a federal model based on federated states determined by ethnic concentration would have contributed to further fragmentation within the political body. Consequentially, the idea of constructing the political body's unity meant creating a unitary state with a de-ethnicized constitution and re-mapping the decentralized government.[50]

In terms of the actual government structure, at the start of the negotiations, the ANC's constitutional model consisted of a President of the Republic elected by Parliament who would exercise executive power in conjunction with the government and the Prime Minister, who would be responsible to Parliament. The Parliament would have been a bicameral body including the National Assembly and the Senate. However, the cornerstone of the ANC's constitutional system was a Bill of Rights – influenced mainly by the Canadian Charter of Rights and Freedoms – that included a list of fundamental individual and group rights, the violation of which could be directly punished.[51] The objective of maximum enforcement of the Bill of Rights led to constitutionalizing the principle that everyone, as an individual or as a group, has the right to direct protection of the rights contained therein (s. 38 of the 1996 Constitution).[52]

Introducing a centralized system of constitutional justice with the institution of the Constitutional Court is another distinguishing element of the ANC's liberal-democratic constitutionalism.[53] These constitutional guidelines began to be formalized by the ANC at the end of the 1980s in the Lusaka statement of 1 March 1988, at a time when the organization was still banned.[54]

National Party's and Inkatha Freedom Party's Relativist Constitutionalism

The NP and the Inkatha Freedom Party (IFP) (the Zulu nationalist party) were two of the most important protagonists of the pre-constitution-making negotiations. They both gave voice to a similar constitutional model, which was the opposite of the ANC's.

The NP set out to defend the Afrikaner population's economic privileges and top government positions. During the negotiations, it focused on the problem of reforming the structure of the public administration. As mentioned above, choosing between a federal or unitary state was the central issue of the political debate. The NP proposed a decentralized system that would give the provinces a wide range of exclusive competences and broad financial and fiscal autonomy. Within this framework, Afrikaner constitutionalism intended to give the central state sole powers regarding defence, national security and foreign policy. All the other competences were to be left to the provinces, including drafting provincial constitutions, unicameral legislative bodies and executive bodies under a Prime Minister. Any potential review of the national constitution on the matters of provincial competences and powers could be exercised only with the agreement of the provincial parliaments through a two-thirds majority vote. The President of the Republic's powers under the NP's constitutional model was quite limited, and the national executive power was based on the model of power sharing (or consociational model). The national legislative body would be elected according to a purely proportional system.[55] According to this model, executive power would have been shared by the main political actors within the political body and subject to the veto of political parties represented in the government. During the drafting of constitution proposals to be presented at the negotiations, the NP and the IFP were influenced by the important public law scholar Arendt Lijphart. Lijphart's theories often turn to federal and power sharing models as the only effective constitutional paradigm for societies with multicultural or multiethnic components and an extremely fragmented political body.[56]

The IFP and its political leader Buthelezi embraced this constitutional model at the beginning of the 1980s.[57] As a result, Afrikaner and Zulu nationalism found common territory in constitutional proposals: shared political intentions requiring a precise political and constitutional form. Continuity with differentialist logic is evident here. The issue of protecting minorities and collective rights was used to depict a society conceived of as a mosaic of groups to which individuals would be bound by birth. However, South Africa had already experienced the latent risks in terms of instability and conflict of this type of society.

Unity through Fragmentation of the Constituent Act

The constitution-making process and procedure are respectively composed of facts and acts; the former are social, political and military, whereas the latter are legal and constitutional.

South Africa's constitution-making procedure was regulated by interim and definitive constituent acts. These legal measures defined the decision-making methods for the definitive Constitution, the mechanisms for attributing constituent power, fundamental content of the new text as well as indicating a court (the Constitutional Court) entitled to check that the negotiated rules of the constitution-making procedure were respected.

A more thorough understanding of this transitional element calls for an examination of the concept of *decision-making*. The fact that the norms regulating the procedure were not previously codified but were deliberately not in compliance with the rules of the 1983 Constitution in force, means that they were in discontinuity with past legal orders from a substantive point of view. In other words, from a constitutional point of view, the new democratic constitutional order was not the result of an Amendment procedure, but it was a clean break from the past.

This dynamic seems to have provided the constitution-making process with the scope to gradually reduce the violent contrast between opposing positions. As such, it became an instrument for merging the different relativist points of view into a shared political and constitutional vision.

The main question is who had the power to make decisions during the constitution-making procedure and based on what norms? Our analysis will focus on the actions of different organizations that exercised de facto powers (including the government in power) and that mutually recognized each other as actors in the constitution-making procedure.

The procedure was agreed upon through negotiation without any normative reference to the previous legal and constitutional order. For this reason, the procedure seems to be a kind of suspension of or exception to the rules in force, a typical feature when creating a new order. It does not belong to an area in which events can be foreseen and governed on the basis of formalized rules (positive legal norms that tend to control events). Instead, in this phase positive legal norms are not yet operative, as they are still under construction. The scenario is left to the action of charismatic forces, decisions of constitution-making entities (political parties, liberation movements, lobbies)[58] and extraordinary facts occurring only at the constituent moment. In this framework, it is important to reflect on the concept of decision-making. Referring to Carl Schmitt's work seems inevitable, especially regarding the connection made by him between decision and sovereignty.[59]

The discontinuity and continuity with the previous political and constitutional order reveal the legal void between the two contradictory moments of the South African constitution-making experience. On the one hand, a radical break was made from the apartheid constitutional order; on the other hand, some elements of the segregationist regime remained. Even though the constitution-making procedure actually took place in a normative void because no reference was made to the previous regime's positive legal norms, the negotiations were held by the apartheid government (elected under the 1983 Constitution that institutionalized the segregationist regime) just as the tricameral Parliament elected in 1990 (under the apartheid regime) guaranteed ordinary state administration up until the first universally elected Parliament (1994) came into power. Even the judiciary (though subject to severe criticism) continued to exercise judiciary power, incorporating criminal law reforms that gradually erased the innumerable discriminatory and illiberal norms of the criminal law system.

This course of events created an underlying ambiguity: the old segregationist regime's institutions officially participated in dismantling the apartheid constitutional order and in building the new order, whereas producing 'rules on the rules' took place in a legal void. Two almost parallel activities seem to be at work here: the constitution-making process and procedure gradually produced facts and acts that, in turn, gave form to constitutional material. The constitutional material was immediately applied in part by the old institutions and, simultaneously, in part by the new institutions created before the adoption of the definitive Constitution. It is interesting to note that the main institutions of the apartheid state (government, parliament and judiciary) participated in their own dismantling.[60] Negotiations (and therefore also politics) filled the gap separating the country's deconstruction and construction. As a result, looking at strictly normative tools for an in depth understanding of the constitution-making process is not entirely effective.[61] For this reason, it is important to analyse the various decision-making moments that led to constituent facts and in turn produced legal formalizations that can be defined as constituent acts.[62]

The need for a constitution-making procedure defined this way was rooted in the transitional political context in which a state of political paralysis had to be resolved. The ANC proposed a procedure in a series of steps which would later be described, regulated and formalized as follows: 1) the organization of a multiparty conference that would set out the rules for instituting a Constitutional Assembly; 2) the approval at the conference of an interim constitution that would be the basis for holding the first universal elections. These elections would create the new Parliament, which would then form the Constitutional Assembly for drafting and adopting the definitive constitution; 3) the consociational adoption through the multiparty conference of a series of meta-constitutional principles that would define the exercise of constituent power.

We can subdivide the constitution-making process into three moments in which constituent facts or acts predominated. The first moment consisted of decisions concerning the redefinition of political crimes and political prisoners. The purpose of this phase was to enable leaders of the national liberation movements and the organizations to which they belonged to become constituent actors. The second moment comprised a series of decisions for keeping political violence under control. Constituent facts dominated these two phases. The third moment was characterized by decisions that produced interim and definitive constituent acts. The actual adoption of the definitive Constitution in 1996 took place in a subsequent phase, which began with the transformation of the Parliament elected in 1994 into the Constitutional Assembly. The Assembly adopted a decision-making policy similar to the legislative process. The constitutional text was in fact discussed, adopted and sanctioned according to a law-making process that we could define as a constitutional-legislative procedure, subject to review by the Constitutional Court.

Phases Dominated by Constituent Facts

It is difficult to identify the moment at which the decision was made to create a new constitution and at which, as a result, the political transition began. President F.W. De Klerk's historical opening speech before Parliament on 2 February 1990 is generally considered to be the process's symbolic beginning. De Klerk announced his government's decision to transform the apartheid regime, to rescind the prohibition of national liberation movements and to release Nelson Mandela. The date of 10 December 1996, the day on which Nelson Mandela as President of the Republic signed the definitive Constitution, is usually considered to be the process's end. Nevertheless, constituent facts preceded and followed these six years that led to the Constitution's adoption.

Many historical studies have demonstrated the political importance of the secret negotiations between the apartheid government and the ANC, which began in the late 1980s.[63] These negotiations took place in England, Switzerland and Zambia and slowly built a climate of trust between adversaries, demonstrating that negotiation was the only kind of change possible.[64] While discussing his *Five Years Plan of Action* during the 1989 electoral campaign, De Klerk mentioned wanting to negotiate a new constitutional order with those who 'desire peace'.[65] The NP did not easily accept De Klerk as candidate for the presidential elections after P.W. Botha (a staunch supporter of apartheid) had abandoned politics, especially considering the new political plan. The ANC echoed this statement in its famous Harare Declaration.[66] The convergence of these two intentions can be traced back to a fundamental constituent fact: creating a new constitutional order. Even if the decision to transform the segregationist regime appears to be a unilateral NP decision, that decision can be examined only in light of the positive response to the objectives (a new constitution and dismantling apartheid) of other de facto constituent actors such as Mandela's ANC. The manifestation of will similar to a contract turned into a fundamental form of acceptance.

The First Phase: Removal of Obstacles

The transition's 'removal of obstacles phase' was a series of important constituent facts in the form of agreements. The first agreements regarding negotiations had the following objectives: a) to enable organizations to be constituent actors; b) to dismantle the laws and legal system of apartheid; c) to prepare the first phase of transitional justice.

Regarding the first objective, negotiations redefined the notions of political crime and common crime in order to legalize *ex post* behaviour and offences (the militancy of banned liberation movements, the expression of political ideas, civil disobedience, etc.) that were considered to be crimes under apartheid. These constituent facts belong to the redefinition of legality under the segregationist constitutional order.

This was a politically delicate and agitated phase: the NP, under pressure from public opinion and the Afrikaner nationalist right, had an ambivalent approach. On the one hand, it negotiated the freedom of political prisoners and the return of exiles; on the other hand, still formally running the government, it delayed enforcing the agreements. Prisoners and exiles remained political criminals and not victims of apartheid. This phase was finally completed due to threats by the liberation movements to use means of radical opposition; it culminated with the legal formalization of two agreements (the Groote Schurr Minute and the Pretoria Minute) and Parliament's approval of amnesty laws for freeing political prisoners.[67]

The Groote Schurr Minute was signed by De Klerk's government and the ANC during negotiations in May 1990 in Cape Town. This agreement formalized the government's commitment to freeing political prisoners and enabling exiles to return. The main problem was defining the legal criteria for determining who would benefit from these measures.[68] The Pretoria Minute included further details about the May 1990 terms of agreement and recorded the commitment, made by Nelson Mandela, to continue the negotiations peacefully and unilaterally suspend all armed actions.[69] On 2 February 1991 another agreement was signed: the Malan Accord. This agreement helped to define the terms of the disarmament process. These two agreements were put into effect through the two Indemnity Acts.[70]

There were important requirements for receiving immunity benefits. Every single request for a benefit in accordance with Law 35/90 had to be investigated; the potential recipients of this legal measure included not only the freedom fighters, but also members of the regime's military and police forces. The concept of a political crime was immediately used for all actors of the apartheid 'war'. On the one hand, this reflected the political nature of the negotiations; on the other, it foreshadowed the TRC's rationale four years later. In order to obtain the release of many militants, the ANC had to accept similar measures that also benefited members of the regime's military and police force. The contradictory nature of the NP's political conduct (with rather dangerous results) can be seen in a provision unilaterally passed by the tricameral Parliament with executive intervention: the Further Indemnity Act 151 of October 1992.[71] This legislation set out to annul the limitations of Law 35/90 so that the government could protect military and police force members from future criminal trials for crimes committed during apartheid. In fact, according to Act 151/92, the President of the Republic could independently grant amnesty after consulting the National Council of Indemnity (the members of which were nominated by the President). This unilateral gesture fostered unrest and brought the negotiations to a halt. The amnesty procedure provided by this law created contempt and disdain for its secretive decision-making (as well as the secretive hearings in which the applicants were heard), the lack of control over De Klerk's actions and the dropping of obligations to investigate and make the 'pardoned' crimes public, obligations provided by the previous law (the only remaining obligation was the publication of the names of those who benefited from the law). Only Mandela's political authority and strength managed to bridge the ever-widening gap.[72] All of these facts reinforce the underlying argument of this book: transitional justice was a fundamental factor within the constitution-making process. The political framework during this phase in matters of indemnity, remission, pardon and release is both controversial and ambiguous. According to statistics released in March 1995 by the Office for Indemnity, Immunity and Release, a total of 14,002 applications were filled. However, it is difficult to figure out precisely how many people received these benefits and for what offences; in reality, all the parties involved had an interest in concealing the proceedings with flexible and incomplete laws. The following factors made the TRC's activity more difficult: 1) many criminals were already protected from criminal trials; 2) it was impossible to calculate how many would have actually fallen under the TRC's definitive amnesty process; 3) each faction practised a policy of political protection. As a result, some did not present themselves before the TRC in the hopes of less tumultuous forms of amnesty at the conclusion of the Commission's work. [73]

Regarding the second fundamental objective of redefining apartheid's legality, in May 1990 the state of emergency was lifted (except for the province of Natal), apartheid in hospitals was abolished and the multiracial schooling legislation was passed. The following year (June 1991), the tricameral Parliament passed the Abolition of Racially Based Land Measure Bill, which abolished the Land Acts of 1913 and 1936, the 1966 Group Areas

Act and the 1950 Population Registration Act: the legislative foundation stone of apartheid was abrogated.

The Second Phase: Political Violence and Transition Obstacles

The second phase of the process was dominated by the problem of curbing political violence. Historians and sociologists have identified two types of political violence: the conflict between the government and the national liberation movements as well as black on black violence. The latter was a characteristic of the internal conflict within the black community in South Africa, especially between the ANC and the IFP, and between 1989 and 1994 much blood was shed as a result of it.[74]

Black on black political violence was exploited at length by the apartheid government (and the Afrikaner nationalist right) in order to justify the black majority's inadequacy to lead the country. The government had given military support to the IFP to increase the conflict between the two main national liberation movements. Polarization within the black majority was useful for taking away precious energy from the confrontation with the NP government.[75] The investigations of the Commission of Inquiry Regarding the Prevention of Public Violence and Intimidation (known as the Goldstone Commission, the last name of its chairman)[76] and the TRC's investigations later revealed the government's manipulation of the conflict between the ANC and the IFP. Nevertheless, the phase ended with the signing of an agreement: the National Peace Accord of 14 September 1991.[77] It contained a series of fundamental decisions for confining internal conflicts and for reaching a stage in which constituent power could be exercised effectively.

Notes

1. See C. Bonvecchio. 2000. 'Il mito dell'unità e il destino della differenza', in U. Regina (ed.), *La libertà nell'unità delle differenze*. Padua: Il poligrafico, pp. 147–60.
2. On the issue of contractualism, see J.W. Gough. 1956. *The Social Contract. A Critical Study of Its Development*. Oxford: Clarendon Press; G. Duso (ed.). 1993. *Il contratto sociale nella filosofia politica moderna*. Milan: Franco Angeli (in particular the introduction 'Patto sociale e forma politica', pp. 7–49); N. Bobbio. 1980. *Il Contratto sociale oggi*. Naples: Guida; F. Atger. 1906. *Essai sur l'histoire des doctrines du contrat social*. Paris: Alcan. Debates arising from the religious wars in sixteenth- and seventeenth-century Europe and from the seventeenth- and eighteenth-century revolutions led to developments in political philosophy, which in turn provided the theoretical groundwork for the idea of coexistence between deeply fragmented social groups. How to avoid a civil war (Hobbes's state of nature) and how to create bonds that would protect the political body's unity (the social contract according to Hobbes, Locke and Rousseau) were the core issues of modern political and legal philosophy up until the nineteenth century. The modern state's evolution from absolutism to liberal democracy has been accompanied by the constant challenge of maintaining the stability of the political body. For a general overview, see G. Sacerdoti. 2002. *Sacrificio e sovranità. Teologia e politica nell'Europa di Shakespeare*

e Bruno. Turin: Einaudi. Carl Schmitt's writings on Thomas Hobbes are particularly interesting; see C. Schmitt. 1936–37. 'Der Staat als Mechanismus bei Hobbes und Descartes', *Archiv für Rechts- und Sozialphilosophie*, 30 *et seq*; C. Schmitt. 1982. *Der Leviathan in der Staatlehre des Thomas Hobbes. Sinn und Fehlschlag eines politischen Symbols*. Cologne: Hohenheim Verlag; C. Schmitt. 1952. 'Dreihundred Jahre Leviathan', *Universitas*, 7 *et seq*; C. Schmitt. 1965. 'Die Vollendete Reformation Bemerkungen und Hinweise zu neuen Leviathan-Interpretationen', *Der Staat*, 4 *et seq*. See also C. Galli (ed.). 1986. *Carl Schmitt. Scritti su Thomas Hobbes*. Milan: Giuffrè. Pierre Rosanvallon has made a significant contribution to the debate (P. Rosanvallon. 1998. *Le peuple introuvable*. Paris: Gallimard; P. Rosanvallon. 2000. *La démocratie inachevée*. Paris: Gallimard). For an overview of German scholarship on the idea of a people, see M. Ricciardi. 1990. 'Linee storiche sul concetto di popolo', *Annali dell'Istituto storico italo-germanico in Trento* 16: 303–69. On the same concept in the US Declaration of Independence, see T. Bonazzi. 1999. *La Dichiarazione di indipendenza degli Stati Uniti d'America*. Milan: Marsilio, pp. 21–25. On the different ways of defining people (as a foundation stone of the state), see T. Bonazzi. 1998. 'Civic Nation and Ethnic Nation', in A. Krasteva (ed.), *Communities and Identities*, Sophia: Petekston, pp. 64–85.

3. For important insight on the legal, theological or religious inclusion of an individual in a community, see T. Bonazzi (ed.). 2003. *Riconoscimento ed esclusione. Forme storiche e dibattiti contemporanei*. Rome: Carocci.
4. See L. Mezzetti. 2003. *Teoria e prassi delle transizioni costituzionali e del consolidamento democratico*. Padua: CEDAM, pp. 275–422; J. Oloka Onyango (ed.). 2001. *Constitutionalism in Africa. Creating Opportunities, Facing Challenges*. Kampala: Fountain; R. Sacco. 2000. 'Il costituzionalismo africano', *Rivista di diritto pubblico comparato ed europeo* 1: 3–10. G. de Vergottini. 1998. *Le transizioni costituzionali*. Bologna: Il Mulino. pp. 131–32; F. Venter. 1998. 'The Emergence of Constitutionalism in Southern Africa in the Late Twentieth Century', in V. Piergigli and I. Taddia, *International Conference on African Constitutions*. Turin: Giappichelli, pp. 11–24. R. Sacco et al. 1996. *Il diritto africano*. Turin: Utet; P.F. Gonidec. 1996a. 'Constitutionnalismes Africains', *Revue juridique et politique indépendance et coopération* 50: 23–50; P.F. Gonidec. 1996b. *Les systèmes politiques africains*. Paris: Librairie Générale de Droit et de Jurisprudence. For an empirical and theoretical study of the genesis of African states during decolonization and the problematic process of constitutionalization, see D.M. Lavroff. 1976. *Les systèmes constitutionnels en Afrique noire. Les Etats Francophones*. Paris: Pedone; A. Cabanis and M.L. Martin. 1999. *Les Constitutions d'Afrique francophone. Évolutions récentes*. Paris: Karthala. Another interesting study is V.T. Le Vine. 1997. 'The Fall and Rise of Constitutionalism in Africa', *The Journal of Modern African Studies* 35(2): 181–206; and A. Bourgi. 2002. 'L'évolution du constitutionnalisme en Afrique: du formalisme à l'effectivité', *Revue frança̧iase de droit constitutionnel* 52: 721–48.
5. For an analysis of post-apartheid South African citizenship, see V. Federico. 2003. 'La cittadinanza nell'esperienza sudafricana', *Quaderni costituzionali* 1: 113–43.
6. The ethnic and linguistic composition of the black population will be discussed in more depth in the following pages.
7. Numerous studies on South Africa's political and constitutional transition use the word 'miracle' in reference to the gradual reconsideration of the catastrophic previsions made by international analysts on the eve of the negotiations. Many feared an explosion of retaliatory violence towards the population of European origin; see H. Adam and K. Moodley. 1993. *The Negotiated Revolution: Society and Politics in Post-apartheid South Africa*. Johannesburg: Jonathan Ball; J. Cameron-Dow. 1994. *The Miracle of a Freed Nation (South Africa 1990-1994)*. Cape Town: Don Nelson; S. Friedman and D. Atkinson (eds). 1994. *The Small Miracle. South Africa's Negotiated Settlement*. Johannesburg: Ravan Press; A. Sparks. 1994.

Tomorrow Is Another Country. The Inside Story of South Africa's Road to Change. Chicago: University of Chicago Press; M. Lobban. 1997. 'Un accord négocié: le processus constitutionnel en Afrique du Sud depuis 1991', *Revue de droit public* 1: 71–110; P. Olivier. 1995. 'Constitutionality and Society in South Africa: What Sort of Democracy', in G. Conac, F. Dreyfus and J. Montero (eds), *L'Afrique du Sud en Transition. Réconciliation et coopération en Afrique Australe.* Paris: Economica, p. 90. H. Ebrahim. 1998. *The Soul of a Nation. Constitution Making in South Africa.* London, Cape Town: Oxford University Press; R. Spitz and M. Chaskalson. 2000. *The Politics of Transition. A Hidden History of South Africa's Negotiated Settlement.* Johannesburg: Witwatersrand; P. Strand. 2000. *Decisions on Democracy. The Politics of Constitution – Making in South Africa 1990–1996.* Uppsala: Uppsala University Press.

8. See J. de Lange. 2000. 'The Historical Context, Legal Origins and Philosophical Foundation of the South African TRC', in C. Villa-Vicencio and W. Verwoerd (eds), *Looking Back Reaching Forward.* Cape Town: Cape Town University Press, pp. 26 *et seq.*
9. At the end of the constitutional transition, criticism of the ANC establishment in power increased due to its neoliberal policies. These policies were gradually criticized because they seemed to lead to a new form of apartheid based on economic asymmetry. The 'miracle' was replaced by the idea of a betrayal of the ideals behind the struggle for freedom. A wide survey of experiences demonstrates the dramatic economic hardship of the black people today; see A. Desai. 2002. *We Are the Poors. Community Struggles in Post-apartheid South Africa.* New York: Monthly Review Press; H. Marais. 1998. *South Africa: Limits to Change: The Political Economy of Transformation.* London: Zed Press; T. Bramble and F. Barchiesi. 2003. *Rethinking the Labour Movement in the 'New South Africa'.* Aldershot: Ashgate; and N. Nattrass. 1994. 'Controversies about Capitalism and Apartheid in South Africa: an Economic Perspective', *Journal of Southern African Studies* 17: 654–77.
10. For an analysis of Hobbes's complex and fascinating concept of representation behind the idea of the political body's unity and its identification with the sovereign, see C. Galli. 1998. 'Immagine e rappresentanza politica', in C. Galli, *Modernità. Categorie e profili critici.* Bologna: Il Mulino, pp. 53–78. See also B. Accarino. 1999. *Rappresentanza.* Bologna: Il Mulino.
11. For an analysis of these different ways of producing the unity of the political body, see C.E. Vaughan. 1939. *Studies in Political Philosophy before and after Rousseau.* Manchester: Manchester University Press.
12. From the point of view of legal positivism, the most effective theoretical approach for describing the concept of unity referred to here is H.L.A. Hart's theory on the validity of rules and the legal system based on the idea of acceptance of 'secondary' legal rules; see H.L.A. Hart. 1994. *The Concept of Law*, 2nd ed. Oxford: Oxford University Press. In Hart's system, the primary or basic rules are rules establishing that 'human beings are required to do or abstain from certain actions, whether they wish to or not', whereas the secondary rules 'provide that human beings may by doing or saying certain things introduce new rules of the primary type, extinguish or modify old ones, or in various ways determine their incidence or control their operations' (see p. 81). The secondary rules (also called rules of recognition) are used for determining the primary rules of obligation. From this perspective, according to Hart, the fact that primary rules are obligatory (in terms of threat – sanctions – force) does not make a legal system valid. Rather, we should think in terms of the foundation of secondary rules that allow for the creation or modification of primary rules of obligation. According to Hart, the foundation of secondary rules lies in social acceptance or collective sharing of certain rules. At the beginning of Chapter 6, Hart claims that: 'the foundations of a legal system consist of the situation in which the majority of a social group habitually obey the orders backed by threats of the

sovereign person or persons, who themselves habitually obey no one. This social situation is, for this theory, both a necessary and a sufficient condition of the existence of law' (p. 101). Criticizing this idea, Hart demonstrates its inability to account for the salient features of a modern national legal system. In Hart's opinion, in a complex social situation there are secondary rules of recognition that identify primary obligatory or binding rules. For this reason, if secondary rules can identify primary rules, the primary rules' 'validity' (as well as the legal system's validity) is based on respecting criteria provided by secondary rules of recognition. Furthermore, these secondary rules, in the end, are part of the legal system. For an in depth study of the idea of social acceptance of the rules of identification regarding fundamental rights, see G. Palombella. 2002. *L'autorità dei diritti*. Bari: Laterza. On the rules of recognition, see also L. Ferrajoli. 1989. *Diritto e ragione. Teoria del garantismo penale*. Bari: Laterza, p. 353; and M. Atienza and J.R. Manero. 1998. *A Theory of Legal Sentences*. Dordrecht: Kluwer, p. 152.

13. For example, the effort made during the definitive constitution's drafting to include members of different communities and individual citizens in writing the common rules, soliciting comments and suggestions as part of a campaign to spread the constitution-making process; see R. Simeon. 1998. 'Considerations on the Design of Federations: the South African Constitution in Comparative Context', *South African Public Law* 13: 43. See also the documents on public involvement in the Constitutional Assembly's 1996 annual report.
14. Reference is specifically made to ANC. 1989. 'Constitutional Guidelines for a Democratic South Africa', *South Africa Journal on Human Rights* 5; ANC. 1992. *Ten Proposed Regions for a United South Africa*. Cape Town: Centre for Development Studies, University of Western Cape; ANC. 1992. *Constitutional Principles and Structures for a Democratic South Africa*. Cape Town: Centre for Development Studies, University of Western Cape; ANC. 1992. *ANC Regional Policy*. Cape Town: Centre for Development Studies, University of Western Cape; ANC. 1993. *Draft Bill of Rights*. Cape Town: Centre for Development Studies, University of Western Cape.
15. Founded in 1912, the ANC drafted the Freedom Charter as a political manifesto in 1955. On its contents regarding the issue of ethnicity, see A.J.G.M. Sanders. 1989. 'The Freedom Charter and Ethnicity – Towards Communitarian South African Society', *Journal of African Law* 33: 105–15. Black intellectual political tradition and ideas that had been the driving force of the ANC's action for decades are in many ways connected to the liberationist tradition. This ideology formally entered the South African political scene in 1943 with the ANC's adoption of the document Africans' Claims in South Africa and the 1955 adoption of the Freedom Charter. The egalitarian approach was one of the fundamental elements of the liberationist tradition, which called for the state's active role in the redistribution of and access to resources. The liberationist discourse was not limited to collectivism and socialism. The backbone of the liberationist ideology was the idea of having a judicial system capable of reinforcing the individual basic rights written in a Bill of Rights (which also recognized social and economic rights).
16. See D. Darbon (ed.). 1995. *Ethnicité et nation en Afrique du Sud. Imageries identitaires et enjeux sociaux*. Paris: Karthala; S. Ellmann. 1994. 'The South African Constitution and Ethnic Division', *Columbia Human Rights Law Review*, 5 *et seq*; and G. Mare. 1993. *Ethnicity and Politics in South Africa*. London: Zed Books. Even though the NP consistently demanded constitutional recognition of the ethnic identity issue for the entire course of the constitutional transition, the South African Law Commission repeatedly expressed itself to the contrary; see South African Law Commission. 1991. *Project 77: Constitutional Models*.
17. See L. Pegoraro and A. Rinella. 1995. 'Repubblica del Sudafrica: il Constitution Act del 1993 tra "federalismo" e "regionalismo"'. *Quaderni Costituzionali*, 277 *et seq*.
18. See Simeon, 'Considerations on the Design of Federations', pp. 42–71.

19. See J. Degenaar. 1993. 'Nosizwe: the Myth of the Nation', *Indicator South Africa* 10(3): 11–16; R. Wilson. 1996. 'The Siza Will Not Go Away. The Truth and Reconciliation Commission, Human Rights and Nation Building in South Africa', *African Studies* 55(2): 1–20.
20. See H. Adam. 1994. 'Ethnic versus Civic Nationalism: South Africa's Non-Racialism in Comparative Perspective', *South African Sociological Review* 7(1): 15–30. For a general view, see R. Toniatti. 1994. 'Minoranze e minoranze protette: modelli costituzionali comparati', in T. Bonazzi and M. Dunne (eds), *Cittadinanza e diritti nelle società multiculturali*. Bologna: Il Mulino; T. Bonazzi, 'Civic Nation and Ethnic Nation', pp. 64–85. Theoretical problems related to pluralist or multiethnic societies in which there are conflicts related to the variety of values held by each group are analysed in J. Habermas. 1996. *Die Eineziehung des Anderen. Studien zur politischen Theorie*. Frankfurt am Main: Suhrkamp Verlag; and C. Taylor. 1992. *The Politics of Recognition*. Princeton: Princeton University Press. See also P. Carozza. 1994. 'Nazione', *Digesto delle discipline pubblicistiche*, pp. 126–59.
21. Galli's analysis of political myths emphasizes Voegelin's definition of the same concept as a 'political religion' as well as Schmitt's definition from a political/ theological point of view (political and theological categories having similar functions). See C. Galli. 1996. *Genealogia della politica. Carl Schmitt e la crisi del pensiero politico moderno*. Bologna: Il Mulino, p. 547. For a reading of South African political history in terms of mythology, see L. Thompson. 1985. *The Political Mythology of Apartheid*. New Haven: Yale University Press.
22. The relationship between term 'invention' and the concepts of people, identity and nation demonstrates important consequences. Over the past decades, the fields of deconstructivist anthropology, history and sociology have produced numerous studies on the issue of ethnic identity, tradition and culture; for example, see E. Balibar and I. Wallerstein. 1988. *Race, nation, class. Les identités ambiguës*. Paris: La Découverte. For an anthropological point of view, see J.L. Amselle and M'Bokolo. 1985. *Au coeur de l'ethnie*. Paris: La Découverte; A.M. Gentili. 1995. 'Etnia, etnicità e rappresentazioni del conflitto etnico in Africa', *Africa e Mediterraneo* 2: 4–11; for a historical approach, see E. Hobsbawn and T. Ranger. 1983. *The Invention of Tradition*. Cambridge: Cambridge University Press; B. Anderson. 1991. *Imagined Communities*, London: Verso. Anderson claims that nationalism as the glorification of the bond between an individual and a particular community appeared relatively recently as a result of invention and manipulative and creative identity processes. In this context, the artificial concept of the nation and the notion of tradition would no longer be rooted in ancient history, as commonly believed. Analysing the process that led to the concept of nation and its radical extension, nationalism, Anderson notes that these concepts never evolved in Europe; instead, they appeared in geopolitical areas colonized by Europe where different colonial cultures of European origin mixed together and integrated elements of the native cultures with they had contact. This alchemy of identity began to produce an 'image of itself' as a distinct community or nation from the original motherland. Gradually, in an attempt to free themselves culturally and economically, the new nations clashed against the colonial powers that they came from. Anderson, Hobsbawn and Ranger have all helped to reveal the constantly changing mechanism of notions such as nation and tradition. These two in particular are subject to constant manipulation, invention and re-creation for political purposes (see also Carozza, 'Nazione'). This broad perspective enables us to gather more information that is useful for understanding the social *enjeux* of post-apartheid South Africa. In other words, the ANC's attempt to impose a universalist and unified vision of the people falls within the dynamics of imagining or redefining the characteristics of a particular political body's identity. Some South African historians stress the importance of identity redefinition processes during the constitution-making process. They also underline the interdependence, even if

asymmetrical, discriminatory and conflicting, that historically unified South African society. Further thought on the mechanisms of constant transformation and manipulation of social categories can be found in P.A. Taguieff. 1987. *La force du préjugé* Paris: La Découverte.

23. See Degenaar, *The Myth of the Nation*, p. 15.
24. For an analysis of the collective rights in the 1996 Constitution *Bill of Rights*, see R. Orrù. 1998. *La Costituzione di tutti. Il Sudafrica dalla segregazione razziale alla democrazia della Rainbow Nation*. Turin: Giappichelli, pp. 210–11.
25. The census taken in October 1996 counted 40.58 million inhabitants of South Africa. 76.7% classified itself as African; 10.9% as white; 8.9% as coloured and 2.6% as Indian/Asian. The second post-apartheid census was taken in October 2001. The South African population is made up of the following ethnolinguistic groups: Nguni people (which includes the Zulu, Xhosa, Ndebele and Swazi), about two-thirds of the entire population. Then there is the Sotho-Tswana population, which includes Southern, Northern and Western Sotho (Tswana); the Tsonga; the Venda; Afrikaners; the English; Coloureds and Indians in addition to numerically marginal populations of Asian and European origin (which nevertheless maintain a strong cultural and linguistic identity). According to the census, the languages spoken in South Africa are: isiZulu (first language of 22.9% of the population), isiXhosa (17.9%), Afrikaans (14.4%), Sepedi (9.2%) and English (8.6%). This does not change the fact that English is the real lingua franca of South Africa, studied and spoken as a second language by a very large percentage of South Africans. See V. Saks. 1997. 'Multiculturalism, Constitutionalism and South African Constitution', *Public Law* (Winter), 672–92; N. Kamwamgamalu. 1998. 'Aspects of Multilingualism in Post-Apartheid South Africa', *Journal of Cross-Cultural and Interlanguage Communication* 17(2/3): 119–328; G.E. Devenish. 1999b. 'Minority Rights and Cultural Pluralism. The Protection of Language and Cultural Identity in the 1996 Constitution', *Tydskrif vir Hedendaagse Romains-Hollandese* 62: 201–25; L. Du Plessis. 1998. 'Statutory Multilingualism and Textual Conflict Under the 1996 Constitution', *Tydskrif vir Hedendaagse Romains-Hollandese* 61: 276–84; P.J. Visser. 1997. 'Public Schools Based on a Common Language, Culture or Religion not Constitutionally Sanctioned', *Tydskrif vir Hedendaagse Romains-Hollandese* 60: 341–48; L. Du Plessis. 2002. 'Legal and Constitutional Means Designed to Facilitate the Integration of Diverse Cultures in South Africa: a Provisional Assessment', *Stellenbosch Law Review* 3: 369–72.
26. The provisions of s. 6 should be read in conjunction with the measures of Schedule 4 of the 1996 Constitution entitled 'Functional Areas of Concurrent National and Provincial Legislative Competence'. Among these concurrent competences, Schedule 4 expressly includes 'language policy and the regulation of official languages to the extent that the provisions of section 6 of the Constitution expressly confer upon the provincial legislatures legislative competence'.
27. These languages include: '(i) the Khoi, Nama and San languages; and (ii) Sign language; and (b) promote and ensure respect for all languages commonly used by communities in South Africa, including German, Greek, Gujarati, Hindi, Portuguese, Tamil, Telegu and Urdu; and Arabic, Hebrew, Sanskrit and other languages used for religious purposes in South Africa'.
28. See L. Du Plessis. 1999. 'South Africa. Report on Language and Law', in E. Jaime (ed.), *Langue et Droit. XV Congrée International de Droit Comparé*. Brussels: Bruylant, pp. 44–45.
29. These sections determine the Commission's competence regarding monitoring, developing and coordinating nationally the policies for protecting and promoting the rights of cultural, religious and linguistic communities. For an analysis of the functions, compositions and procedures of these bodies, see A. Lollini. 2004b. 'L'isola e l'arcipelago: la Francia ed il Sudafrica post-apartheid come modelli antitetici di

tutela costituzionale di lingue minoritarie e regionali', in A. Lollini (ed.), *Pluralismo linguistico e costituzioni. Un'analisi comparata*. Bolzano: Alpha-Beta, pp. 66–73.

30. The post-apartheid South African experience allows us to reflect on a parliamentary model's ability to confront the problem of building a common ground of shared values and principles when having to start out with extreme social polarization due to the presence of ethnic, religious, linguistic and cultural particularisms within the political body. The problem in South Africa was providing instruments and procedures that could support Parliament's actions as a special body appointed for constructing a general will. During the constitution-making process, the opponents to constructing a unified political body indirectly and unconsciously supported Carl Schmitt's criticism of the parliamentary model (and the liberal model in general). As Schmitt provokingly claims in *Die geistesgeschichtliche Lage des heutigen Parlamentarismus*, the parliamentary system cannot resolve the paradox of relativism and fragmentation that characterizes mass democracies merely by words, dialogue and debate. Simple mediation of rational public discussion and balancing Parliament interests and opinions cannot alone produce the generalization of particularist opinions and reasons. For an analysis of the problems regarding political mediation and representation, see Galli, *La genealogia della politica*.
31. The constitution-making process has often been defined as a 'battle over the Constitution'; see A. Sachs. 1986. 'Towards the Constitutional Reconstruction of South Africa', *Lesotho Law Journal* 2; and S. Gloppen. 1997. *South Africa: the Battle Over the Constitution*. Aldershot: Dartmouth.
32. Italian scholars who have analysed the constitution-making process include Orrù, *La Costituzione di tutti*; and L. Pegoraro and A. Rinella. 1997. 'La nuova Costituzione della Repubblica del Sudafrica (1996-1997)', *Rivista trimestrale di diritto pubblico* 2: 517–52.
33. An analysis of how constituent power is exercised in different constitution-making processes can be found in C. Klein. 1996. *Théorie et pratique du pouvoir constituant*. Paris: Presses Universitaires de France.
34. Adam and Moodley. *The Negotiated Revolution*; Cameron-Dow, *The Miracle of a Freed Nation*; and Z. Yacoob. 1996. 'The Constitution Making Process: An Overview', *The Human Rights and Constitutional Law Journal of Southern Africa* 1(1): 18–24.
35. See Friedman and Atkinson, *The Small Miracle*; Ebrahim, *The Soul of a Nation*; and Spitz and Chaskalson, *The Politics of Transition*.
36. Civil war and the state of nature are looked at jointly by Sacerdoti, *Sacrificio e sovranità*, pp. 15 *et seq*.
37. See N. Mandela. 1991. 'Opening Address to the 48th National Conference of the African National Congress', Durban. Retrieved 31 March 2008 from http://www.anc.org.za/ancdocs/history/mandela/1991/sp910700-02.html. Also quoted in Lobban, 'Un accord négocié', p. 72.
38. On the phenomenon of political violence in South African history and that inevitably marked the political transition, see W. Beinart. 1992. 'Political and Collective Violence in Southern African Historiography', *Journal of Southern African Studies* 18: 455–86; M.E. Bennun. 1993. 'Boipatong and After: Reflections on the Politics of Violence in South Africa', *International Journal of the Sociology of Law* 21: 49–72; C. Manganyi and A. du Toit (eds). 1990. *Political Violence in South Africa*, London: MacMillan; A. Minnaar, I. Liebenberg and C. Schutte (eds). 1998. *The Hidden Hand: Covert Operations in South Africa*, Pretoria: HSRC; A. Rok. 1992. 'Political Violence in South Africa: A Rejoinder to Morris and Hindson', *Review of African Political Economy* 55: 67–83; A. Minnaar, T. Keith and S. Pretorius. 1994. *Unsuspecting Targets – An Analysis of Massacres in South Africa*. Pretoria: HSRC.
39. See D. Heather. 1999. *South Africa Reborn: Building a New Democracy*. London: UCL.

40. See Republic of South Africa Constitution Act 110/1983.
41. With the Boers' defeat in the South African War (called the Anglo-Boer War before the dismantling of apartheid) and the Treaty of Vereeniging (1902), the Cape, Natal (1840), Transvaal (1856) and Orange Free State (1854) colonies formed the Union of South Africa. These territories had previously had forms of self-government created by Boer populations migrating to the North and East (the famous Great Trek) after losing the Cape Colony to the British. The Union adopted a constitutional text that was formally enacted on 31 May 1910 with the South Africa Act approved by the British Parliament. The Constitution followed a Westminster model with an emphasis on parliamentary authority. Legislative power was exercised by the House of Assembly with 121 members (all belonging to the white population), and by a Senate with 40 members. Just like the constitutions of other colonies, the right to vote was based on property (see D. Marais. 1991. *South Africa: Constitutional Development: a Multi-Disciplinary Approach*. Halfway House: Southern Book Publishers). The Union's Constitution was not, however, the first constitutional text to be enforced in the territories today comprising South Africa. The Cape and Orange Free State colonies had already approved two constitutions in 1854, which contained elements of French, American and German constitutionalism. The Cape Colony Constitution provided a system for accessing political rights (in particular the right to vote) without racial discrimination but based on property. The result of course was that few non-Europeans actually had the right to vote for representatives in the legislature. The Orange Free State's Constitution was much more limiting; it did not allow for any equalization between the black and white populations in terms of civil and political citizenship, creating a system with the seeds of institutionalized discrimination. At the end of the century, the union of the Cape Colony, Natal, Transvaal and the Orange Free State was the most important political objective. The violent war between the British and the Boers (1899–1902) acted as an impetus for unification and ultimately led to the Union of South Africa in 1910. The Union came into being under the political, legal and cultural influence of Great Britain (the war's victor). The polarization between the Anglophone population of British origin and the Afrikaners of Dutch origin was already evident. The former wanted to keep the common law constitutional and legal model, whereas the latter demanded a constitutional system based on Roman-Dutch law (see L. Thompson. 1960. *The Unification of South Africa 1902–1910*. London: Oxford Clarendon Press; H.R. Hahlo. 1960. *The Union of South Africa: the Development of Its Laws and Constitution*. London: Stevens & Sons; L. Du Plessis. 1992. *An Introduction to Law*. Cape Town: Juta, pp. 51 *et seq*. In Italian, see P. Biscaretti di Ruffià. 1946. *La Costituzione dell'Unione del Sud-Africa*. Florence: Sansoni). Some forms of discrimination give rise to the Afrikaners' desire to have the Afrikaner language among the Union's official languages (for how the opposition between the British and the Afrikaners later led to the segregationist system and contributed to apartheid's creation once the Boer people were freed from British political power, see L. Thompson, *Political Mythology*). Simultaneously, the ANC, founded in 1912, began to organize the political struggle for defending the rights of non-Western populations (the native and Indian populations). The groundwork of the ANC's constitutionalism began to form in this period. The ANC's political fight, which became concrete with the creation of the United Democratic Front, first aimed to acquire civil and political rights. It is easy to see how the ANC's political ideas were considered subversive throughout the twentieth century up until the democratic transition that began in 1990. The year 1948 marked the electoral victory of the NP, the party representing the Afrikaner electorate, and the transfer of power from the British establishment. For the Afrikaners it was a political and moral revenge which was followed by the transformation of the Union to the Republic of South Africa in

1961. See Pegoraro and Reposo, 'Repubblica del Sudafrica', pp. 197 *et seq*; R. Orrù, *La Costituzione di tutti*, pp. 52–55.

42. See D.L. Horowitz. 1991. *A Democratic South Africa? Constitutional Engineering in a Divided Society*. Berkeley: University of California Press.

43. The first signs of the mixture of these two traditions can be seen in the two Charters of Justice. In 1827 and 1832, two texts containing mostly penal measures were introduced in the Cape Colony. These were legal rules of Roman-Dutch origin applied within an adversarial criminal trial (the British 'trial by jury') system. See H. Hahlo and E. Kahne. 1991. *The South African Legal System and Its Background*, 6th ed. Cape Town: Juta, pp. 237–40 and 575. See also (though somewhat dated but still full of insight) G.T. Morice. 1905. *English and Roman-Dutch Law: Being a Statement of the Differences between the Law of England as Prevailing in South Africa and Some Other of the British Colonies*. London: Butterworths. Ever since, the Charters of Justice elements of these two different legal cultures continued to interact with one another in South Africa, producing important consequences on a strictly constitutional level: see X. Philippe. 1997–98. 'Common Law et droits coutumiers dans le nouvel ordre constitutionnel sud-africain', *Annuaire des pays de l'Océan Indien* XV: 259–81. Philippe stresses how the Constitutional Court, instituted under the new constitutional order, constantly has to harmonize the differences between these two traditions when interpreting the Constitution. Additional elements of indigenous customary law, now constitutionalized in the 1996 Constitution (Chapter 12, s. 211–12), make the Court's work even more complex (*Constitutional Court*: *ANC* v. *Minister of Local Government and Housing KwaZulu Natal, Minister of Traditional and Environmental affairs KwaZulu Natal, Chairman of Traditional Leaders* (1998) (4) BCLR 399 (CC); *Premier of KwZn, Executive Council of Traditional Leaders (KwZn) v. State* (1995) (12) BCLR 1561 (CC); *Bhe v. Magistrate, Khayelitsha and Others* (2004) (1) BCLR 27 (C), in which the Court had to decide on the compatibility of customary succession law with constitutional principles of non-discrimination). On the problem of the hybrid nature of South Africa's legal system, see also G.J. van Niekerk. 1998. 'A Common Law for Southern Africa: Roman Law or Indigenous African Law?', *Comparative and International Law Journal of Southern Africa* 31: 158–73; and A. Lollini. 2005. 'Pluralismo giuridico e ordinamento costituzionale: i Traditional Leaders nella Costituzione della Repubblica del Sudafrica', in S. Baldin (ed.), *Diritti tradizionali e religiosi in alcuni ordinamenti contemporanei*. Trieste: EUT, pp. 9–26.

44. See H. Webb. 1998. 'The Constitutional Court of South Africa: Rights Interpretation and Comparative Constitutional Law', *University of Pennsylvania Journal of Constitutional Law*, 205–83; M. Du Plessis. 2000. 'The Legitimacy of Judicial Review in South Africa's New Constitutional Dispensation: Insights from the Canadian Experience', *The Comparative and International Law Journal of Southern Africa* 33: 227–47.

45. See ANC. 1995. 'Building a United Nation: Discussion Paper and Policy Proposal'. Johannesburg.

46. On the importance of majority rule, see V.J. Belfiglio. 1983. 'How Will Majority Rule Come About in Azania/South Africa?', *Journal of Modern African Studies* 21(3): 509–21.

47. See M.C. Malose Motimele and I. Mmakwena Semenya. 1993. *Constitution for a Democratic South Africa*. Johannesburg: Skotaville.

48. See M.P. Voster, M. Wiechers and D.J. van Vuuren. 1985. *The Constitution of Transkei, Bophuthatswana, Venda, and Ciskei*. Durban: Butterworths. These were actual ethnic nations that gradually received self-government and administration abilities. As compensation for not having political and social citizenship in white South Africa, the black population received forms of citizenship just within the

homelands, resulting in institutionalized segregation. Eventually the Bantustans were granted 'full independence' under apartheid: Transkei in 1976, Bophuthatswana in 1977, Venda in 1979 and Ciskei in 1981.

49. On the dynamics of gradually closing the gap between positions during the negotiations before drafting the constitution, see R. Humphries, T. Rapoo and S. Friedman, 'The Shape of the Country: Negotiating Regional Government', in Friedman and Atkinson (eds), *The Small Miracle*, pp. 148–81; Sparks, *Tomorrow Is Another Country*; Lobban, 'Un accord négocié', pp. 71–110. See also Pegoraro and Rinella, 'Repubblica del Sudafrica', pp. 279 *et seq*.
50. The sociopolitical implications related to a federal model have been analysed by Canadian constitutional scholars due to the complications that the Canadian federal model began to demonstrate. See R. Simeon. 1982. 'Criteria for Choice in Federal Systems', *Queen's Law Journal* 18: 131–57.
51. See N. Haysom. 1991. 'Democracy, Constitutionalism and ANC's Bill of Rights for a New South Africa', *South African Journal of Human Rights* 7: 103 *et seq*.
52. 'The right to approach a competent court, alleging that a right in the Bill of Rights has been infringed or threatened, and the court may grant appropriate relief, including a declaration of rights.' The subjects entitled to ask for court relief for the violation of those rights are: 'a) anyone acting in their own interest; b) anyone acting on behalf of another person who cannot act in their own name; c) anyone acting as a member of, or in the interest of, a group or class of persons; d) anyone acting in the public interest; e) an association acting in the interest of its members.'
53. Among the scholars who contributed to the creation of this vision is Albie Sachs (a supporter of John Rawls's point of view). Sachs, 'Towards the Constitutional Reconstruction of South Africa'; A. Sachs. 1989. 'Post-Apartheid South Africa a Constitutional Framework', *World Policy Journal* 6(3): 503–29; A. Sachs. 1990. *Protection of Human Rights in South Africa*. Cape Town: Oxford University Press; A. Sachs. 1992a. *Advancing Human Rights in South Africa*. Oxford: Oxford University Press; A Sachs. 1992b. 'Affirmative Action and Good Government', in P. Hugo (ed.), *Redistribution and Affirmative Action. Working on the South African Political Economy*. Pretoria: Southern Book Publishers.
54. During this phase, the ANC had already modified its basic constitutional ideas by letting go of a constitutional order rigidly based on the Westminster system and majority rule and embracing the idea proposed by the NP of a rigid constitution (see Friedman and Atkinson, *The Small Miracle*, pp. 7 *et seq*; H. Giliomee and L. Schlemmer. 1989. *From Apartheid to Nation Building*. Cape Town: Oxford University Press). The ANC had already reformulated its Marxist ideology and socialist constitutional model, leaving behind the idea of establishing a socialist economic model. In *The ANC's Discussion Document on Economic Policy* published in 1990, the organization expressly stated that it accepted a mixed model of economic development based on the freedom of economic enterprise and the protection of private property (principles all later constitutionalized) with amendments supporting economic redistribution (see Spitz and Chaskalson, *The Politics of Transition*, pp. 16–18). In order to get the white population to accept a unitary political body, clear economic guarantees had to be made. The ANC's political victory did not lead to expropriation; otherwise the ANC might have risked losing international political support that it had received during apartheid. Placing the new South Africa within the dynamics of the international economic market also had an important role. See J. Dugard. 1978. *Human Rights and the South African Legal Order*. Princeton: Princeton University Press.
55. A. Lijphart. 1987. 'Choosing an Electoral System for Democratic Elections in South Africa, an Evaluation of the "Principal Options"', *Critical Choices for South African Society* 2: 2–13.

56. See A. Lijphart. 1984. *Democracy. Patterns of Majoritarian and Consensus Government in Twenty-one Countries.* New Haven: Yale University Press; A. Lijphart. 1985. *Power Sharing in South Africa.* Berkeley: University of California; A. Lijphart. 1989. 'The Ethnic Factors and Democratic Constitution Making in South Africa', in E.J. Keller and L.A. Picard (eds), *Domestic Change and International Conflict.* Boulder: Rienner; A. Lijphart. 1991. 'Constitutional Choices for a New Democracy', *Journal of Democracy* 2(1): 72–84; A. Lijphart. 1992. *Parliamentary Versus Presidential Government.* Oxford: Oxford University Press. The consociational constitutional model based on ethnic groups is analysed in L.J. Boulle. 1984b. *South Africa and the Consociational Option. A Constitutional Analysis.* Johannesburg: Juta. On the implications of a power sharing model in South Africa, see M. Macdonald. 1992. 'The Siren's Song: the Political Logic of Power Sharing in South Africa', *Journal of Southern African Studies* 18(4): 709–25.
57. See R. Southall. 1983. 'Consociationalism in South Africa: the Buthelezi Commission and Beyond', *Journal of Modern African Studies* 21(1): 77–112.
58. According to Olivier Beaud, constituent actors, called *instances constituantes*, are '*les autorités qui prennent des décisions*' within the context of a constitution-making procedure; see O. Beaud. 1994. *La Puissance de l'Etat.* Paris: Presses Universitaires de France, p. 266. Constituent actors are in reality representatives of the different South African peoples that have not yet formed a unitary political body. In this phase, the black majority could not even be considered a voting body since it had never received civil and political rights.
59. See Galli, *Genealogia della Politica*, especially notes 7 (p. 423), 12 (p. 425) and 72 (p. 443).
60. Beaud poses an important question: '*comment peut-on étudier juridiquement la procédure constituante puisque la constitution antérieure ne peut pas, par nature, prescrire la forme et le contenu de la constitution ultérieure qui l'abroge?*' (Beaud, *La puissance de l'Etat*, p. 264). The French scholar, in an effort to resolve the paradox of continuity and discontinuity with the previous order, uses Maurice Hauriou's thesis according to which: '*le droit va du discontinu au continu et chaque fois qu'un événement le rejette dans la discontinuité il recommence à s'orienter vers la continuité qui n'est peut-être, ici, qu'une forme de l'inertie. Les destinées du pouvoir constituant n'ont point échappé à cette loi*' (M. Hauriou. 1965. *Précis de droit constitutionnel*, 2nd ed. Paris: Centre National de la Recherche Scientifique, pp. 254–55). Carl Schmitt also deals with the break between de-constituent and constituent moments which he traces back to the origin of modernity's 'crisis'. The people's iconoclastic decision to dismantle a political system – an act that manifests the people's existence – eventually dies when forced to choose a form of representation, causing the people to disappear from the system. Therefore, if the decision to dismantle a system implies the existence and identity of a people (an active role), representation signifies the people's absence (a passive role). This dynamic can also be seen in South Africa: a) if the black people can be considered a constitution-making energy (that sometimes expressed itself through violence); b) if the same people, due to their lack of political citizenship, could be considered a people only in a normative sense; c) and if the constitution-making process marks the moment when the black population becomes a legitimate political actor, by the same token we cannot ignore the fact that their identity was almost entirely absorbed by the representation bestowed on the main mass political movements (the ANC, PAC and IFP) guiding the constitutional negotiations. This demonstrates the fundamental role of the political elite in whom the black people vested unlimited representation.
61. In 1945, Costantino Mortati demonstrated how the creation of a state cannot be limited to just normative criteria. According to Mortati, normative elements are always a part of a broader system of material forces and political principles. See C. Mortati. 1992. 'La teoria del potere costituente', in P. Pombeni. (ed.), *Potere*

costituente e riforme costituzionali. Bologna: Il Mulino, pp. 183–93. See also Klein, *Théorie et pratique du pouvoir constituant*; A. Pace. 1997. *Potere Costituente, rigidità costituzionale, autovincoli legislativi*. Padua: CEDAM; G.U. Rescigno. 1996. 'La discussione nell'Assemblea costituente del 1946 intorno ai suoi poteri, ovvero del potere costituente, delle assemblee costituenti, dei processi costituenti', *Diritto Pubblico*, pp. 23 *et seq*; M. Dogliani. 1989. 'Costituente (potere)', *Digesto delle discipline pubblicistiche* 4. Turin: Utet, pp. 280 *et seq*; M. Dogliani. 1986. *Potere costituente: seminario di diritto costituzionale*. Turin: Giappichelli; P.G. Grasso. 1985. 'Potere costituente', in *Enciclopedia del diritto*. Milan: Giuffrè, vol. 34, pp. 646 *et seq*; G. Zagrebelsky. 1984. *Il sistema costituzionale delle fonti del diritto*. Turin: Eges; P. Barile. 1966. 'Potere costituente', in *Novissimo digesto italiano*. Turin: Utet, vol. 13, pp. 443–50. See also A. Negri. 2002. *Il Potere costituente. Saggio sulle alternative del moderno*. Rome: Manifestolibri.

62. According to Beaud, there are two main types of decisions: a) pre-constituent decisions; and b) constituent decisions. The former '*expriment la volonté politique de recourir à une nouvelle constitution; elles organisent la transition constitutionelle en préparant la procédure constituante proprement dite. Ce sont des décisions "préparatoires" à la constitution finale*'. In Beaud's opinion, pre-constituent decisions are further divided: '*d'un côté, la décision de recourir à une nouvelle constitution et, de l'autre, une ou des décisions, qui interviennent sur le fondement de cette décision globale, d'enclencher un processus constituant, dont l'objet est de prescrire au futur pouvoir constituant, des formes (procédure et compétence) et quelquefois des principes de fond.*' In Beaud's view: '*La décision même de recourir à une noucelle constitution (ou ensemble de décisions), qui est à l'origine de toute la procédure, sera qualifiée de* décision d'initiative pré-constituante', whereas the second type of pre-constituent decisions can be defined as '*décision attributive du pouvoir constituant*'. The second category, the constituent decisions, refers to the adoption of '*loi constitutionnelle*'. They seem to imitate the normal legislative process (proposal, discussion, adoption, ratification and enactment). Their character depends on when they intervene and the capacity of the constituent moments that make those decisions. From this perspective, they include: 1) decisions determining the project's status (*décision d'initiative constituante*); 2) decisions of *dernier ressort* (involving the issue of sovereignty). The latter can be definitive or non-definitive, that is, '*les décisions qui statuent de manière non définitive sur le projet ou la proposition de constitution sont des actes d'*adoption constituante. *En revanche, les décisions qui ratifient par un acte définitif ce projet ou cette proposition préalablement adopté sont des* sanctions constituantes'. Beaud, *La puissance de l'Etat*, pp. 265 *et seq*.
63. See Sparks, *Tomorrow Is Another Country*; Adam and Moodley, *The Negotiated Revolution*; D. Ottaway. 1993a. *Chained Together: Mandela, De Klerk, and the Struggle to Remake South Africa*. New York: Times Books; M. Ottaway. 1993b. *South Africa. The Struggle for a New Order*. Washington, DC: Brookings Institution; M. Benson. 1994. *Now Is the Time: a Personal Account of South Africa's Historic Transition from Apartheid to Democracy*. Sydney: Australian Broadcasting Corporation.
64. See Spitz and Chaskalson, *The Politics of Transition*, pp. 14–18.
65. See Lobban, 'Un accord négocié', p. 74.
66. See ANC, 'Constitutional Guidelines'.
67. The Indemnity Act 35/1990; Indemnity Amendment Act 124/1992 and Further Indemnity Act 151/1992.
68. Immunity was given immediately to the members of the ANC's National Executive Committee and other exiled members. The Working Group instituted with the agreement establishes that those who had illegally left the country and had belonged to banned political organizations would have benefited from the President's Pardon Power (s. 6 of the 1983 Constitution), Law 35/1990 and s. 69 of the 1959

Correctional Services Act. The text of the Groote Schurr Minute has been analysed in Ebrahim, *The Soul of a Nation*, pp. 44–55. The notion of a political crime (and, as a result, of a political prisoner who may receive immunity or have his punishment cancelled) follows the famous Norgaard Principles (incorporated in s. 20(3) of the TRC Act), which were made law for the same purpose during Namibia's transition (see note 14 in Chapter 2).

69. See Ebrahim, *The Soul of a Nation*, pp. 57–62; 'Pretoria Minute'. 1990. *South African Journal on Human Rights* 6: 322–23; F. Kutz. 2001. *Amnestie für politische Straftäter in Südafrika*. Berlin: Arno Spitz GmgH.
70. See Government Gazette 12470, 1990. The text was signed on 15 May 1990 and became effective on 18 May. The law made temporary immunity and permanent indemnity (after evaluating the gravity of the act) possible. The first forty-eight political prisoners were released in June of 1990. Also according to the Guidelines for Defining Political Offences in South Africa of November 1990, to be able to benefit from these measures, the political crime had to have been committed before 8 October 1990. Where the law makes no specification, the benefits for political prisoners were also extended to the regime's security forces and military, unleashing violent arguments and disdain (see J. Sarkin. 2004. *Carrots and Sticks: The TRC and the South African Amnesty Process*. Antwerp: Intersentia, pp. 36–41).
71. See Government Gazette 14401, 1992. De Klerk used a particular procedure called the deadlock breaking institution (a power of the President's Council, which he had full control of) to combat the refusal of the House of Delegates (the Indian House) to approve this legislation, which clearly set out to protect members of the regime's institutions from criminal trials.
72. See N. Kollapen. 1993. 'Accountability: the Debate in South Africa', *Journal of African Law* 37(1): 1–9; P. Parker. 1996. 'The Politics of Indemnities, Truth Telling and Reconciliation in South Africa. Ending Apartheid without Forgetting', *Human Rights Law Journal* 17(1–2): 1–13; R. Keightley. 1993. 'Political Offences and Indemnity in South Africa', *South African Journal on Human Rights* 9: 334–57; TRC. 1998. *TRC Final Report*, London: MacMillan, vol. 1, pp. 49–53; Kutz, *Amnestie für politische Straftäter in Südafrika*.
73. Data on the number of applicants who received benefits and on the number of prisoners released are presented by A. du Bois-Pedain. 2007. *Transitional Amnesty in South Africa*. Oxford: Oxford University Press, pp. 40–43. See Sarkin, *Carrots and Sticks*, pp. 40–49.
74. See Adam and Moodley, *Negotiated Revolution*; Adam and Moodley. 1992. 'Political Violence, Tribalism and Inkatha', *Journal of Modern African Studies* 30: 485–510.
75. See Minnaar, Liebenberg and Schutte, *The Hidden Hand*, p. 199.
76. The Commission, chaired by Richard Goldstone and in accordance with the Prevention of Public Violence Act 139/1991, was one of the bodies instituted by the National Peace Accord. The Commission preceded the creation of the TRC and conducted investigations on violent events such as the Boipatong massacre and the death of activist Chris Hani; see R. Goldstone. 1996. 'Justice as a Tool for Peace-Making: Truth Commission and International Criminal Trials', *Journal of International Law and Politics* 28(3): 485–503; I. Liebenberg. 1996. 'The Truth and Reconciliation Commission in South Africa: Context, Future and Some Imponderables', *South African Public Law* 11(1–2): 123–60 (in particular pp. 138–40).
77. See P. Gastrow. 1995. *Bargaining for Peace. South Africa and the National Peace Accord*. Washington, DC: United States Institute for Peace Press.

2

CONSTITUENT ACTS

Multiparty Assemblies: Gradual Predominance of Constituent Acts

The third phase of the transitional process saw the gradual replacement of constituent *facts* with strictly constituent *acts* and marks the transition to the constitution-making procedure. Its main components are: the three multiparty assemblies, that is, CODESA (Convention for a Democratic South Africa) I and II and the Multi-party Negotiating Process (MPNP); the writing of the Interim Constitution of 1993 and the 34 Constitutional Principles, without which constituent power could not be exercised; the 1994 democratic elections and the summoning of the Constitutional Assembly; the institution of the Constitutional Court before the adoption of the definitive Constitution and the institution of the TRC. This phase consists of a series of significant decisive moments. For this reason, we will analyse CODESA I and II and the MPNP in order to understand when and how fundamental decisions were made.[1]

The autumn of 1991 (29–30 November) marked the beginning of this phase. An organizational committee made up of representatives of twenty political organizations met in order to define the procedure of the multiparty convention. On 20–21 December 1991, CODESA I began; 228 delegates from nineteen political organizations tried to negotiate the Constitution.[2] The convention was chaired by three important jurists: Michael Corbet, Petrus Shabort and Isamil Mahomed. Gerrit Viljoen, Minister of Constitutional Development, defended the NP government's position and aimed to keep control of certain decision-making mechanisms so as to be able to veto decisions. The government was acutely aware of the demographic power in the hands of the black majority's political organization; it thus used a delaying strategy so that the white oligarchy would have control over the power to decide the outcome. The main negotiating tactic used by the NP – even years later – was to write the Constitution in a multiparty assembly with a fixed number of representatives for each accredited political organization. The purpose of this tactic was to eliminate the weight in numbers of the political organizations representing the black electorate, thereby avoiding the situation where the power to write the Constitution would be given to a body based on a national proportional election. The ANC instead preferred the immediate summoning of a Constitutional Assembly elected with universal suffrage, which would have inevitably marginalized the political organizations representing the country's white minority. Even if work had already been organized and begun,[3] disagreements about the procedure that CODESA I was to follow and contrasts between extremely different constitutional plans[4] led to a halt in negotiations in 1992; however, before the negotiations broke down, an agreement was signed by all participants – the Declaration of Intent – except for the independent province Bophuthatswana and the IFP.[5] The government seemed to still have control over the decision-making. The ruling Parliament would have the power to ratify the decisions made during the assemblies, which was a type of protection that the NP wanted. In reality, this principle denied CODESA the status of constituent body.[6]

Negotiations resumed on 15–16 May 1992 with CODESA II. Differences had still not been resolved: debate revolved around defining the majority necessary in the Constitutional Assembly for approving the Constitution. The NP tried to influence the end result of the Constitution's adoption process. In fact, De Klerk's party demanded a 75 per cent quorum as opposed to the two-thirds usually required. The ANC was willing to accept a quorum of 66.6 per cent or even 70 per cent. The NP, on the one hand, wanted to extend the validity of the Interim Constitution (which contained a power sharing system), which, based on agreements made previously, would have been adopted by a multiparty assembly; on the other hand, it wanted to strain relations between Mandela and his people by trying to undermine his authority.

A purely juridical reading of the constitution-making procedure does not provide a full picture of the facts that led to the breakdown of CODESA II. On 17 June 1992, a group of attackers, which witnesses reported included white men, killed at least forty-five people in Boipatong; the ANC, as a gesture of protest against the government's ambiguous conduct, unilaterally interrupted the negotiations. The negotiation slowly began to resume with informal bilateral meetings. On 26 September 1992, these efforts were rewarded with the Record of Understanding signed by the government and the ANC.

This agreement, whose key negotiators were Cyril Ramaphosa representing the ANC and Roelf Mayer for the NP, was a pivotal moment in the constitution-making process.[7] The agreement was the basis for further important decisions about containing political violence as well as about the constitution-making procedure by formalizing the terms for the future Constitutional Assembly. The Assembly would be elected on the basis of universal suffrage and would operate with a constituent power bound to principles contained in an interim constitution; it would also have two years from the moment it convened to write the definitive constitution. The agreement also required that rules be drafted for the Constitutional Assembly and a quorum for approving various dispensations. The Constitutional Assembly would also have ordinary legislative functions based on the interim constitution.[8] In addition, the Record of Understanding formally decided a fundamental issue: the first post-apartheid legislature (with a five-year term) would be a Government of National Unity (GNU) composed of members of political parties that acquired more than five per cent of the vote in the multiracial democratic elections.

These agreements brought about the acceptance of a temporary coalition government, which was proposed by the leader of the South African Communist Party, Joe Slovo; together these provisions were called the sunset clause.[9] This called for a much more gradual (and therefore acceptable) change; due to the uncertainty regarding the immediate ability of the black people to produce political leaders, the proposed system would have guaranteed that the state's bureaucratic and administrative functions would continue. Over the course of the five-year GNU, the public administration personnel of the old regime would gradually be integrated with staff from the black population (belonging to different political organizations).[10]

The signing of the Record of Understanding began an intense phase of dealing with proposed constitutional models, including the use of comparisons with foreign models. For example, the ANC began to contact German constitutional scholars in order to study the federal model; some documents published later with the slogan 'unified State but not over centralised' demonstrate how the ANC constitutional model slowly began to include the idea of dividing competences between the state and local bodies. The agreement also set out to spark debate on the interim provisions regarding the executive branch and established the need to make ad hoc legal measures in the future. An agreement was made for a transitional government, the Transitional Executive Council (TEC), of four 'committees': security, finances, foreign affairs and local government; two other committees dealt specifically with the problems of the media and organizing elections.[11]

It is still difficult to separate constituent facts from acts in this phase. In any event, some of the decisions adopted during this period deeply influenced the creation of the new constitution.

Interim and Definitive Constituent Acts

The third multiparty assembly, the MPNP, marked the beginning of the procedure phase dominated by the adoption of constituent acts; some were interim while others were definitive. The following took place within the MPNP: a) adopting the Interim Constitution; b) formally giving constituent power to a future Constitutional Assembly, which would be bound by 34 Constitutional Principles (CPs); c) laying the groundwork for the institution of the Constitutional Court before the adoption of the definitive constitution; d) resolving the issue of transitional justice with a system of case-by-case amnesty to be administered by the Truth and Reconciliation Commission (TRC). All these decisions were formally incorporated into the Interim Constitution as well as in the definitive Constitution. The decisions regarding transitional justice were included with the concluding provisions of the 1993 Interim Constitution, that is, in the Postamble under the heading 'National Unity and Reconciliation'. The MPNP was a moment in which de facto constituent power was exercised;[12] the radical break from the previous constitutional order and the new constitutional order began to take shape. The decision-making phase of the MPNP was a moment linking the past with the future.

The facts described above allow us to read the South African constitution-making process as a succession of constituent acts within a subdivided and extended constitution-making procedure.[13] This type of constitution-making procedure, in fact, was experimented with in another constitutional transition around the same time: Namibia.[14]

The Negotiation Planning Conference was convened on 4–5 March 1993 in order to organize work. First, a resolution was passed that called for the resumption of the CODESA II negotiations. The MPNP officially began on 1 April 1993 according to the agreements made at CODESA II. The MPNP was organized as follows: 1) the Negotiating Council with two delegates for every accredited political organization; 2) the Plenary Body with the leaders of those organizations; 3) the Negotiating Forum, acting as a link between the two other bodies, composed of four negotiators for each organization; 4) the Planning Committee responsible for the proper execution of the negotiations; 5) three subcommittees with executive responsibilities.[15] On 7 May 1993, the Negotiating Council agreed on the creation of seven technical committees that would discuss and study specific issues: 1) political violence; 2) constitutional issues (Interim Constitution and Constitutional Principles); 3) fundamental human rights (especially during the interim period); 4) the creation of an independent electoral commission (a fundamental body for the first multiracial elections); 5) the creation of an independent media commission and telecommunications authority; 6) abrogation of discriminatory legislation; 7) the Transitional Executive Council (TEC).[16] The adoption of the 'sufficient consensus' decision-making procedure limited the power of minority positions to block measures and therefore provided a way of circumventing the problem of delaying tactics.[17]

Deciding Who Decides

One of the most delicate issues was designating which de facto constituent political actors could be admitted to the decision-making group. Studying the rules that determined which *constituent actors* could participate at the negotiations is fundamental to understanding the strategy of inclusion, the foundation stone of constructing the new political body's unity.

The status of the main political actors at the constitutional negotiations was very different. On the one hand, the government, formed under the previous constitutional system, represented and had the legitimacy of only the white population that had voted for it. De Klerk also had a popular mandate to continue the constitutional negotiations following a referendum (which was held on 17 March 1992 and in which only the white population could vote). In this phase, in fact, the bitter opposition of the radical Afrikaner right against De Klerk's politics threatened the transition. Without a mandate, De Klerk would not have been able to continue the negotiations; however, 68.6 per cent of the voters were in favour of the President and continuing the negotiations.

On the other hand, there was the archipelago of non-governmental actors in the constitution-making procedure. The ANC was the most obvious in terms of size, importance and legitimacy, but there were also many other important political organizations (the IFP, SACP, AZAPO, PAC) as well as religious organizations. For the former national liberation movements in particular (most of all the ANC), de facto historical and social legitimacy gave them the right to participate in writing the new constitution. Though the government was still connected to the old segregationist constitutional order and the ANC represented a break from that order, they did recognize each other as legitimate participants in the constitution-writing process.

Bearing in mind the importance of the MPNP's decisions, the complexity of the constituent actors' representativity emerged. This problematic issue related to the power to make decisions regarding requests to participate in the constitution-writing process. The power to exclude, which at this phase could have been used without any formal criteria or control, became the power to silence different voices and visions regarding the new constitution. Analysis of the rules for participating in the constitution-writing process (which were called the standing rules)[18] shows how they were originally unbound by positive law or previously formalized procedures. This was the moment in which a radical break was made from the previous constitutional order.[19]

Even if a group of standing rules had already been adopted for CODESA I and II, the new rules were different due to the changed composition and political objectives of the multiparty assemblies.[20] The MPNP's standing rules were more intricate because of the important constituent decisions that it had to make. The prerequisites for admission included the formal commitment of the applicant to participate in the following multiracial elections, criteria which aimed to filter out political organizations formed for the express purpose of disturbing the negotiations. The parties and the organizations aspiring to be accredited had to prove that they had support on a national level, the so called 'substantial support in a national context'. The applicants' intention to peacefully participate in the constitutional transition also had to be examined.[21] From a formal point of view, the applying organizations had to fill out a questionnaire with the names and functions of their delegates (providing a list of active members was sufficient for demonstrating national political support); the meetings in which the organization participated; a demonstration of financial independence and the geographic area where they were active. Once again, the objective was to prevent, as much as possible, the formation of ad hoc groups that attempted to negatively influence the negotiations. It is interesting to note that the 'traditional leaders' were admitted to the negotiations.[22] The MPNP's standing rules therefore included the participation of the traditional leaders; the issue of the real representativity of these delegations required specific procedures for evaluating the traditional leaders' applications, both for the Negotiating Council and the Planning Committee. These bodies could decide not to accept these applicants if there were doubts about their formation, actual existence and their representativity of certain traditional indigenous communities.[23]

These rules were codified autonomously by the constituent actors at the negotiations. The MPNP's admission rules and the assembly's procedures were self-produced by the participants without any type of external control or the help of any rule that had previously been made positive law by the state. The normative void in which these decisions were made is a common feature of the creation phase of a new political and legal system that takes shape in absence of pre-established positive rules. The decision-making power to include or exclude the assembly's participants dominated this *constituent moment* just as the strength and political weight of the individual organizations gave shape to this procedure. In this situation, aside from the IFP's radical position, the standing rules and the criteria for inclusion and exclusion encountered no opponents; collective acceptance and self-regulation were widely agreed upon. In fact, no one threatened to use external powers due to disagreement about these rules. Moreover, the effectiveness of these rules is demonstrated by the fact that some organizations were excluded from the negotiations because they failed to satisfy the prerequisites, even if later they were granted the status of observers.[24] The setup of the rules of inclusion in and exclusion from constitutional negotiations seems to demonstrate that mutual recognition and mutual legitimacy as political actors in adopting the new constitution were necessary for collective survival and suspending political violence.

The Constitutional Principles

Codifying the 34 CPs was a significant political and legal-constitutional compromise; the definitive Constitution would be written by an elected body (just as the ANC demanded), but its constituent power would be bound by the Principles adopted in the MPNP by multiparty delegations. The delegations were composed of an equal number of representatives (as the NP requested in order to limit the black population's demographic power).

The CPs were much debated; they created a framework for the Constitutional Assembly's activity and limited its *constituent function*. They were added to the 1993 Interim Constitution (Schedule 4) and were defined as the pre-Constitution.[25] For some scholars, the CPs were a 'solemn pact between parties' and the core of the constitutional system.[26] Given that the Constitutional Court would be called on to verify the definitive Constitution's compliance with the CPs, these principles appear to be imbued with the power to resist change and, as a result, they are at the top of the hierarchy of constitutional sources. The South African constitutional scholar François Venter subdivides them in the following five categories: 1) constitutional fundamentals; 2) the state's general characteristics; 3) the Constitution's characteristics; 4) the Constitution's structure; and 5) the political and constitutional transition.[27]

The first category incorporates: the principle of equality; a comprehensive breakdown of fundamental rights (separated from the principle of equality, which has a unique place); the principles dealing with the notion of 'diversity' and the principle of self-determination (a fervent demand of the Afrikaner nationalists). The formal and substantive principle of equality – the cornerstone of the post-apartheid order – is spread across a number of other principles: Principle I asserts gender and racial equality; Principle III prohibits any other form of discrimination for the express purpose of constructing the political body's unity; Principle V codifies equality before the law (and places emphasis on a fair legal process as a tool for combating the social asymmetry created by the segregationist regime). How the principles of diversity are defined is also very interesting; theoretically, they seem to be in contrast with the principles of equality. This ambiguity is explained by the opposing interests that created these principles through negotiation; the principles of equality were formalized as a break from apartheid logic, whereas the principles of diversity were codified to protect ethnolinguistic and cultural differences. The concept of unity was not limited to uniformity, but it also rejected the creation of a hierarchy of cultural identity. In creating unity, it was necessary for the state to actively protect differences, creating connections between the 'islands' of South Africa's social 'archipelago'.

Pluralism had to be recognized and promoted with active policies; Principles XI and XX enacted this new fundamental quality of post-apartheid constitutionalism.[28] From this perspective, the right to self-determination introduced in Principle XII (which the Afrikaner community wanted), in compliance with the Constitution, is a corollary of the right to difference. The expression of this right had to be balanced with the principle of equality. Recognition of differences would prevent future discrimination regarding the rights recognized by the Constitution. Formalizing the principle of equality had important effects in terms of making a radical break from the segregationist order. As many studies have shown, substantive criminal law and the structure of the South African trial contributed immensely to the implementation of oppressive and discriminatory policies; affirming the principles inherent in the concept of a fair trial and equality before the law was an expression of the will to eradicate the apartheid ideology.

Numerous principles dealt with other fundamental rights: Principle II stems from mid twentieth-century liberal-democratic constitutionalism and endorses legal protection of fundamental rights. Simply declaring the principles is not sufficient: the legal system's express protection is also part of making fundamental rights effective. In connection to this rationale is Principle VII, which provides for the immediate creation of the Constitutional Court responsible for the traditional activities of studying and interpreting the constitutional text and safeguarding fundamental rights (including by direct application of individual citizens in the interest of justice). Principle IX codifies freedom of information as a fundamental constitutional principle. Principle XIII recognizes traditional leaders and indigenous customary law. The new constitutional order appears to endorse the idea that common law of British origin and indigenous customary law should be formally protected by the Constitution and the judiciary. Principle XXVIII calls for the freedom of association and the right to join trade unions, to collective bargaining and to fair labour conditions, all fundamental issues for the trade unions and organizations that sided with the liberation movements in the fight against apartheid.

Principle I obliges the future Constitutional Assembly to create a democratic government; further details are provided in Principle VIII: 'There shall be representative government embracing multiparty democracy, regular elections, universal adult suffrage, a common voters' roll, and, in general, proportional representation.'[29] Going back to Venter's first category of constitutional fundamentals, Principles XIV, XVI and XVII are to be read jointly. They establish the general structures of the decentralized state and the division of powers and functions between the national and provincial governments.

Venter's second category of principles pertains to the general characteristics of the state. Principle I establishes the sovereignty of a unitary state with a common citizenship. Principles VI and VII sanction the separation of powers.[30] Principle IX confirms the right to government information: the transparency of public bodies was considered fundamental to the new order.[31] Principle X sets the obligation of determining legal procedures in the next *constituent phase*, on a national and provincial level. The decentralized local bodies receive legislative power in this phase (and, as a result, the issues falling under their responsibility), while provisions determining how that power is to be exercised are still to be defined. All of this demonstrates how the *constituent activity* did not end with the MPNP, as there were still many fundamental elements to determine.[32] Principles XXV, XXVI and XXVII guarantee the fiscal autonomy of the provincial and local governments.

Venter's third category relates to characteristics of the constitution; these principles include Principle IV, which states that the Constitution is the supreme law of the state.[33] Principle VII states that South Africa shall be a constitutional state with a constitutional justice system. These principles reinforce the rigid nature of the Constitution, which could be amended only by procedures involving special majorities – to be defined by the Constitutional Assembly.[34]

The Constitution's structure is the fourth category and includes principles defining the relationship between powers both vertically (national and provincial bodies) and horizontally (the various bodies of the Provinces). Principles XVI–XXVII subdivide the legislative powers and functions of each level of government and provide that there shall be democratic representation at every level. The future Constitutional Assembly would have to establish the exclusive and concurrent powers when cooperation between state and province is required (Principle XXI(6)).[35]

The last group of principles define the procedures for completing the constitutional transition. Principle XXXII gives constitutional value to the MPNP's decision that South Africa would have a GNU for the whole course of the first legislature.

The Bill of Rights

During the MPNP, signing the agreement on the text of the chapter entitled 'Fundamental Rights' was undeniably one of the most important constituent acts of the constitution-making procedure.[36] The Canadian Charter of Rights and Freedoms[37] was its main source of inspiration; the list of fundamental rights was later adopted with a few changes in the definitive Constitution, where it was formally entitled the Bill of Rights. This section will deal with this evolution. CP II states that the Constitution must contain 'universally accepted fundamental rights, freedoms and civil liberties'; the CPs laid down other provisions regarding fundamental rights that were later grouped together and organized as the Bill of Rights. Drafted and described in detail, the Bill of Rights also includes the criteria for how fundamental rights are to operate and be interpreted, and a clause specifying the limits, suspension and protection of these rights. Though the rights dealing with the principle of equality (s. 9) – the real landmark of the post-apartheid system – dominate this part of the Constitution, the Bill of Rights also contains classic liberal rights (as limits to public power) and social rights (which define broad areas of state intervention in welfare matters). Third generation rights also receive ample attention, such as the rights to life (s. 11), human dignity (s. 10), safe environment (that is not harmful to health and not exploited solely for economic purposes, so as to also benefit future generations (s. 24)), information and the protection of privacy (s. 14), child protection (s. 28)[38] and just administrative actions (s. 33).[39] The thirty-nine sections of the Bill of Rights are to be read in connection with the Preamble of the 1996 Constitution and the six sections of the Founding Provisions (s. 1–6). This important beginning part of the 1996 text embodies the principle of a unified state founded on the values of democracy, human dignity, advancement of human rights, non-racialism and non-sexism. This part also provides for the supremacy of the Constitution in the context of a rule of law, common citizenship and multilingualism.

The Bill of Rights expressly forbids torture and inhuman and degrading treatment (s. 12), slavery and forced labour (s. 13), and guarantees freedom of movement and residence on national territory (s. 21). Shadows of the past can clearly be seen in these provisions, expressly breaking the limits imposed by the apartheid regime on movement and residence as well as the violence that the regime enforced. The Bill of Rights contemplates individual economic and social protection in terms of solidarity and redistribution of economic resources. This is such a vast section of the Bill of Rights that it could be viewed as potentially developing policies invading the personal sphere. A great number of constitutional provisions recognize and protect the social state. Two of the most interesting of these provisions are s. 26, the right to housing (rather important considering the poor living conditions in which the majority of the black population finds itself today) and s. 27, entitled 'Health Care, Food, Water and Social Security', which recognizes a number of rights regarding health care services, access to water resources and food distribution within the limits of the state's economic resources. The objective of these provisions is to gradually make it possible for each of these rights to be enjoyed, a fact that would symbolize the completion not only of a political and constitutional transition but also, and perhaps more importantly, of an economic transition (in terms of a horizontal redistribution of resources).[40] The social dimension of the Bill of Rights also includes s. 29, which recognizes and protects the right to an education and basic schooling services. As for socioeconomic provisions, the complex group of rules regarding labour relations (s. 22–23) and the rights of association and union protection is connected to the freedom of economic enterprise (especially s. 25 protecting private property) in order to properly balance protecting workers and developing a free market. The Bill of Rights, just like the entire text of the Constitution, was influenced by the dialectic between an individualist/universalist vision of fundamental rights and a collectivist/relativist vision, which can be seen in the spelling out of individual and collective rights.[41] As an example of this, s. 3 recognizes the right to protecting linguistic diversity and multilingualism (s. 30–31) and the right of association (s. 18).

Section 8(2) lays out an innovative, horizontal application of the Bill of Rights in relations between private persons,[42] while s. 36 contains the criteria for limiting fundamental rights as well as the criteria according to which they could be balanced. The breadth of the Constitution's fundamental rights requires criteria for limiting and balancing them through hermeneutics. Rights may be limited if 'reasonable and justifiable in an open and democratic society based on human dignity, equality and freedom', and the following must be accounted for: 'a) the nature of the right; b) the importance of the purpose of the limitation; c) the nature and extent of the limitation; d) the relation between the limitation and its purpose; e) less restrictive means to achieve the purpose.' This section's provisions clearly state that the limitation is justifiable only 'in terms of law of general application' and in such a way that the right is limited as little as possible and is reasonable, proportional and adequate for the purpose to be achieved.[43] From this perspective, s. 37, entitled 'States of Emergency', lays out a special table of non-derogable rights. These rights cannot be derogated from even if a threat to the country calls for Parliament to adopt special restrictive measures. The non-derogable (and therefore absolute) rights include equality, human dignity, life, personal freedom and due process of law, prohibition of slavery and force labour, and children's rights.

The criteria and means for the Constitutional Court's interpretation of the Bill of Rights are also highly innovative. Section 39 provides that the court is obliged to consider international public law and may also consider foreign law and jurisprudence. Constitutionalizing instruments that expose the South African constitutional order to other systems when interpreting the Bill of Rights is perhaps the greatest innovation of post-apartheid constitutionalism.[44]

A Break from the Past

In addition to the 34 CPs and the Bill of Rights, the MPNP also produced, on 22 December 1993, the Interim Constitution. This group of texts marks a formal break with the political and constitutional order of apartheid.[45] This break consists of, as can be read from the Interim Constitution's Preamble, the construction of a 'non-racial and non-sexist democracy', founded on the principle of equality and the banning of discrimination. Together, these new provisions outline a new constitutional state (as provided in s. 4(1) and (2)) that embodies a rigid concept of the constitution, the supreme law of the state. The fundamental rights are protected by the judiciary and the Constitutional Court. A complete break from the past is made; apartheid was an authoritarian system based on group exclusion, discrimination and hierarchy. The white Afrikaner oligarchy's historical, political and religious justifications[46] and its lack of criticism towards the state allowed a regime to develop that politically and economically excluded the 'non-white, non-male, non-middle-class'.[47] The founding values of the new state, the government's form and the overall organization of institutions were all a radical change to the previous structure. Constitutional justice was introduced, the protection of fundamental rights was revolutionized and a break was even made from the British Westminster model, which had been a feature of the apartheid constitutional order and determined the sovereignty or supremacy of Parliament. Introducing the supremacy of the Constitution (protected by the Constitutional Court) and amendment procedures based on qualified majorities for its modification aimed to limit 'the omnipotence of law', which had been used in the past in order to justify the segregationist ideology.[48]

The Interim Constitution introduced changes to the presidential and parliamentary system. The President of the Republic is both the Head of State and the chief executive (s. 76). He is responsible to Parliament (s. 87) just as the cabinet must have the legislature's confidence (s. 93). The interim constitutional system called for a GNU composed proportionally of ministers nominated from each party that reached five per cent in the first multiracial elections. A totally different type of parliamentarism from the previous system was adopted; under the Interim Constitution, it consisted of a National Assembly (400 members as provided by s. 40–47) and a Senate (10 senators for each province). Discontinuity with apartheid also meant changing the voting system: finally, and for the first time, a multiparty system with universal suffrage. The National Assembly is elected for a five-year term using a proportional method, as set out by Schedule 2 of the 1993 Constitution and the Electoral Act 1993 (s. 40(1)). Instead the Senate is composed of delegates nominated by the parties represented in the provincial legislatures (also using the proportional method) of each province (s. 48–54).[49]

All these elements point to the political objective of the constitutional transition: constructing the new political body's unity. The GNU represented executive power shared by all the political groups elected in 1994. The Senate's structure, in which each province was represented on an equal basis, satisfied the opposing requests of the ANC and the NP (for a unitary or federal state). It also created a balanced and equal relationship between the different geographical areas so as not to accentuate the pre-existing demographic and socioeconomic disparities of the provinces.

Chapter 8 of the Interim Constitution (s. 110–23) institutes a series of constitutional bodies for enforcing the rights established by the Bill of Rights and therefore making the symbolic and political break from the previous system a reality. The most important bodies enacted for gradually reducing inequality and mistrust towards the state's bureaucratic apparatus[50] are the Public Protector, the Human Rights Commission, the Commission on

Gender Equality and the Commission on Restitution of Land Rights. As such, concrete legal and formal elements that represent the discontinuity with the previous order were created during this phase of the constitution-making process. Apartheid no longer exists, but the new democratic order has yet to be completely established. Many other constituent acts still have to be drawn up.

The Genesis of the Truth and Reconciliation Commission

The MPNP not only saw the creation of *constituent decisions* analysed in the previous sections, but it also produced fundamental decisions that formally make transitional justice part of the constitution. Generally speaking, transitional justice refers to the instruments (whether judicial, quasi-judicial, alternative or complementary to criminal trials) for dealing with crimes committed under a previous political system. Transitional justice, as will be explained in more depth in the following chapter, was extremely important to the post-apartheid political and constitutional order, and it appears to be a fundamental part of the constitution-making process in all countries that were formerly criminal states.[51] The MPNP helped to create the conditions for resolving this delicate and important issue of the constitution-making procedure, laying the groundwork for future decisions regarding constitutional rules on transitional justice. The *constituent decision* made here was to opt for a form of justice that was complementary to criminal justice and that incorporated restorative justice methods limiting the new state's ability to take penal action.[52] The MPNP drafted some rules placed at the end of the Interim Constitution under the title 'National Unity and Reconciliation'; these provisions set the general criteria of the amnesty process for crimes with a political scope committed during apartheid (and the TRC would be the body authorized to hold those proceedings). It reads:

> This Constitution provides a historic bridge between the past of a deeply divided society characterised by strife, conflict, untold suffering and injustice, and a future founded on the recognition of human rights, democracy and peaceful co-existence and development opportunities for all South Africans, irrespective of colour, race, class, belief or sex. The pursuit of national unity, the well-being of all South African citizens and peace require reconciliation between the people of South Africa and the reconstruction of society.
>
> The adoption of this Constitution lays the secure foundation for the people of South Africa to transcend the divisions and strife of the past, which generated gross violations of human rights, the transgression of humanitarian principles in violent conflicts and a legacy of hatred, fear, guilt and revenge.
>
> These can now be addressed on the basis that there is a need for understanding but not for vengeance, a need for reparation but not for retaliation, a need for ubuntu but not for victimisation.

> In order to advance such reconciliation and reconstruction, amnesty shall be granted in respect of acts, omissions and offences associated with political objectives and committed in the course of the conflicts of the past. To this end, Parliament under this Constitution shall adopt a law determining a firm cut-off date, which shall be a date after 8 October 1990 and before 6 December 1993, and providing for the mechanisms, criteria and procedures, including tribunals, if any, through which such amnesty shall be dealt with at any time after the law has been passed.

At the end of the MPNP, the TRC was not yet formally created, even if a decision was already made about a *constitutional suspension of a strictly criminal approach* and incorporated into the Constitution; the genesis of the Commission coincided with the creation of a rather controversial constitutional rule. Mandela's party proposed the idea of an ad hoc judicial body for crimes committed under apartheid while preparing its platform for the 1994 multiracial elections. Prior to the MPNP, the government was concerned about legal action that could be taken against members of the apartheid regime (which was fuelled by the case against former defence minister Magnus Malan)[53] and counterattacked by accusing the ANC of committing crimes, especially in the camps in other African countries for activists exiled by the apartheid government. Using criminal justice against past crimes could have been a real obstacle for the transition and the transfer of political power to the black population. The white oligarchy, even if slowly accepting the rules for transferring political power, was not willing to be subject to criminal trials for past crimes. The ANC's response to the NP's accusations began as an internal party investigative commission that was to shed light on the crimes reported by the NP. When the first report was published, the ANC's political opponents expressed doubt about the Commission's impartiality.[54] A second investigative body was appointed and the results of its investigation were submitted to the ANC's National Executive. Numerous criminal episodes were attributed to ANC activists in exile and tainted the perception of the methods used in the national liberation movement;[55] there was a real risk that the liberation movement would lose its good standing, especially on an international level,[56] hence the idea of the political establishment connected to Mandela: the creation of an ad hoc commission that would deal with the truth about the past and the redistribution of responsibility in order to provide the post-apartheid political body with an official version of the past. Two important conferences were organized in relation to this proposal: 'Dealing with the Past' and 'Truth and Reconciliation'. A number of Latin American specialists (where important political transitions from authoritarian regimes had just been concluded using the experimental Truth Commission Models) were invited. Afterwards, Chilean and Argentinian specialists were asked to work with the drafters of the Commission's statute. Public debates were organized across South Africa for the discussion of this delicate problem with the purpose of involving public opinion as much as possible, including even the most marginal rural areas.[57] The concepts of reconciliation, national unity, amnesty, forbidding revenge and compensation for victims were discussed during these debates; simultaneously, the need for determining an official version of the past began to manifest itself in public opinion. Numerous documents containing criticism and general evaluations were gathered and given to Parliament, which was working on the statute of the future TRC. A parliamentary committee on justice was also set up; this body was appointed with the task of analysing the documents and proposals in order to define the functions and responsibilities of this new body. This led to Parliament passing the National Unity and Reconciliation Act 34/1995, which formally established the TRC and regulated its procedural code.[58]

The next problem was selecting and nominating the TRC members. Mandela decided to make a list of twenty-five names from a list of 299 candidates suggested by citizens, NGOs, religious and secular organizations. There was much discussion about the committee of twenty-five. Once again, in the inclusive spirit of the constitution-making process, public hearings were organized; having consulted the members of the executive, the charismatic and authoritative President selected seventeen commissioners of the newly-instituted TRC.[59]

The nomination process for the TRC commissioners was different from the procedures used in other countries where similar commissions had been set up. In most cases, the commissioners were chosen directly, depending on the constitutional model, by heads of state or government. An even more important fact is that the laws, functional rules, procedures and methods were prepared by the commissioners nominated by the president or the government and thereby were not subject to parliamentary control. The degree of democratic legitimacy of these bodies is somewhat inferior in comparison to the TRC.[60] The advantage of a commission created with the procedure analysed here (based on a legislative text passed by Parliament, composed of members indicated by the political body and chosen with transparent methods) is that it is generally an independent instrument which will better respect democratic principles as part of the 'constituent mandate' assigned to it.[61]

The Institution of the Constitutional Court: the Paradox of a Constituted Body Co-participating in the Constituent Process

The decision to institute the Constitutional Court before the adoption of the definitive Constitution had some rather interesting implications. This court assisted in the process of gradually eliminating laws influenced by segregationism from the legal system. These laws were passed under the old constitutional system and could not be immediately abrogated, an act that could have paralysed the state. As a result, the Constitutional Court made a substantial contribution to making a break from the previous constitutional order.[62]

Another unique element enriched post-apartheid constitutionalism. While still in the constitution-making process it was decided that, once the Interim Constitution was approved, the Constitutional Court would be immediately set up with a series of very important responsibilities. In addition to verifying the compatibility of the definitive Constitution with the CPs issued by the MPNP, the Court also had to start interpreting the interim text. This fact created another dynamic of the segregationist system's transformation. Scrutinizing case-by-case the constitutionality of old laws under the new post-apartheid system, the Court helped to remove those laws that were not compatible with the new principles; the constitution-making process worked from above and below. In fact, while important judgments determined the constitutionality of symbolic and discriminatory provisions (such as gradually declaring criminal laws and criminal procedural laws unconstitutional), the MPNP and the Constitutional Assembly were simultaneously designing the new constitutional order. In addition, an intense dialogue developed between the Constitutional Court and the Constitutional Assembly, especially when the definitive text was being evaluated for certification.

Thus, the old legal system's transformation through court decisions coincided with the writing of the new definitive Constitution; this justifies the hypothesis that the Constitutional Court profoundly affected the constitution-making process.[63] This process could not have been completed without simultaneously activating a group of bodies that were able to work alongside the writing process of the new constitution. The 'supplementary constituent bodies' acted as a kind of interdependent and coherent network. In other words, each body (instituted by interim constitutional rules) made a specific contribution to the exercise of constituent power by developing constitutional matters in relation to its sphere of responsibility.

On 14 September 1993, the MPNP's Negotiating Council agreed on instituting the Constitutional Court before passing the definitive Constitution.[64] On 12 November 1993, the government and the ANC presented a document that would become Chapter 7 of the 1993 Constitution.[65] The system of judicial review, which was first introduced by CP VII, was officially authorized in s. 98 of the 1993 Constitution, giving South Africa a system of centralized judicial review.[66]

The Different Forms of Judicial Review Procedures

Putting together all the constitutional provisions that brought about the institution of the Constitutional Court is a rather complex task. In addition to the interim constitutional rules (s. 97–100), the new Parliament, meeting as the Constitutional Assembly, passed the law creating the Constitutional Court before drafting the Constitution.[67] The Court made its first decisions in 1995 under the transitional regime; this section, however, refers to the provisions of the definitive 1996 Constitution: s. 166, 167, 172, 174, 175, 176, 177, Schedule 6 (16)(a) and (b), s. 79, 121, 80 and 122, regulating the procedures of preventive judicial review, and s. 144, listing the persons entitled to raise a question about validity.

The post-apartheid judicial review system has many shapes. It provides for abstract and preventive review of the laws passed by the national and provincial legislatures as well as concrete *ex post* judicial review that gives citizens a means of direct recourse.[68] There are two methods of preventive abstract judicial review of laws depending on whether the question has been raised by the President of the Republic, provincial Premiers or by members of the legislature. Section 167 of the definitive Constitution confirms that the Constitutional Court is the highest court on constitutional issues.[69] Subsection (4)(a) gives the Constitutional Court a monopoly on decisions regarding constitutional matters, conflicts between central and provincial bodies, certification of the provincial constitutions[70] and the constitutionality of the amendments made to the Constitution, as well as the power to verify the President's constitutional obligations. Subsections (b) and (c) lay down the procedures for preventive abstract judicial review of national and provincial laws. Sections 79 and 121 (procedure for national laws), 80 and 122 (procedure for provincial laws) are expressly mentioned in Section 167.

The first preventive abstract judicial review procedure is similar both for national and provincial legislation during the phase prior to the President's (for national laws) or Premier's (for provincial laws) signature of the bill (s. 79).[71]

If the President has doubts about the constitutionality of a law passed by the National Assembly, he may order the legislature to re-examine it. The reconsideration procedure may also involve the National Council of Provinces if the bill includes contents whose responsibility the Constitution assigns to the provinces. If the bill passes again after reconsideration and the President once again refuses to sign it, it is up to the Constitutional Court to decide on its constitutionality. Section 121 states the same procedure for the provincial legislature, in which the Premier of the province starts preventive judicial review. If the disagreement between the Premier and the legislature continues, the Constitutional Court will decide.[72] If the Court decides that law is not unconstitutional, then the President (or Premier) must sign it.

Sections 80 and 122 provide for a second kind of preventive abstract judicial review. Once again, it is a similar procedure on a national level (s. 80) and on a provincial level (s. 122). For the former, at least a third of the members of the National Assembly is required in order to apply to the Court to decide on the constitutionality of national law, within thirty days of the President's signature; for the latter, twenty per cent of the provincial legislature's members is required. Further requirements are: a) the presence of a general interest of justice; and b) that the application has a reasonable prospect of success, that is, it has legal grounds and is not simply a means of political opposition.[73]

Section 167(4) provides for procedures of concrete *ex post* judicial review (s. 172(2)).[74]

Judicial review of a law in force starts out with an Order of Constitutional Invalidity issued by the Supreme Court of Appeal or the High Court acting as lower court judges; the court suspends the proceedings until a decision has been made by the Constitutional Court, the only body that can confirm and make a valid Order of Constitutional Invalidity.[75]

Section 167(6)(a) and (b) of the 1996 Constitution also provides for judicial review by direct access.[76]

Rule 18 of the Constitutional Court Rules lays down the procedure for direct access to the Constitutional Court in the interests of justice.[77] An application for direct access filed with the Court's Registrar is accepted if it contains: a) the grounds of the claim of unconstitutionality; b) whether the dispute can be decided 'without the hearing of oral evidence' or if the procedure according to Rules 11–13 is to be followed; c) how the evidence in favour of the request is produced and how 'conflicts of facts' can be resolved. Just like all other judicial review methods, opposition may be made against this claim of unconstitutionality.[78]

The complexity of South Africa's system of judicial review can be seen in the analysis of the procedure mentioned in the paragraph above. This procedure merges direct access with elements of indirect review or incidenter proceedings. In fact, section 167(6)(b) provides the following: 'to appeal directly to the Constitutional Court from any other court.' This final possibility of accessing constitutional justice allows for application to the Court regardless of whether a competent court has issued an Order of Constitutional Invalidity. Rule 19 of the Constitutional Court Rules states that every dispute about a decision, other than an order of constitutional invalidity, regarding a constitutional matter may be directly appealed against before the Constitutional Court by the parties aggrieved by the decision. However, the claim must contain an interest of justice,[79] without which it will not be admitted.

Rule 20 of the Constitutional Court Rules also provides the possibility of questioning the unconstitutionality of a decision made by the Supreme Court of Appeal.

The Constitution gives the Constitutional Court the power to evaluate the compatibility of judicial review procedures and, according to s. 144, the power to certify provincial constitutions. Section 167(4)(e) provides that the Constitutional Court also verifies that the President fulfils his constitutional obligations, acting as a body in conjunction with Parliament that checks the executive branch.

The range of possibilities for accessing constitutional justice makes the Constitutional Court an important institution in the new post-apartheid order. How the judges are appointed helps to demonstrate this body's independence. Section 176(1) provides that the Court be composed of nine judges, appointed for a twelve-year term, but that they must retire at the age of seventy, in addition to the Chief Justice of South Africa and Deputy Chief Justice. Their appointment is part of a procedure that directly involves the President and a special constitutional body: the Judicial Service Commission (JSC). According to s. 174(3), the President appoints the Chief Justice and Deputy Chief Justice after having consulted the party leaders of the National Assembly and the JSC, whereas the remaining judges are appointed by a procedure according to s. 174(4), in which the President chooses from a list prepared by the JSC. This list must contain three more names than the number of judges to be appointed. The President must choose based on consultations with the Chief Justice and the party leaders of the National Assembly. Even though the President may advise the JSC on the acceptability of the candidates, it is always up to the JSC to prepare the list that limits the President's room for manoeuvre. The JSC's composition, according to s. 178(1), is a key factor for designating Constitutional Court judges and is to be made up of legal professionals, executive and legislative branch members.[80]

The different ways of applying to the Court could appear to create a vast number of requests. However, the statistics published annually by the *South African Journal on Human Rights*,[81] though a useful tool, do not help in assessing this information. In fact, it refers to a significant number of cases that the Court dismisses, but does not provide an exact number. In any event, we can imagine the reasoning behind such broad judicial review. First, it was part of making the post-apartheid system's formation uniform in addition to giving it substance. In fact, the Constitutional Court has an important instructive function as a body for the enforcement of the new constitutional logic of the Constitution's judicial protection (a concept alien to the previous system, which was based on British constitutionalism). Post-apartheid constitutionalism (especially that of the ANC) tends to enforce constitutional norms through legal proceedings. The justiciability of rights is a primary instrument for making long-lasting social changes; rebalancing and redistributing resources; a shift from political demands (which can turn into violent conflicts) to legal demands. Moreover, there is the idea that providing broad access to justice (including constitutional justice) can help to direct dissent and demands within society away from violent methods (which in some urban areas of South Africa can become quite serious) to legal method, introducing democratic principles based on state instruments for resolving conflicts.[82]

The Constitutional Court's Constituent Influence

The exercise of constituent power can normally be traced back to when a body appointed with the power to write a new constitutional text begins the constitution-writing process. In addition to this formal factor, there is also a material factor, which at times seems to predominate: constituent activity can be seen in the transformation of a system that makes a radical break from the principles and form of the previous constitutional order.[83] The break from the past can be a transformation that makes the previous order 'unrecognizable' or a negation of basic characteristics of the constitutional order by starting a new constitution-making process. Defining this idea in concrete terms is no simple task; in fact, scholars have often dealt with the problem of the limits of constitutional revision in order to differentiate the process of amending and interpreting constitutional rules from the rewriting of the state's basic rules.[84]

This issue, which will not be dealt with here in detail, is important for understanding the Constitutional Court's operation, especially its first rulings. In this context, we can see how the Court's first decisions helped to repeal and replace laws that were connected to the apartheid constitutional order. These court decisions made a break from the previous order just as multiparty assemblies and the Constitutional Assembly did. The South African constitutional experience seems once again to confirm the idea that the constitution-making process is a process that can be subdivided into a number of constituent facts and acts adopted by a number of bodies; in some cases these bodies exercised de facto constituent power, while in others they were given the ability to exercise portions of constituent power.

An analysis of the Court's first decisions supports this hypothesis; judicial review of criminal, administrative and civil law resulted in a formal and concrete rejection of the previous constitutional order while the new Constitution was being written, almost as if they were inseparable macro- and micro-constituent activities that enabled the pending constitution-making process to gradually penetrate deeper. In other words, replacing the previous system's principles, rules and laws with a democratic model took place through politics and negotiations and also through court decisions made by the Constitutional Court.[85]

In 1995, the Constitutional Court ruled on fourteen of the twenty-two constitutional disputes under examination. The following year, the Court issued forty rulings on delicate matters regarding the application and interpretation of the Bill of Rights, such as abolishing the death penalty, the unconstitutionality of corporal punishment, abolishing imprisonment for debt and banning inhuman or degrading treatment, all of which had been cornerstones of the apartheid ideology.[86] There are two symbolic cases of the Court's first period of activity: *S. v. Zuma and Others*[87] and *S. v. Makwanyane and Another*.[88]

The Zuma case dealt with the constitutionality of s. 217(1)(b)(ii) of Criminal Procedure Act 51 of 1977, which governed the controversial issue of the right to silence and the authenticity and voluntary nature of confessions obtained under duress, intimidation or forms of physical or psychological pressure. The central problem that the Court had to decide on regarded confessions taken by members of the police force without any requirement of repeating them during the trial, something that was legitimate according to apartheid criminal law. Section 217's provisions contained elements that are traditionally absent in British common law (the basis of the South African criminal law), which considers a confession valid only if obtained by a judge. The Court was called to rule on the constitutionality of the law's automatic reversal of the burden of proof, something extremely harmful to a defendant's rights and to the principle of the presumption of innocence. In fact, it would be up to the person confessing to prove that the confessions obtained by members of the police force were done so with the use of violence or duress. In particular, the provision places on the accused the burden of proving that the confession recorded by the magistrate was not 'free and voluntary', placing an onus on the accused which must be discharged on a balance of probabilities. In other words, merely raising a doubt does not discharge the onus.

It is easy to imagine how provisions like these were helpful to the apartheid regime's repression and criminalization of dissent and how they were aimed mainly at the black population. With this decision the Court had its first opportunity to deal with the mechanisms activating judicial review codified in the 1993 Interim Constitution and, consequentially, with the problem of declaring jurisdiction. The *Zuma* case contained two separate mechanisms of judicial review: decentralized concrete *ex post* procedure[89] and direct access to the Court in the interests of justice.[90]

In the unanimous judgement drafted by Justice Sydney Kentridge, the Court decision stated that the right to silence, the rights of the accused, the inadmissibility of compelled confessions and the presumption of innocence have been recognized by the common law applied in the colonial territories (today corresponding with South Africa) ever since 1830. The segregationist system gradually erased these rights starting in the second half of the twentieth century, creating an illiberal order through provisions of this kind. The Court therefore declared s. 217 unconstitutional on the grounds of s. 25 of the Interim Constitution (s. 12 of the Bill of Rights in the 1996 Constitution), helping to end one of the criminal realities of apartheid. In fact, the judgement made a shift from a 'confession based' criminal procedure to an 'evidence based' procedure that integrates all the elements of a fair trial.

The interpretive methods used for resolving many of the issues in the *Zuma* case were further developed with the *Makwanyane* case, a landmark case in which the Court declared, through the main opinion written by President Arthur Chaskalson, that capital punishment was unconstitutional according to the new constitutional order. This court decision was a historic one, because of all the new issues the Court had to confront and its innovative approach. First, the Court demonstrated its own autonomy in the face of political power and public opinion (largely in favour of keeping the death penalty)[91] and in its legal and constitutional choices. These choices oriented future interpretations of the post-apartheid Constitution, making the new constitutional order a markedly liberal-democratic order. At the heart of the decision is the judgment of the constitutionality of capital punishment (s. 277(1)(a) of the Criminal Procedure Act 51 of 1977) in relation to s. 8 (equality before the law), s. 9 (right to life), s. 10 (protection of human dignity) and s. 11(2) of the 1993 Constitution. The provisions of this last section establish the unlawfulness of cruel, inhuman or degrading treatment and punishment. In a decision that used many foreign constitutional decisions[92] as a means of comparison, the Court ruled that the death penalty was a cruel and degrading treatment and a constitutionally illegitimate limitation to the right to life. The break from the past is also evident in this case. The significance of this judgment to the constitution-making process can be seen in the Court's reasoning, according to which in South Africa the race issue and poverty were factors that had to be considered. A very high percentage of death sentences concerned blacks belonging to the poorest social classes. Cultural deficiency had often led to linguistic difficulties during these trials, which, even when translation was used, undermined the right of a defence. The way in which capital punishment was also used to silence dissidents certainly cannot be overlooked.

This decision had effects that went beyond merely the basic function of interpretation. The decision's value can be deduced from a series of considerations. The 1993 Constitution (and later the 1996 Constitution) contains an important rule that expressly forbids satisfying impulses of 'vengeance and retaliation'. This provision adopted the policy of transitional justice regarding apartheid crimes (being the foundation stone of the TRC), and it also established important ethical and legal criteria of the new constitutional system. Its objective was to neutralize any vindictive force for crimes of the past and to help reconstruct interracial coexistence.

By the same token, the provision tried to avoid triggering uncontrollable spirals of revenge based on race.[93] These provisions became a general source of inspiration for the new constitutional order through a total reconfiguration of criminal law (an area where the state had traditionally shown its authoritarian and illiberal nature).

In addition, the *AZAPO* case[94] is a decision where the Court's interpretive function produced important effects. In this judgement, the Court ruled on the constitutionality of the TRC and the amnesty proceedings for crimes committed under apartheid. By declaring the constitutionality of the TRC, the Court de facto 'ratified and co-participated' in the decision to *suspend a strictly criminal approach* for crimes of the apartheid past.

The Conclusion of the Constitution-making Procedure

The conclusion of the constitution-making procedure consisted of the following phases: 1) the adoption of the 1993 interim text; 2) the first multiracial democratic elections in April 1994; 3) the Constitutional Assembly's passing of the definitive text and the Constitutional Court's declaration of the text's compliance with the CPs.

From a chronological point of view, on 18 November 1993 the participants in the constitution-making procedure, gathered at the MPNP, approved the Interim Constitution; Parliament, elected while the segregationist system was still in force, ratified it on 22 December during an extraordinary session.[95] Some important political actors like the IFP and the Freedom Front (FF), which had created a coalition called the Freedom Alliance (FA), abandoned the negotiations before the text's final approval;[96] Buthelezi threatened to not participate in the elections. Once again, this act confirms the importance of including all political actors in the constitution-making process and in the new political body, otherwise political violence and conflict would have been triggered. On 25 April 1994, the FA agreed to sign the Interim Constitution *in extremis* just a few days before the multiracial elections and only after several amendments had been approved.[97] On 27 April, the first democratic elections with universal suffrage were held.[98] With the ANC's overwhelming victory and the nomination of Nelson Mandela as President of the Republic, the black population's long struggle for civil rights reached a historic milestone; however, there was still a journey ahead towards obtaining fair access to economic resources. As had been previously agreed, the GNU[99] was nominated, and the newly-elected Parliament convened as the Constitutional Assembly in order to draft the definitive Constitution. Once the Interim Constitution was adopted, the constitution-making procedure continued in the form of constitutional provisions to be inserted in the interim text (s. 73).[100]

The 1993 Constitution was a text with limited temporal validity; constituent power was transferred from the MPNP to the new Parliament (which would turn into the Constitutional Assembly) which received instructions on the procedure, time and majority for adopting the definitive Constitution.[101]

Scholarly debate on the nature of this body shows that it is not unanimously considered a Constitutional Assembly. In fact, for some, it is a *constituent body* which had limited constituent power and simply refined the constitutional choices already made.[102] Others believe, through careful analysis of the Constitutional Assembly's work, that it exercised co-ownership of the constituent power, which led important elements of South Africa's post-apartheid government to be redesigned. For this reason, the 1996 Constitution was different in terms of form and substance from the interim text.[103] Reformulating the 34 CPs in detailed constitutional rules gave the body considerable creative activity.

The Assembly had to adopt the definitive constitutional text within two years of its formation;[104] it was divided into six committees, which finished drafting the definitive text on 8 May 1996; a majority of eighty-six per cent approved. Considerable effort was made to include the South African population in this last phase of the process;[105] the method used was public discussion, including sending written documentation directly to the Assembly.[106] The Constitutional Court also accepted citizens' opinions on the two occasions that it ruled on the definitive Constitution's compliance with the CPs.

In a chronological perspective, it is important to stress how the Court rigorously performed its constitutional mandate by refusing to certify the Constitution and sending it back to the Constitutional Assembly due to the many dissimilarities found, the most important of which dealt with territorial autonomy.[107] The Assembly, once it renegotiated the parts in question, sent the text back to the Court for a certification of compliance, which was confirmed on 4 December 1996. The Constitution's compliance was certified definitively, but it was officially signed by President Mandela on 10 December.

The constitution-making procedure thus ended with a legal act, both inside and outside the process. There is an evident paradox in the latter. A *constituted body* made a judgment on a *constituent body* in exercising constituent powers. On the one hand, this would support the idea that the Assembly was not a true constituent body; on the other hand, it would confirm the hypothesis that the constituent act was fragmented in a series of acts similar to a legislative act. From this perspective, the constitution-making procedure gradually diluted the constituent power to the point that the adopted measures became similar to ordinary legislation.

It is important to remember that no constitutional provision called for a referendum, which would have given the people the final decision. It seems that the constituent elite chose to exercise broad mediation between the political body and the constitution-making process. While ample regard was paid to public opinion and the public were encouraged to participate in the debate on adopting the new Constitution, the possibility of directly sanctioning the constitutional text was taken away; once the 1994 elections granted representation to Parliament members, the people disappeared from the constitution-making procedure and made room for the Constitutional Assembly representatives and the Constitutional Court. One possible interpretation of this complex legal and political dynamic can be traced back to the political elite's awareness of the fragmentation within the political body. At this stage, political mediation was more necessary than ever; the cultural and economic divisions as well as the risks of conflict persuaded the *constituent actors* to use a final constituent polity, cutting off the people and replacing them with the Constitutional Court. In doing so, a powerful political mythology was employed: the idea of the Rainbow Nation. However, merely formally adopting a new constitutional text would not be enough to construct the political body's unity. Reaching this distant objective would require new powerful instruments.[108]

Notes on the Post-apartheid State and Government Forms

Post-apartheid South Africa is a constitutional state with a rigid Constitution expressly stating the supremacy of the Constitution in Section 2. The radical break from the previous order can be seen in the parliamentary form of government (with an asymmetrical setup of competences and functions between the National Assembly and the National Council of Provinces),[109] protection of the democratic form with broad pluralistic connotations such as constitutional recognition of indigenous customary law and traditional leaders, multipartyism, recognition of linguistic, religious, ethnic and cultural groups and the principle of equality as the cornerstone of the new constitutional order.

The executive power is exercised jointly by the President of the Republic, who is elected by the National Assembly and who is also the head of state, and by the Cabinet. They must have the legislature's confidence and are responsible before the National Assembly (the President individually, each Minister and the Cabinet as a whole).[110] Codified in a long and very detailed text, the government's form is a parliamentary model (with proportional representation) with a presidential government; this form is rather unusual, combining elements of parliamentarism and presidentialism. The South African model does not seem to be a semi-presidential form because it has a Parliament that nominates the President, that may revoke its confidence and that cannot be dissolved by a presidential act. Because the head of state is not directly elected and has a diarchic relationship with the executive branch, the lower house has a markedly central role.[111]

The decentralized system and territorial autonomy are more complex and were difficult to organize. They were the result of a delicate negotiation between constitution-making parties in favour of a centralized system and those wanting a form of federalism. Though the Interim Constitution appeared to recognize a system based on federalism, the 1996 Constitution contains a clear recentralizing force, which, however, was not enough to make the system a simple regional state. South Africa is in fact divided into nine provinces that have legislative powers (and thus with elected legislatures) on matters that Schedule 4 (Functional Areas) establishes as exclusive. The Constitution recognizes their right to an executive branch (coordinated by a Premier) within the scheme of the functions assigned, as well as the right to draft provincial constitutions, which must be certified by the Constitutional Court.[112]

The recentralizing thrust that the ANC had given to the Constitutional Assembly because of the large majority it obtained after the 1994 elections can be seen in the constitutionalization of cooperative government (s. 41); this concept implied collaborative procedures for governing relations between the state and territorial bodies before starting proceedings before the Constitutional Court. The post-apartheid system's suspension between weak federalism and federal regionalism can also be seen in the creation of an upper house of the national parliament, the National Council of Provinces (NCOP), with a fixed number of delegates nominated by the provincial legislatures. This body participates in all national legislative procedures regarding matters assigned to the provinces, but the executive branch is not accountable to it, just to the National Assembly. Territorial bodies co-participated in constitutional revision procedures through the NCOP.[113] The Constitution recognizes three distinct but interdependent levels of territorial decentralization:[114] national and provincial bodies and municipal councils. The Constitution lists the competences of the municipal councils, which also have legislative and executive powers for these competences.

Generally speaking, the new constitutional order was founded on the principle of democracy, the institution of multiple mechanisms for checking and limiting public authorities (Watch Dogs),[115] on universal suffrage with common electoral rolls and elections every five years. The underlying values promoted as a symbolic and substantive differentiation from the apartheid regime were human dignity, social justice, formal and substantive equality, and no discrimination based on race, ethnicity or gender. Another important feature is the recognition of collective rights within a broad and innovative multilingual system. Introducing centralized judicial review with preventive abstract and concrete *ex post* methods, along with other constitutional provisions, are a break from the Westminster model used in segregationist South Africa ever since it became a Republic in 1961. A final comment should be made on the nature of the post-apartheid legal system. As scholars have repeatedly pointed out, South Africa combined British common law and Roman-Dutch law concepts. Traces of this fusion of two models is evident today; for example, though the use of the Constitutional Conventions (typical of British common law) has been neutralized by constitutionalizing some of them (limiting the direct application of those that are not expressly stated in the Constitution), the principle of the binding precedent still remains in force.

The Post-apartheid Constitution as a Peace Treaty

In addition to shedding light on some important and innovative elements of post-apartheid constitutionalism, studying the constitution shows how the post-apartheid constitution is a peace treaty between long-standing adversaries that sets down the rules for living together in the same territory.

The text of the new democratic constitution was negotiated at length between political entities that had previously been engaged in a war and can be considered as the formalization of a peace agreement.[116] The Constitution gives legal and constitutional form to an idea of peace that requires legal instruments in order to develop over time and to gradually create the political body's unity so that it may become a nation. Unity is not magically created by formalizing the new political form in the constitution, but requires a process. In this context, the constitution becomes a set of tools for continuing the work of a social and cultural melting pot that today, despite the many important steps already made, is still not complete. The new shared democratic principles, the new institutional setup and the special constitutional bodies all have the function of constructing a unitary political body; the lack of this type of unity has in fact been part of the failure of other constitutional projects in Africa.[117]

Peace treaty similarities can be seen in many of the elements analysed thus far. From the signing of the 1993 Interim Constitution created by the MPNP (its final provisions fall under the heading 'National Unity and Reconciliation)' to constitutional engineering embodying opposing visions and needs, it seems clear that a choice was made to build mechanisms that would encourage social unity (trying to oppose trends of social fragmentation). In this context, the new Constitution, both in terms of substance and how it was produced, became a kind of vessel containing peace agreements.

Post-apartheid constitutionalism is characterized by the idea of instituting spaces (such as the TRC, the Constitutional Court and the other constitutional bodies analysed) for the dialogue between opposing visions of society, values and politics. During the constitution-making process, these spaces were supposed to soften the centrifugal and conflicting forces in order to create a shared position. The participation of different segments of South Africa's social and political fabric and the sheer number of issues that were regulated support reading post-apartheid constitutionalism as a series of agreements between opposing sociopolitical entities. The purpose of these agreements was to encourage peaceful relations and social unity.

Though economic redistribution and access to resources are today the main problems in making this effort for peace effective, the manipulative and forced quality that sometimes marks the inclusion process should not be overlooked.

Notes

1. See R. Orrù 1998. *La Costituzione di tutti. Il Sudafrica dalla segregazione razziale alla democrazia della Rainbow Nation*. Turin: Giappichelli; A. Rinella. 1995. 'Il Constitution of the Republic of South Africa Act 1993', *Quaderni costituzionali* 1: 147–66; L. Pegoraro and A. Rinella. 1997. 'La nuova Costituzione della Repubblica del Sudafrica (1996-1997)', *Rivista trimestrale di diritto pubblico* 2: 517–52; see also L. Scaffardi. 1996. 'La "rivoluzionaria" tutela dei diritti fondamentali della nuova Costituzione del Sudafrica', *Giurisprudenza costituzionale*, 604 *et seq*.
2. The PAC boycotted CODESA because it argued that the convention should have been held outside of South Africa and under a neutral chairman. The IFP's President Buthelezi demanded additional Zulu delegations including the monarchical leaders, and the IFP acted ambiguously, keeping a low profile. The Conservative Party and the Azanian People's Organisation (AZAPO) were also absent from the convention; see M. Lobban. 1997. 'Un accord négocié: le processus constitutionnel en Afrique du Sud depuis 1991', *Revue de droit public* 1: 71–110, p. 89. The NP and the ANC were

present, as well as the other parties of the Tricameral Parliament. The parties elected in the non-independent homelands of Kwazulu, KaNgwane, KwaNdebele, Lebowa, Qwaqua and Gazankulu accepted the invitation, as did representatives of the independent homelands (Transkei, Venda, Bophuthaswanai and Ciskei).

3. CODESA was divided into five working groups. The first working group had to create a 'free and fair' climate for the transition. The second group dealt with drafting the constitutional principles and the rules concerning the relationship between powers of the central state and those of the local agencies. The third group studied interim measures. The fourth group had the task of reforming the Homelands, and the fifth group, the Gender Advisory Committee, was appointed with studying anti-discrimination measures regarding gender. See S. Friedman. 1993. *The Long Journey: South Africa's Quest for a Negotiated Settlement*. Braamfontein: Ravan Press, pp, 34–128.
4. The NP maintained an aggressive position, which in some cases demonstrated its ambiguity about really wanting to build a constitutional order that would unify the political body. Just as CODESA I began, De Klerk stated at congress in the province of Trasvaal: 'The reality of the people and communities to remain themselves and be able to preserve the values that are precious to them – so the whites can each feel secure in their own distinctiveness.' The ideas the NP expressed at CODESA showed that it still wanted to create a system founded on the constitutionalization of the 'identity obsession'. As part of this intention, during the negotiations it proposed a bicameral parliament: one house with 300 members elected nationally and the second with 130 members, 10 for each of the ten 'Federal Provinces' as well as 10 members for each of the three groups 'represented constitutionally' (English, Afrikaners, Asians).This was absolutely unacceptable to the ANC. According to the power sharing model, there would be a rotating presidency and the decisions would be made consociationally. The Swiss constitutional model was the model referred to; see H. Codrer. 1994. 'Towards a South African Constitution', *The Modern Law Review* 57(4): 491–533; A. Sparks. 1994. *Tomorrow Is Another Country. The Inside Story of South Africa's Road to Change*. Chicago: University of Chicago Press, p. 126. The first negotiation 'skirmishes' were followed by documents illustrating the different constitutional views. In April 1991, the ANC published *The Structure of a Constitution for a Free South Africa* and, later, *Constitutional Principles for a Democratic South Africa*. They called for a unitary state founded on a constitution with a long list of fundamental rights. In September 1991 the government published *Constitutional Rule in a Participatory Democracy*. Simultaneously, the Law Commission published *Report on Constitutional Models*; see G. Carpenter. 1994. 'The Republic of South Africa Constitution Act 200 of 1993: An Overview', *South African Public Law* 9: 222–32; H. Ebrahim. 1998. *The Soul of a Nation. Constitution Making in South Africa*. London: Oxford University Press, pp. 73–97.
5. The Declaration of Intent is a significant legal text restating the form that the constitution should take: unitary state, a non-racial and non-sexist multi-party democracy; the supreme law of the constitution; the introduction of judicial review, a Bill of Rights and a system of checks and balances. A detailed analysis of the Declaration can be found in Orrù, *La Costituzione di tutti*, pp. 72–73.
6. A comparative study of constitutional assemblies made by Jon Elster offers a few points to reflect on (J. Elster. 1996. 'Constitution Making in Eastern Europe: Rebuilding the Boat in the Open Sea', in G. Zagrebelsky, P.P. Portinaro and J. Luther (eds), *Il futuro della Costituzione*. Einaudi: Turin, pp. 209–28). From a historical point of view, Elster's study demonstrates how in France the Estates-General of 1789 consisted of 300 representatives of the nobility and the clergy and 600 representatives of the Third Estate. During the first meeting in May, the assembly discussed for six weeks whether to vote by orders or by poll (one vote per person); the second

option prevailed. In Elster's opinion, this change basically transformed the Estates-General into the Constituent Assembly (see also F. Furet. 1988. *La Révolution 1770-1870*. Paris: Hachette; M. Gauchet. 1995. *La Révolution des pouvoirs. La souveraineté, le peuple et la représentation 1789-1799*. Paris: Presses Universitaires de France, pp. 55–57; and R. Martucci. 2001. *L'ossessione costituente. Forma di governo e costituzione nella Rivoluzione francese (1789-1799)*. Bologna: Il Mulino, pp. 103 *et seq*); in particular, see L. Jaume. 2007. 'Constituent Power in France: The Revolution and its Consequences', in M. Loughlin and N. Walker (eds), *The Paradox of Constitutionalism: Constituent Power and Constitutional Form*. Oxford: Oxford University Press, pp. 67–86. Members of CODESA I and II acted expressly for the groups they represented and for the specific interests of political organizations; the assemblies at this stage were still far away from being an assembly equipped with constituent power.

7. This phase of negotiations is in fact called the Ramaphosa-Meyer Channel. The diplomatic skill and importance of these two men had a positive effect even for the Constitutional Assembly (see P. Gastrow. 1995. *Bargaining for Peace. South Africa and the National Peace Accord*. Washington, DC: United States Institute for Peace Press, pp. 99 *et seq*; Ebrahim, *The Soul of a Nation*, pp. 588–94.
8. The results of these agreements were constitutionalized in s. 36–37 of the Interim Constitution approved in 1993: the bicameral Parliament (the National Assembly and the Senate) would draft the definitive Constitution.
9. J. Slovo. 1992. 'Negotiations: What Room for Compromise?', *African Communist* 3/4: 36–40; N. Mandela. 1994. *Long Walk to Freedom. The Autobiography of Nelson Mandela*. Boston: Little Brown, p. 562; R. Spitz and M. Chaskalson. 2000. *The Politics of Transition. A Hidden History of South Africa's Negotiated Settlement*. Johannesburg: Witwatersrand, p. 87; T. Eloff. 1994. 'The Process of Giving Birth', in B. de Villiers (ed.), *Birth of Constitution*. Cape Town: Juta, pp. 12 *et seq*.
10. The norms enacted to guarantee that the new state would function were very significant. Both the realism and responsibility of the ex-Freedom Fighters can be read in the words of Joe Slovo: 'We can win political office, but won't have political power' (cited in Sparks, *Tomorrow is Another Country*, p. 182).
11. I. Sarakinsky. 1995. 'Rehearsing Joint Rule. The Transitional Executive Council', in S. Friedman and D. Atkinson (eds), *The Small Miracle: South Africa's Negotiated Settlement*. Johannesburg: Ravan Press, pp. 60–91; Lobban, 'Un accord négocié', p. 81.
12. The significant decisions made by the MPNP regarding constitutional matters were fundamental to establishing the new post-apartheid constitutional order; see F. Venter. 1994. 'Milestones in the Evolution of the New South African Constitution and Some of its Salient Features', *South African Public Law* 9: 219; C. Jung and I. Shapiro. 1995. 'South Africa's Negotiated Transition Democracy, Opposition and the New Constitutional Order', *Politics and Society* 23(3): 269–308; J. Sarkin. 2000b. 'L'écriture de la Constitution sud-africaine de 1996: approche formelle et matérielle', *Revue française de droit constitutionnel* 44: 747–67.
13. See R. Orrù, *La Costituzione di tutti*, p. 94. There are problematic aspects of the concept of a fragmented constituent act. It has implications for the study of constitution-making processes and for the analysis of how constitutional orders function. Regarding the former, this theory criticizes the idea of a constitution *se fait d'un seul coup*, but it also argues that the interpretive work of the constitutional judges – putting ideas into words and therefore revitalizing the written text – is a constant activity of creation. This interesting and controversial approach was developed in reference to rather stable constitutional orders such as in France by O. Cayla. 1999. 'La chose et son contraire (et son contraire, etc.)', *Les Etudes philosophiques* 3: 307 *et seq*. Analysing the issue of law interpretation (even when contradictory), in particular the *Conseil d'Etat*'s jurisprudence, Cayla states that: '*la Constitution, en tant*

que discours doté de signification normative, n'est pas dans le texte de la Constitution qui est muet, mais seulement dans la parole de sa lecture. Or, il peut y avoir, [...], une pluralité de lectures successives et de sens différents par un même lecteur: la signification constitutionnelle, contrairement à ce que la fixité de son support textuel laisserait supposer, n'est donc pas stable mais éminemment muable, et susceptible de connaître des infléchissements porteurs de contradictions' (p. 306). Cayla claims that: '*Dans ces conditions, où la Constitution n'existe, en tout cas pour le sujet de sa juridicité, que dans l'actualité du déroulement de chacune des lectures qui lui en est faite par une multiplicité d'interprètes 'authentiques', rien n'est jamais constitué*' (p. 307). Therefore, in the author's opinion: '*est la réitération infinie du texte par des vocalisations renouvelées qui l'actualisent et l'altèrent sans cesse (...) si bien que c'est d'un processus permanent de constitutionnalisation*' (p. 307). Cayla's idea enriches thought on the relationship between the constitution-making process and the constitution by suggesting new elements. In particular, ambiguity of the word 'constitution' is at play. This word contains different meanings: *ordo ordinans* (a constituent moment that implies movement) and *ordo ordinatus* (the result of the constituent moment that expresses stability and fixedness). The South African constitution-making process as a succession of constituent acts makes a break from the traditional idea of a constitution that is the result of a *fiat lux*. There are two reasons for considering this approach. First, the construction of the political body's unity is a process demanding stable constituent energy to neutralize the constant centrifugal forces at play within society. This is an especially delicate factor from a theoretical point of view as well as from a formal and legal point of view, since defining the beginning and end of a constitution-making process is fundamental for creating a stable legal system (a prerequisite for its validity, existence and efficacy). Second, apartheid was a complex legal and administrative system, and in a transition the previous system cannot be totally abrogated at once. As a consequence, the apartheid system could not simply be abolished while making the change to the new system (see the following sections).

14. The same South African government led by the NP and De Klerk played a fundamental role in Namibia's negotiated transition. This transition also included the United Nations, Namibian liberation movements, Canada, the USA, France, the UK and Germany. The Namibian experience could be considered as a kind of laboratory that created a model later applied to the South African transition. During the course of the South African transition, this model evolved into a more complex and defined procedure. Therefore, the South African procedure was not entirely new, but was the evolution of a previous political, legal and constitutional experience. See M.G. Erasmus. 2000. 'The Impact of the Namibian Constitution on the Nature of the State, Its Politics and Society: the Record after Ten Years', in O. Manfred et al., *The Constitution at Work. 10 Years of Namibian Nationhood*. Windhoek: University of Namibia Press-Oxford African Book Collective, p. 6. The complex and dramatic history of Namibian independence was an international case between the UN and South Africa. In the 1970s, South Africa attempted to extend its territorial, military and administrative control over the Territory of West Africa (future Namibia) while the UN sought to create an independent state through international mediation (for a legal and historical view, see J. Dugard. 1973. *The South Africa/Namibia Dispute*. Berkeley: University of California Press). Under the UN's auspices, the Western Contact Group (WCG – the USA, Canada, France, the UK and Germany) organized a multilateral conference that in 1982 approved a series of Constitutional Principles. The conference's participants included the UN, the WCG and Namibian political actors who had long opposed South Africa's interference – in particular SWAPO (South West Africa People's Organisation). This political and military organization had fought a violent liberation war against South African militias. SWAPO was

recognized by the UN in 1973 as a key political player. Prior to writing the Constitutional Principles, in 1978 the UN Security Council had approved the famous Resolution 435, which set down the guidelines and procedure for settling the Namibian problem. Resolution 435 was approved based on a report drafted by the WCG after the first negotiation phase with South Africa, SWAPO, Zambia, Angola and Botswana (the main countries of Southern Africa). The 1982 Constitutional Principles were approved within the procedure laid out in Resolution 435 as a first step in the peace process. From a constitutional point of view, the Principles contained the following measures: 1) respecting the result of democratic elections; 2) adopting a Bill of Rights; 3) instituting a constitutional court to certify and enforce the Bill of Rights (once drafted); 4) protecting property rights in the face of expropriation for lack of compensation; 5) an independent judiciary; 6) preserving multi-party democracy. Legal scholars have discussed these Principles at length and whether they should be considered 'supra-constitutional' rules or merely guidelines. In studying elements recurring in South Africa's post-apartheid constitution-making procedure, it is important to note that, once Namibia gained independence and its Constitution was approved, the Security Council published a report judging the compliance of the constitutional text with the 1982 Principles. Even if in reality applying the principles was delayed, in 1989 democratic elections were held; thereafter, when the Constituent Assembly was convened, the Principles were translated into constitutional law. This process ended in 1990 with the Constitution's approval. For more details, see D. van Wyk. 1991. 'The Making of Namibian Constitution: Lessons for Africa', *CILSA* 24: 341–51; M. Wiechers, 'Namibia: the 1982 Constitutional Principles and Their Legal Significance', in Manfred et al., *The Constitution at Work*, pp. 1–21; G.J. Naldi. 1995. *Constitutional Rights in Namibia.* Cape Town: Juta.

15. See D. van Wyk. 1994. 'Introduction to the South Africa Constitution', in D. van Wyk et al., *Rights and Constitutionalism: The New South Africa Legal Order*. Cape Town: Juta, pp. 131 *et seq*.
16. See TEC Act 151/1993; R. Orrù, *La Costituzione di tutti*, pp. 95–96; J. Heunis. 1994. 'Transitional Executive Council', in B. de Villiers (ed.), *Birth of a Constitution*. Cape Town: Juta, pp. 20 *et seq*; I. Sarakinsky, 'Rehearsing Joint Rule', pp. 60–91. Each technical committee had to evaluate and process the summary documents to facilitate the Negotiating Council's operation. These committees did not function as bodies representing political parties and organizations, but as technical bodies appointed for summarizing and working out the various positions expressed. In June 1993, the differences, especially regarding the list of fundamental rights, spurred the creation of an ad hoc committee of the political organizations in disagreement about specific items.
17. Since no quorum was set, if there were contrary votes, an evaluation was made if there was sufficient consensus in favour of a single provision, unless the contrary votes were cast by the two main actors: the ANC and the NP.
18. These were defined as standing rules of procedure, as they were to govern the working procedures of the bodies within the multi-party assemblies.
19. Labelling these rules as 'autopoietic' is a source of controversy. This notion was subject to an in depth analysis by Gunther Teubner in a study on the theory of law. The author's thoughts are based on an unresolved juxtaposition of a strictly normative and analytical approach (which tends to maintain normative law as a closed, self-justified and autonomous system) with a sociological approach (which tends to look at the interaction between a legal system and other external sources of positive law); see G. Taubner. 1993. *Le droit, un système autopoïétique*. Paris: Presses Universitaires de France. Creating rules as important as those determining the constituent actors who could participate in the negotiations appears to be influenced by extra-legal variables as opposed to previously created positive law. For this reason, this process

seems to fall under Romano's category in which de facto establishment of a new order takes place neither through an antijuridical nor a juridical procedure; that is, it follows a procedure outside the rules in force at the time of the new order's establishment. In the author's opinion, this is possible when 'in the life of the state there are sometimes moments of crisis in which the efficacy of the law, if not destroyed, is at the very least suspended. In this way, the state is held up by energies that do not come from the law but from energies outside the law until the crisis is resolved'; see S. Romano. 1950. 'L'instaurazione di fatto di un ordinamento costituzionale e la sua legittimità', *Scritti Minori*, Milan: Giuffrè, vol. 1, p. 134. This change is also discussed and developed further in A. Pace. 1997. *Potere Costituente, rigidità costituzionale, autovincoli legislativi.* Padua: CEDAM, p. 102.

20. CODESA's standing rules called for a Steering Committee (StC) that was composed of members from the leading political organizations of the transition and that had the task of deciding the admission applications to the negotiations. Section 1 of the rules included the following participants: De Klerk's government, the political parties, the authorities and organizations listed in an additional document. The StC could decide also on admitting other 'candidates'; 12 members was the mandatory number for each delegation (see *Official Standing Rules of Procedure for Plenary Sessions of CODESA*). The interpretation of these rules created a lot of tension, which emerged when the IFP asked for a higher number of Zulu delegates. After bitter discussion, the IFP request was refused. The following participated at CODESA: the government, the ANC, the government of the independent Homelands, the Democratic Party, the IFP, the Dikwankwetla Party, the Inyandza National Movement, the Intando Yesizwe Party, the Labour Party of South Africa, the Natal/Transvaal Indian Congress, the NP, the National People's Party, Solidarity, the SACP, the United People's Party and the Ximoko Progressive Party. Among the parties with national importance, only the PAC was absent (*Negotiations News*, 20 October 1992). See also note 2 of this chapter.
21. See Article 9.1, 'Participation', s. IV (Procedural Issues) of the *Standing Rules of the Multi-Party Negotiating Process*. Article 9.1.2 states that applicant political parties and organizations must submit all information and documentation requested to demonstrate their political activity on a national level.
22. The traditional leaders were constitutionalized in Chapter 11 (s. 181–84) of the 1993 Constitution, later adopted in s. 211(1), (2) and (3); 212(1) and (2) of the 1996 Constitution, as well as in the 1993 Government Transition Act.
23. In addition to the political parties that had participated in CODESA I and II, seven other organizations were admitted to the negotiations: the Afrikaner Volksunie, the Konservatiewe Party, the Cape Traditional Leaders, the KwaZulu Government, the Orange Free State Traditional Leaders, the Pan Africanist Congress of Azanian and the Transvaal Traditional Leaders.
24. The applicants excluded were: the People's Democratic Christian Party, the United Federal Party, the Sindowonye Progressive Party, the Reform Party of South Africa, the Insika National Party, the National Forum, the African Democratic Movement, the People's Progressive Party, the Merit People's Party, the National Seoposengwe Party, the Third Force Nationalist Party, the Green Party of South Africa, the Sofasonake Party, the Free Cape Movement and the United Asian Movement. See *Standing Rules of the Multi-Party Negotiating Process*, Article 9.1.3. Important authors like Spitz and Chaskalson have stressed that the South African population's heterogeneity was well-represented in the MPNP; see Spitz and Chaskalson, *The Politics of Transition*, p. 46.
25. Codrer, 'Towards a South African Constitution', p. 500; F. Venter. 1995. 'Requirements for a New Constitutional Text: the Imperatives of the Constitutional Principles', *South African Law Journal* 112: 32–44.

26. See E. van Huyssteen. 2000. 'The Constitutional Court and the Redistribution of Power in South Africa', *African Studies* 59(2): 254.
27. Venter, 'Requirements for a New Constitutional Text', 33 and 39; F. Venter. 1997. 'Aspects of the South African Constitution of 1996: An African Democratic and Social Federal Rechtsstaat?', *Heidelberg Journal of International Law* 57: 52–82. For a detailed analysis, see Orrù, *La Costituzione di tutti*, pp. 87–95; and Rinella, 'Il Constitution', pp. 50 *et seq.*
28. For more information regarding plurilingualism, see A. Lollini. 2004b. 'L'isola e l'arcipelago: la Francia ed il Sudafrica post-apartheid come modelli antitetici di tutela costituzionale di lingue minoritarie e regionali', in A. Lollini (ed.), *Pluralismo linguistico e costituzioni. Un'analisi comparata*. Bolzano: Alpha-Beta, pp. 25–84.
29. See P. Strand. 2000. *Decisions on Democracy. The Politics of Constitution – Making in South Africa 1990 – 1996*, Uppsala: Uppsala University Press, p. 189; Z. Yacoob. 1996. 'The Constitution Making Process: An Overview', *The Human Rights and Constitutional Law Journal of Southern Africa* 1(1): 18–24.
30. See J.D. van der Vyver. 1993. 'The Separation of Powers', *South African Public Law* 8: 190 *et seq.*
31. See S. Alkema. 1996. 'The Right to Access to Information: A Fundamental Right?', *Human Rights and Constitutional Law Journal of Southern Africa* 1(1): pp. 32 *et seq.*
32. This issue is analysed in Spitz and Chaskalson, *The Politics of Transition*, pp. 79–80.
33. See Venter, 'Milestones', pp.211–22.; Sarkin, 'L'écriture de la Constitution sud-africaine', p. 767.
34. See A. Lollini. 2007c. 'Revisione e manutenzione della Costituzione sudafricana', in F. Palermo (ed.), *La "manutenzione" costituzionale*. Padua: CEDAM, pp. 405–35.
35. On decentralized cooperation, see C. Murray and R. Simeon. 2002. 'Eight Years of Decentralisation in South Africa', *Second International Conference on Decentralization 25–27 July 2002*. Manila: Philippines; L. Pegoraro and A. Rinella. 1995. 'Repubblica del Sudafrica: il Constitution Act del 1993 tra "federalismo" e "regionalismo"', *Quaderni Costituzionali* 277–85, p. 280.
36. The interim Constitution formally calls them Fundamental Rights (Ch. 3). The title Bill of Rights was adopted only during the approval of the definitive 1996 Constitution (Ch. 2). On the symbolic, political and legal value of a separate list of fundamental rights placed at the beginning of the constitutional text, see G. Bognetti. 1987. 'Bill of Rights', in *Digesto delle discipline pubblicistiche*. Turin: Utet, vol. 2, pp. 358 *et seq.* This becomes all the more significant for South Africa where none of the preceding constitutions had a complete list of rights. In addition to this structural factor, the substance of the Bill of Rights represented a break from the previous system's values.
37. See F. Venter. 2000. *Constitutional Comparison. Japan, Germany, Canada and South Africa*. Cape Town: Juta-Kluwer Law International, pp. 127–92. See G.A. Beaudoin and E. Mendes. 1996. *The Canadian Charter of Rights and Freedoms*. Toronto: Carswell, pp. 1–4. For very important studies on the matter, see D. Atkinson, 'Insuring the Future? The Bill of Rights', in Friedman and Atkinson (eds), *The Small Miracle*, pp. 121–47.
38. See B. Goldblatt and S. Liebenberg. 2004. 'Giving Money to Children: the State's Constitutional Obligation to Provide Child Support Grants to Child Headed Households', *South African Journal on Human Rights* 20: 151–64.
39. See L. Routenbach and E. Malherbe. 1999. *Constitutional Law*. Durban: Butterworths, pp. 319 *et seq*; H. Cheadle, D.M. Davis and N.R.L. Haysom (eds). 2002. *South African Constitutional Law: The Bill of Rights*. Durban: Butterworths; G. Devenish. 1999a. *A Commentary on the South African Bill of Rights*. Durban: Butterworths.
40. The interpretation and implementation of socioeconomic rights require some clarity. The South African Constitutional Assembly adopted a realistic approach; redistribu-

tion is effective only if within the new state's economic capacity. In fact, the Bill of Rights calls for progressive realization with resources available so as not to feed impossible expectations (see M. Wesson. 2004. 'Grootboom and Beyond. Reassessing the Socio-Economic Jurisprudence of the South African Constitutional Court', *South African Journal on Human Rights* 20: 284–308). A series of decisions made by the Constitutional Court supported this interpretation of socioeconomic rights: *Soobramoney v. Minister of Health, KwaZulu Natal* (1998) (1) SA 765 (CC); *Government of the Republic of South Africa v. Grootboom* (2001) (1) SA 46 (CC); *Minister of Health Care v. Treatment Action Campaign* (2002) (5) SA 721 (CC). This last judgement reconfirmed the *Grootboom* decision, which limited the application of socioeconomic rights in as much as the state is actually able to concretely fulfil the constitutional principles, and dealt with the controversial issue of the distribution of antiretroviral pharmaceuticals. The Treatment Action Campaign (TAC), an important organization led by the famous activist Zackie Achmat, attacked the government for having refused to distribute the pharmaceuticals for free. Mbeki's government, claiming that the HIV pharmaceuticals could be toxic, continued to refuse to distribute the antiretroviral drug Navirapine; despite this, after much fighting, the pharmaceutical companies decided to lower the pharmaceutical's cost considerably. After a long and dramatic fight, the TAC decided to make use of the judicial tools available and appealed to the Constitutional Court, which confirmed its status as a fundamental body for the implementation of the new principles (see M. Tveiten. 2003. 'The Right to Health Secured HIV/Aids Medicine. Socio-Economic Rights in South Africa', *Nordic Journal of International Law* 72: 41–71; C. Ngwena. 2003. 'Access to Antiretroviral Therapy to Prevent Mother-to-Child Transmission of HIV as a Socio-economic Right, an Application of Section 27 of the Constitution', *South African Public Law* 18: 83–102; T.J. Bollyky. 2002. 'Balancing Private Rights and Public Obligations: Constitutionally Mandate Compulsory Licensing of HIV/Aids Related Treatment in South Africa', *South African Journal on Human Rights* 18: 530–69). The Court, although in agreement with the previous decisions regarding socioeconomic rights, called for the provision of pharmaceuticals and experimental programmes (which nevertheless were not enough to resolve the epidemic). Housing programmes and providing electricity and water to the townships were for the most part insufficient. The government's inability to manage contingent expectations and problems created frustration and indifference towards the freedom fighters who were now leading the country.

41. See L. Du Plessis. 1996. 'Evaluative Reflections on the Final Text of South Africa's Bill of Rights', *Stellenbosch Law Review* 7: 283–305; L. Du Plessis and H. Corder. 1994. *Understanding South Africa's Transitional Bill of Rights*. Cape Town: Juta; D. van Wyk. 1994. 'The South African Bill of Rights: an Evaluation', *South African Public Law* 9: 278–86.
42. Section 8(2) confirms that the Bill of Rights is binding not only on public authorities but also on 'natural and juristic persons'. This important innovation of the 1996 Constitution orders compliance with and also the guarantee of fundamental rights in relations between private persons. As Orrù points out (Orrù, *La Costituzione di tutti*, pp. 152 and 202–03), the Constitutional Court in the case *Du Plessis and Others v. De Klerk and Others* (1996) (3) SA 850 (CC); (1996) (5) BCLR 658 (CC) seems to change the German theory of indirect or mediated efficacy on a horizontal level (*Indirekte Drittwirkung*) of the rights enforced by the Bill of Rights. In this particular court case, the Constitutional Court defined the direct application of the Bill of Rights (when a dispute is between a private citizen and a public authority) and indirect application (when between private individuals); see J. van der Walt. 2003. 'Horizontal Application of Fundamental Rights and the Threshold of the Law in View of the Carmichele Saga', *South African Journal on Human Rights* 19: 517–40; C. Sprigman and M. Osborne. 1999. 'Du Plessis is Not Dead: South Africa's 1996

Constitution and the Application of the Bill of Rights to Private Disputes', *South African Journal on Human Rights* 15(1): 25–51; M. Montalti. 2004. 'L'efficacia orizzontale del Bill of Rights sudafricano alla luce di alcune riflessioni comparative', *Diritto pubblico comparato ed europeo* 4: 1714–33.

43. G. van der Schyff. 2005. *Limitation of Rights: A Study of the European Convention and the South African Bill of Rights.* Nijmegen: Wolf Legal Publishers.
44. This is not the appropriate place for a full analysis of this interesting feature of the new constitutional system. See H. Webb. 1998. 'The Constitutional Court of South Africa: Rights Interpretation and Comparative Constitutional Law', *University of Pennsylvania Journal of Constitutional Law* 205–83. The South African model is currently being analysed by international constitutional scholars who study the so called 'constitutional court dialogue' or 'circulation of constitutional hermeneutics'. This theme is studied in particular in the USA, which gives rise to a paradox: though US public law scholars are open to this interpretation practice, the Supreme Court has basically forbidden comparisons with the decisions of other constitutional courts. See S.K. Harding. 2003. 'Comparative Reasoning and Judicial Review', *The Yale Journal of International Law* 28(2): 409–64; C. McCrudden. 2000. 'A Common Law of Human Rights?: Transnational Judicial Conversations on Constitutional Rights', *Oxford Journal of Legal Studies* 20: 499 *et seq*; M. Tushnet. 1999. 'The Possibility of Comparative Constitutional Law', *Yale Law Journal* 108: 1225–309; D. Fontana. 2001. 'Refined Comparativism in Constitutional Law', *UCLA Law Review* 49: 539 *et seq*; V.C. Jackson. 1999. 'Ambivalent Resistance and Comparative Constitutionalism: Opening up the Conversation on "Proportionality" Rights and Federalism', *University of Pennsylvania Journal of Constitutional Law,* 583 *et seq.* The debate received impetus from A.M. Slaughter. 2003. 'A Global Community of Courts', *Harvard International Law Journal* 44: 191–219; S. Choudhry. 1999. 'Globalization in Search of Justification: Towards a Theory of Comparative Constitutional Interpretation', *Indiana Law Journal* 74: 821 *et seq*; B. Ackerman. 1997. 'The Rise of World Constitutionalism', *Virginia Law Review* 83(3): 771 *et seq.*
45. F. Dreyfus. 1994. 'La Constitution Intérimaire d'Afrique du Sud', *Revue Française de Droit Constitutionnel* 19: 410 *et seq*; and G. Conac, F. Dreyfus and J.O. Monteiro (eds). 1995. *L'Afrique du Sud en Transition.* Paris: Economica.
46. The historical hostility between the Dutch and British populations, which led to the British defeating the Afrikaners in a series of military struggles, made it difficult for the Dutch population to develop their cultural, political and linguistic culture autonomously. The military defeats and the search for new territories in which to create an independent political community fuelled the Afrikaners' sense of victimization. Some historians have analysed the role of the events that determined the Afrikaner identity in the creation of the segregationist system. See L. Thompson. 1985. *The Political Mythology of Apartheid.* New Haven: Yale University Press, pp. 31–61; T. Dunbar-Moodie. 1975. *The Rise of Afrikanerdom: Power, Apartheid, and the Civil Religion.* Berkeley: Berkeley University Press; A. du Toit. 1983. 'No Chosen People: The Myth of the Calvinist Origins of Afrikaner Nationalism and Racial Ideology', *American Historical Review* 88: 920–52; I. Hexham. 1981. *The Irony of Apartheid: the Struggle for National Independence of Afrikaner Calvinist against British Imperialism.* New York: Edwin Mellon Press; D. Darbon, 'Les enjeux du "droit des groupes" dans la négociation constitutionnelle en Afrique du Sud', in Conac, Dreyfus and Monteiro (eds), *L'Afrique du Sud en Transition*, p. 138.
47. See A.M. Gentili. 1990. 'Apartheid', in N. Bobbio, N. Matteucci and N. Pasquino (eds), *Dizionario di politica.* Turin: Utet, pp. 37 *et seq.* There are interesting implications regarding the exclusion of the black population from access to economic resources, public administration and the judiciary. The black population is especially held back from accessing the state justice system, when not a defendant; see 'The Truth and Reconciliation Commission, and the Bench, Legal Practitioners and Legal

Academics'. 1998. *South African Law Journal* 115: 15–106. In the Homelands, separate, tradition-based judicial mechanisms were set up (in Italian, see M. Guadagni. 1995. 'Sudafrica', in R. Sacco et al., *Il diritto africano*. Turin: Utet, pp. 351 *et seq*; and in particular the so called 'Legal Pluralism' – R. Wilson. 2001. *The Politics of Truth and Reconciliation: Legitimizing the Post-apartheid State*. Cambridge: Cambridge University Press, pp. 188–222). In light of this, the break from the segregationist system also meant access to the judicial system, now recognized in the Constitution. Section 38 of the Bill of Rights, for example, establishes that any competent court may offer relief for violation of a fundamental right, and it provides a wide range of individuals and entities that may legitimately approach a court for protection of those rights, whether acting on their personal behalf, on behalf of someone else, as a member or in the interest of a group or simply acting in public interest. Increasing the means for directly accessing judicial protection of fundamental rights could appear to weigh down the judicial system and to be a source of consternation. These decisions made by the Constitutional Assembly can be explained by the historical exclusion of the larger part of the population from the law as a form of protection, in a past where the law meant violence and discrimination. In an attempt to correct the past, a system was created that at times seems redundant. Though this may be the case, there are two other points to be made. First, economic and democratic advancement is not conceivable if justice and protection of economic rights are not guaranteed. Any potential growth of capital and labour of a future black middle class required a system of private law protection. Second, there is the need for conflict solution through a judicial system able to protect individual and enforce those rights. The use of law and judicial institutions could channel the conflicting forces present.

48. See Orrù, *La Costituzione di tutti*, pp. 191–92.
49. For an analysis of the electoral system, see Dreyfus, 'La Constitution Intérimaire', pp. 482–83. Regarding the territory's subdivision in provinces, Schedule 1 (Part 1) of the Interim Constitution foresees the creation of nine provinces out of the eleven under apartheid: Natal, Northern Cape, Northern Transvaal, North-West, Eastern Cape, Eastern Transvaal, Orange Free State, Pretoria-Witwatersrand-Vereeniging and Western Cape. In the 1996 Constitution, the province names were changed again to Eastern Cape, Free State, Gauteng, KwaZulu-Natal, Mpumalanga, Northern Cape, North West and Western Cape.
50. On the issue of mistrust towards state institutions, see R. Wilson. 1998. 'Human Rights, Globalisation and Culture. The Experience of the TRC in South Africa', *Transnational Conference, Manchester 16–18 May 1998*, Manchester.
51. On the relationship between constitution-making processes and transitional justice, see A. Lollini. 2004a. 'La "giustizia di transizione": il principio del duty to prosecute come una nuova variabile di eterodeterminazione dei processi costituenti?', in G. Gozzi and F. Martelli (eds), *Guerre e minoranze. Diritti delle minoranze, conflitti interetnici e giustizia internazionale nella transizione alla democrazia nell'Europa Centro-Orientale*. Il Mulino: Bologna, pp. 323–62.
52. On the concepts discussed on the following pages, see R. Claassen. 1996. 'Principles of Restorative Justice', *Conciliation Quarterly* 15(3): 6 *et seq*; L. Walgrave. 2002. *Restorative Justice and the Law*. Portland: Willan Publishing; E.G.M Weitekamp and H.J. Kerner. 2002. *Restorative Justice. Theoretical Foundation*. Portland: Willan Publishing; in Italy, G. Mannozzi. 1996. *Razionalità e 'giustizia' nella commisurazione della pena. Il Just Desert Model e la riforma del sentencing nordamericano*. Padua: CEDAM; G. Mannozzi. 1999. *La mediazione penale*. Padua: CEDAM; G. Mannozzi and E. Paliero. 1992. 'Mediation and Reconciliation Models in Italian Legal Experience', in H. Messmer and H.U. Otto (eds), *Restorative Justice on Trial*. Dordrecht: Kluwer Academic. For the debate on alternative justice models for serious

violations of fundamental rights, see L. Huyse and E. van Dael. 2001. *Justice après des graves violations de droits de l'homme. Le choix entre l'amnistie, la commission de la vérité et les poursuites pénales*. Leuven: University of Leuven, vol. 1–2; S.R. Ratner and J.S. Abrams. 1997. 'Non Prosecutorial Options: Investigatory Commissions, Civil Suits, and Immigration Measures', in *Accountability for Human Rights Atrocities in International Law. Beyond The Nuremberg Legacy*. Oxford: Clarendon Press, pp. 193 *et seq*; J.M. Osiel. 2000. 'Why Prosecute? Critics of Punishment for Mass Atrocities', *Human Rights Quarterly* 22: 118–47. For a philosophical and theological analysis of punishment, see L. Eusebi (ed.). 1989. *La funzione della pena: il commiato da Kant e da Hegel*. Milan: Giuffrè (in particular P. Noll, 'La fondazione etica della pena', pp. 29–56); L. Eusebi and A. Acerbi (eds). 1998. *Colpa e pena? La teologia di fronte alla questione criminale*. Milan: Vita e pensiero. From a (Judeo-Christian) theological point of view, E. Wiesnet's criticism of the retributive punishment is interesting; see E. Wiesnet. 1980. *Die Verratene Versöhnung: zum Verhältnis von Christentum und Strafe*. Düsseldorf: Atmos Verlag.

53. See note 53, Chapter 3.
54. See *TRC Final Report*, 'Historical Context', vol. 1, ch. 2. The name of the ANC's first commission was the Stuart Skweyiya Motsuenyane Commission.
55. See *Commission of Enquiry into Complaints by Former African National Congress Prisoners and Detainees Report*. 1992. Cape Town: University of the Western Cape.
56. In response to this, Mandela spoke publicly before the TRC about crimes committed in the Angola exile camps in the 1970s. Thabo Mbeki, Mandela's successor as President, and other ANC activists filed a controversial collective request for amnesty.
57. The public debate's importance and breadth is stressed by H. van der Merwe, H. Dewhirste and B. Hamber. 1999. 'Non-Governmental Organisations and Truth and Reconciliation Commission: An Impact Assessment', *Politikon* 26(1): 55–79; D. Shea. 2000. *The South African Truth Commission: The Politics of Reconciliation*. Washington, DC: United States Institute of Peace.
58. For the genesis of the TRC, see K. Christie. 2000. *The South African Truth and Reconciliation Commission*, Basingstoke: Macmillan (especially Chapter 3, 'Negotiation the Truth in Times of Transition', pp. 65 *et seq*); R.I. Rotberg. 2000. 'Truth Commissions and the Provision of Truth Justice and Reconciliation', in R.I. Rotberg and D. Thompson (eds), *Truth v. Justice. The Morality of Truth Commissions*. Princeton: Princeton University Press, pp. 3–21. On 17 May 1995, the National Assembly passed the law followed by the Senate on 27 June. Mandela signed the text on 29 July. The new text that provided for conditional amnesty did not change the effects of the 1990 Indemnity Act, the 1992 Indemnity Act Amendment and the 1992 Further Indemnity Act. Law 34/95 did not receive a favourable response from the Freedom Front (a far-right party) or from the IFP because of the famous cut off date. It was originally fixed as 5 December 1993 and could not include amnesty requests for crimes committed during the period leading up to the 1994 elections. The two parties were aware that many of their militants had acted criminally in the period from December 1993 to May 1994. They asked for the date to be extended to 10 May 1994 and it was later changed.
59. This point is discussed in more depth in J. Sarkin. 2004. *Carrots and Sticks: The TRC and the South African Amnesty Process*. Antwerp: Intersentia, pp. 55–58.
60. See N. Aletta. 1999. 'Truth and Reconciliation: the Birth of the Present and the Reworking of History', *Journal of Southern African Studies* 25: 499–519; A. Boraine. 2001. *A Country Unmasked: Inside South Africa's Truth Commission*. Oxford: Oxford University Press.

61. The creation process of the TRC was commented on in A. Krog. 1998. *Country of My Skull. Guilt, Sorrow, and the Limits of Forgiveness in the New South Africa*. New York: Random House, pp. 27–33; and especially in *TRC Final Report*, vol. 1, ch. 3.
62. See H. Klug. 2000. 'Constitutional Court and the Institutional Dynamics of Constitutionalism', in *Constituting Democracy. Law, Globalism and South Africa's Political Reconstruction*. Cambridge: Cambridge University Press, pp. 139–59. On the impact of introducing centralized judicial review in the South African constitutional order, see X. Philippe. 1998. 'La saisine du juge constitutionnel en Afrique Australe', in F. Delperee and P. Foucher (eds), *La saisine du juge constitutionnel aspect de droit comparé*, Brussels: Bruylant, pp. 73–93.
63. Intense dialogue between the Court and the Constitutional Assembly heated up, especially between the first and second evaluation of the definitive Constitution's compliance with the 34 CPs. After the first evaluation, the Court refused to approve the constitutional text and asked the Assembly to make numerous changes. See Venter, 'Requirements for a New Constitutional Text', pp. 32–44. Section 71(1) of the Interim Constitution adopted and constitutionalized the certification of the final constitution's compliance with the CPs.
64. See X. Philippe. 1996. 'La Cour constitutionnelle sud-africaine et le règlement des conflits politiques', *Revue française de droit constitutionnel* 27: 461–91; and R. Pretorius. 1994. 'Enforcement mechanisms in the 1993 Constitution', *South African Public Law* 265–77.
65. Chapter title, 'The Judicial Authority and the Administration of Justice'.
66. Chapter 8, s. 165–80 of the 1996 Constitution covers the judicial system and constitutional justice. According to s. 98(2) of the 1993 Constitution, the Court is called on to certify the definitive Constitution's compliance with the CPs, the final phase of the constitution-making process. The constitutional justice system to be introduced was the subject of much discussion during the negotiations. The ANC's political and constitutional vision of a separate and independent centralized body prevailed. The NP's opposing idea was the creation of a special chamber within the Supreme Court's Appellate Division; see Spitz and Chaskalson, *The Politics of Transition*, pp. 192–96.
67. The Constitutional Court Complementary Act 13/1995 amended by the Constitution of the Republic of South Africa Second Amendment Act 44/1995. Two other legislative texts were later passed: the Public Service Laws Amendment Act 47/1997 and the Constitutional Court Complementary Act 79/1997. As well as the rules of the Constitutional Court approved in 2003, see *Government Gazette* 25726 of 31 October 2003.
68. In general, see Orrù, *La Costituzione di tutti*, pp. 459–99; X. Philippe. 1996. 'La Cour constitutionnelle sud-africaine et le règlement des conflits politiques', *Revue française de droit constitutionnel*, pp. 463 *et seq*. See also L. Pegoraro. 1998. *Lineamenti di giustizia costituzionale comparata*. Turin: Giappichelli.
69. Section 167(4): 'Only the Constitutional Court may a) decide disputes between organs of state in the national or provincial sphere concerning the constitutional status, powers or functions of any of those organs of state; b) decide on the constitutionality of any parliamentary or provincial Bill, but may do so only in the circumstances provided in section 79 or 121; c) decide applications envisaged in section 80 or 122; d) decide on the constitutionality of any amendment to the Constitution; e) decide that Parliament or the President has failed to fulfil a constitutional obligation; f) certify a provincial constitution in terms of section 144. (5) The Constitutional Court makes the final decision whether an Act of Parliament, a provincial Act or conduct of the President is constitutional, and must confirm any order of invalidity made by the Supreme Court of Appeal, a High Court, or a court of similar status, before that order has any force.'
70. See note 108 below.

71. Section 121(1): 'The President must either assent to and sign a Bill passed in terms of this Chapter or, if the President has reservations about the constitutionality of the Bill, refer it back to the National Assembly for reconsideration. (2) The joint rules and orders must provide for the procedure for the reconsideration of a Bill by the National Assembly and the participation of the National Council of Provinces in the process. (3) The National Council of Provinces must participate in the reconsideration of a Bill that the President has referred back to the National Assembly if a) the President's reservations about the constitutionality of the Bill relate to a procedural matter that involves the Council; b) section 74(1), (2) or (3)(b) or 76 was applicable in the passing of the Bill. (4) If, after reconsideration, a Bill fully accommodates the President's reservations, the President must assent to and sign the Bill; if not, the President must either a) assent to and sign the Bill; or b) refer it to the Constitutional Court for a decision on its constitutionality. (5) If the Constitutional Court decides that the Bill is constitutional, the President must assent to and sign it.'
72. Rule 13 of the Constitutional Court Rules (according to the last amendment to the Rules in Government Notice R1603 in *Government Gazette* 25643 of 1 October 2003, effective 1 December 2003) sets forth the adversarial procedure before the Constitutional Court. The President or the Premier of the province must submit to the Court Registrar, the Speaker of the National Assembly (or of the provincial legislature if a provincial Premier raises the issue) and the Chairperson of the National Council of Provinces a document that includes all the provisions that are held to be unconstitutional and the legal motivation for refusing to sign the law. Subrules (3) and (4) of Rule 13 give national and provincial legislators the right to send a written reply to the Court regarding the issues raised by the President or Premier. Rule 11 then regulates the procedure before the Court. The Chief Justice may request at any given moment further documentation or clarification from the parties.
73. Subrules 5 and 6 of Rule 15 of the Constitutional Court Rules give legislature members and ministers (national and provincial) the right to file with the Court Registrar within 15 days from the date of serving the application a notice opposing the procedure. Even though the Chief Justice may request supplementary information or documents at any moment, if no notice of opposition is made, the Court decides on the basis of the documents filed.
74. 'a) The Supreme Court of Appeal, a High Court or a court of similar status may make an order concerning the constitutional validity of an Act of Parliament, a provincial Act or any conduct of the President, but an order of constitutional invalidity has no force unless it is confirmed by the Constitutional Court. b) A court which makes an order of constitutional invalidity may grant a temporary interdict or other temporary relief to a party, or may adjourn the proceedings, pending a decision of the Constitutional Court on the validity of that Act or conduct. c) National legislation must provide for the referral of an order of constitutional invalidity to the Constitutional Court. d) Any person or organ of state with a sufficient interest may appeal, or apply, directly to the Constitutional Court to confirm or vary an order of constitutional invalidity by a court in terms of this subsection.'
75. See S. Jagwanth. 2002. 'The Constitutional Roles and Responsibilities of Lower Courts', *South African Journal on Human Rights* 18: 201–24. Rule 16 of the Constitutional Court Rules states that those entitled to participate in the confirmation of an order of constitutional invalidity are: 'a person or organ of State.' An application opposing or in favour of the order of constitutional invalidity ruled by the lower court must be lodged within 15 days of the order's filing at the Constitutional Court's Registrar; this provision is to be read in conjunction with s. 172(2)(d). The persons entitled to oppose or support an order of constitutional invalidity are those with a 'sufficient interest'. As for the terms for claims and counterclaims in relation to order's confirmation, the procedure used by the Court is provided in Rule 11 of the Constitutional Court Rules.

76. Section 167: '(6) National legislation or the rules of the Constitutional Court must allow a person, when it is in the interests of justice and with leave of the Constitutional Court a) to bring a matter directly to the Constitutional Court; b) to appeal directly to the Constitutional Court from any other court.'
77. See S. Matela. 1998. 'Direct Access to Constitutional Court', *South African Journal on Human Rights* 14: 333 *et seq.*
78. Rule 18 of the Constitutional Court Rules states that even if the Chief Justice asks for supplementary documents at any moment from the parties, the Court may decide immediately based on the documentation presented without debate.
79. Rule 19 then illustrates the terms for the claims and counterclaims of the parties transferring the dispute from a lower court to the Constitutional Court.
80. Section 178: 'a) the Chief Justice, who presides at meetings of the Commission; b) the President of the Constitutional Court; c) one Judge President designated by the Judges President; d) the Cabinet member responsible for the administration of justice, or an alternate designated by that Cabinet member; e) two practising advocates nominated from within the advocates' profession to represent the profession as a whole, and appointed by the President; f) two practising attorneys nominated from within the attorneys' profession to represent the profession as g) one teacher of law designated by teachers of law at South African universities; h) six persons designated by the National Assembly from among its members, at least three of whom must be members of opposition parties represented in the Assembly; i) four permanent delegates to the National Council of Provinces designated together by the Council with a supporting vote of at least six provinces; j) four persons designated by the President as head of the national executive, after consulting the leaders of all the parties in the National Assembly; and k) when considering matters specifically relating to a provincial or local division of the High Court, the Judge President of that division and the Premier, or an alternate designated by the Premier, of the province concerned.'
81. Also based on Juta's Constitutional Law Bulletin and the Faculty of Law of the University of Witwatersrand.
82. The role of law as an instrument for social change in South Africa not just during the transition is stressed by Klug, *Constituting Democracy*, p. 7.
83. In this sense, Mortati, according to whom the condition for 'the appearance of constituent power in a strict sense constitutes a break in constitutional legal relationships'; see C. Mortati. 1972. 'La Costituente' (1945), in *Raccolta di scritti*. Milan: Giuffrè, pp. 26 *et seq*; see also Pace, *Potere costituente*, pp. 97 *et seq* (especially pp. 105 *et seq*).
84. For a comparative overview, see M.F. Rigaux. 1985. *La théorie des limites matérielles à l'exercice de la fonction constituante*. Brussels: Lancier. See also Pace, *Potere costituente*, pp. 121 *et seq*; M.P. Viviani Schlein. 1997. *Rigidità costituzionale. Limiti e graduazioni*. Turin: Giappichelli; A. Cerri. 1991. 'Revisione costituzionale', in *Enciclopedia Giuridica*. Rome: Treccani, vol. 27; G. Silvestri. 1987. 'Spunti di riflessione sulla tipologia e sui limiti della revisione costituzionale', in *Studi in onore di P. Biscaretti di Ruffia*. Milan: Giuffrè, vol. 2, pp. 1205 *et seq*; P. Barile and U. de Siervo. 1968. 'Revisione della Costituzione', in *Novissimo Digesto Italiano*. Turin: Utet, vol. 15. In general, see Loughlin and Walker, *The Paradox of Constitutionalism*.
85. See X. Philippe. 1999. 'Droit Constitutionnel étranger: Afrique du Sud', *Revue Française de Droit Constitutionnel* 37: 159–71; and van Huyssteen, 'The Constitutional Court', pp. 255 *et seq.*
86. See J. Sarkin. 1997. 'The Political Role of the South African Constitutional Court', *South African Law Journal* 114: 135–50; G. Carpenter. 1996. 'The South African Constitutional Court: Taking Stock of the Early Decisions', *The Human Rights Constitutional Law* 1(1): 29 *et seq.*
87. See (1995) (4) BCLR 401 (CC).
88. See (1995) (6) BCLR 665 (CC).

89. See s. 101(6) of the 1993 Constitution, adopted in s. 167(4) and 172(2) of the 1996 Constitution.
90. The Court, in fact, accepted the application of the Attorney General of the Natal Province (Tim McNally) who asked to participate in the dispute before the Court in the interests of resolving this delicate problem of procedural law. According to the Attorney General, the uncertainty about the constitutionality of s. 217 created serious instability in many of the pending criminal trials. This constituted a criterion of 'Interest of Justice', which is a prerequisite for directly accessing the judgment of constitutionality. The Court admitted McNally's application, which had legal grounds in s. 100(2) of the Interim Constitution in combination with the reading of Rule 17(1)(2) of the Constitutional Court. This constitutional provision was later adopted in s. 167(6)(a) and (b). See Webb, 'The Constitutional Court of South Africa', pp. 211 *et seq.*
91. The *Makwanyane* decision had a revolutionary effect and overturned legal, political and cultural characteristics of the past; even public opinion was mostly against abolishing the death penalty. In South Africa, during the 1980s until 1988, hundreds of death sentences were decided or carried out; there were also many waiting on death row for execution. The relationship between the Court and public opinion was much discussed in relation to this judgment; the very idea of creating a centralized body for judicial review as opposed to leaving the Constitution's protection to the Supreme Court is part of the political idea of having a powerful body safeguarding fundamental rights. Symbolically, the Court's headquarters were decorated with murals representing national unity. The judges wear green robes so as to differentiate themselves from ordinary judges. The Court's symbol is the African tree of justice, under which disputes traditionally were settled. The branches of this tree correspond with the South African flag. More important than the symbols, however, is the fact that the Court immediately won the people's trust. In this context, *Makwanyane* represents a break from seeking the approval of black and white public opinion. Even though, as is usual with the Court's commencement, many letters for and against the death penalty were addressed to the Court and read by the judges, the judges expressed themselves in complete autonomy on this very delicate issue. Many have claimed that the Court's decision was a minority stance considering the majority public opinion and was thus in opposition with the principle of a majority democracy. The request for a referendum on the death penalty was later denied. In this critical situation, the hostility and mistrust of some towards judicial review manifested itself. Criticism was grounded in the idea that a few individuals who were not elected decided on a hugely important issue. According to others, the Court's power to control laws voted on by the legislature would be a clear violation of the separation of powers and the autonomy of the legislature's power. See Webb, 'The Constitutional Court of South Africa', p. 233 (note 169); Choudhry, 'Globalization in Search of Justification', pp. 850 *et seq*; M. Zlotnick. 1996. 'The Death Penalty and the Public Opinion', *South African Journal on Human Rights* 12(1): 70–78; P.M. Maduna. 1996. 'Death Penalty and Human Rights', *South African Journal on Human Rights* 12(2): 193–213.
92. See also A. Lollini. 2007b. 'Legal Argumentation Based on Foreign Law. An Example from Case Law of the South African Constitutional Court', *Utrecht Law Review* 3(1): 60–74; A. Lollini. 2007a. 'La circolazione degli argomenti: metodo comparato e parametri interpretativi extra-sistemici nella giurisprudenza costituzionale sudafricana', *Rivista di diritto pubblico comparato* 479–523.
93. The Court expressed doubts about the death penalty as a deterrent (§ 115–127). The problems related to prevention are analysed in § 128, whereas the constitutional ban on retribution and revenge, based on the Postamble 'National Unity and Reconciliation', are in § 129–31.

94. See Case CCT 17/96, *The Azanian People Organization, (AZAPO), Nontsikelelo Margaret Biko, Churchill Mhlleli Mxenge, Chris Ribeiro v. State* (1996) (8) BCLR 1015 (CC). For a detailed analysis, see Chapter 4.
95. The text was then published in the *Government Gazette* 15466, January 1994.
96. The Freedom Alliance is one of the many paradoxes of the South African constitution-making process: the two opposing political parties (Afrikaner and Zulu) were both opponents of the ANC.
97. See Constitution of South Africa Amendment Act 2 of 1994, *Government Gazette* 15550, March 1994.
98. For an analysis of the 1994 elections, see R.W. Johnson and L. Schlemmer. 1996. *Launching Democracy in South Africa. The First Open Election, April 1994*. New Haven: Yale University Press; and R. Southall. 1994. 'The South Africa Elections of 1994: the Remaking of a Dominant-Party State', *The Journal of Modern African Studies* 32(4): 605–29.
99. The GNU was composed of members of political parties that obtained more than 5% of the vote; the law provided for the GNU's dissolution at the end of the five-year legislature; twenty-six members were nominated in proportion to each party's votes. In the spirit of national unity and according to s. 88 and 89 of the 1993 Constitution, the decisions were to be made in order to achieve a consensus (except for a few cases when a majority was required). See Spitz and Chaskalson, *The Politics of Transition*, pp. 87–99; and Friedman, *The Long Journey*, p. 103.
100. '(1) The Constitutional Assembly shall pass the new constitutional text within two years as from the date of the first sitting of the National Assembly under this Constitution. (2) For the passing of the new constitutional text by the Constitutional Assembly, a majority of at least two-thirds of all the members of the Constitutional Assembly shall be required: Provided that provisions of such text relating to the boundaries, powers and functions of provinces shall not be considered passed by the Constitutional Assembly unless approved also by a majority of two-thirds of all the members of the Senate.'
101. See F. Dreyfus. 1994. 'La Constitution Intérimaire d'Afrique du Sud', *Revue Française de Droit Constitutionnel* 19: 410.
102. This opinion is shared by Rinella, 'Il Constitution', p. 155; Pegoraro and Rinella, 'La nuova Costituzione', p. 525.
103. See Orrù, *La Costituzione di tutti*, pp. 91 *et seq*. Orrù notes that the Constitutional Assembly had the characteristics of a constituent body. First, it was a unicameral body with members elected proportionally (see also de Vergottini, *Diritto costituzionale comparato*, p. 147). The fact that this body acted simultaneously as a bicameral Parliament, exercising its normal legislative functions and control over the executive, does not seem out of place. In fact, this setup has often been seen throughout history. From a strictly constitutional point of view, the Assembly redesigned the executive's structure and functioning, creating a system that would replace the power sharing system (confirming the shift from a consociational democracy to a competitive democracy). In addition, it proceeded to redefine the legal relationship between the centre and the outlying areas by adding the cooperative government rule. There were a number of other important changes: the new territorial subdivision of political power, the new bicameralism with the Senate's transformation into the National Council of Provinces (and a different subdivision of the legislative powers), some important changes to the judicial review system (with emphasis on the centralized method), and the change of the chapter titled 'Fundamental Rights' into the Bill of Rights, which broadened protection of socio-economic rights.
104. See Sarkin, 'L'écriture de la Constitution sud-africaine', p. 749; Lobban, 'Un accord négocié', p. 87.

105. See 'Public Participation Kicks Off', *Constitutional Talk*, 10–23 February 1995; 'Towards a New Constitution', *Constitutional Talk*, 30 June–10 August 1995; 'Excellent Results for Constitutional Assembly Media Campaign', *Constitutional Talk*, 22 April–18 May 1996.
106. As of 20 February 1996, 1,500 individual accounts and 248,500 signatures on petitions and memorandums were delivered to the Assembly. See J. Sarkin, 'L'écriture de la Constitution sud-africaine', p. 749. On the Public Participation Programme, see Orrù, *La Costituzione di tutti*, pp. 107–09. On the contribution of Submissions from the general public, see Webb, 'The Constitutional Court of South Africa', p. 205.
107. *In Re Certification of the Constitution of the Republic of South Africa* (1996) (10) BCLR 1253 (CC). For an analysis of the court decision, see M. Chaskalson and D. Davis. 1997. 'Constitutionalism, the Rule of Law, and the First Certification Judgement: ex Parte Chairperson of the Constitutional Assembly in Re: Certification of the Constitution of the Republic of South Africa 1996', *South African Journal on Human Rights* 13: 430–45. For a point-by-point analysis of the dissimilarities that the Court found, see Orrù, *La Costituzione di tutti*, pp. 114–22.
108. For a reflection on the ambiguity of the Constitutional Court's certification, between political control and judicial review, in relation to a limited number of generally formulated rules, see Sarkin, 'The Political Role', pp. 135–50; J. Sarkin. 1998. 'The Effect of Constitutional Borrowings on the Drafting of South Africa's Interim Bill of Rights and the Role Played by Comparative and International Law in the Interpretation of Human Rights Provisions by the Constitutional Court', *Journal of Constitutional Law* 1–2: 176 *et seq*.
109. See Chapter 4 entitled 'Parliament', s. 42–82, which includes the provisions regarding the national legislature's functioning.
110. The rules governing executive power are in Chapter 5, 'The President and National Executive' (s. 83–102).
111. See Orrù, *La Costituzione di tutti*, p. 409, who holds that the elements of parliamentarianism prevail over presidentialism and semi-presidentialism and argues that it is a semi-parliamentary form.
112. See Chapter 6 under the title 'Provinces' (s. 103–50). The certification procedure for provincial constitutions has been used in two circumstances. Only two provinces have submitted constitutional texts to the Constitutional Court: Western Cape and KwaZulu-Natal (KZN). Interestingly, these are the only two provinces not under ANC control. As for Western Cape's constitution, the Constitutional Court issued two judgments. At the first certification procedure (*In Re Certification of the Constitution of Western Cape* (1997) (9) BCLR 1167 (CC)), the Court requested a few changes. When this province's constitution was submitted a second time to the Court, it was approved (*In Re Certification of the Amended Text of the Constitution of the Western Cape* (1997) (12) BCLR 1653 (CC)). In 1996, the Constitutional Court had already ruled against KZN's provincial constitution (*In Re Certification of the Constitution of the Province of KwaZulu-Natal* (1996) (11) BCLR 1419 (CC)). With interesting legal argumentation, the Court pointed out numerous conflicts between the KZN Constitution and the 1993 Interim Constitution, declaring the provincial text unconstitutional.
113. See C. Murray and R. Simeon. 1999. 'From Paper to Practice: the National Council of Provinces after its First Year', *South African Public Law* 14: 96–141.
114. As determined by the measures contained in Constitutional Principle XVI.
115. See Chapter 9, 'State Institutions Supporting Constitutional Democracy', s. 182–94.
116. Elements that support this interpretation can be found in Ebrahim, *The Soul of a Nation*, pp. 170–72; and Gastrow, *Bargaining for Peace*.

117. This problem with African constitutionalism has been pointed out by Sacco, 'Il costituzionalismo africano', pp. 6 *et seq*; Gonidec, 'Constitutionnalismes Africains', pp. 23 *et seq*; and Mezzetti, *Teoria e prassi*, p. 288.

Part II

The Constituent Role of the Truth and Reconciliation Commission

3

The Constitutional Suspension of a Strictly Criminal Approach

Introduction

The unitary political project came about as a result of innovative constitutional experiments led by extremely diverse constituent actors. This project, however, contained underlying ambiguities and, understandably, weaknesses that could not be removed. The unexpected unity that was created continued to be weak; in fact, supplementary constitution-making tools were developed in order to give this fragile unity a chance at being long-lasting.

These tools were created in order to give continuity to the constitution-making process in a material sense and in order to neutralize the centrifugal forces within the social fabric. In other words, these tools were to aid the construction of the new unitary post-apartheid political body by extending the constitution-making process beyond the formal moment of the adoption of the definitive Constitution. These instruments were mechanisms for making the new post-apartheid constitutional principles a reality. While the formal act of writing the constitution was certainly a fundamental condition, it was not enough for handling the radical innovation of a unitary political project and a constitutional transition. One of the most important constitution-making tools, appointed with a very significant supplementary function, is the Truth and Reconciliation Commission (TRC). The second part of this book analyses the activity of one of its bodies: the Amnesty Committee (AC).

The AC was responsible for implementing the Amnesty Process that the Constitution provided for political crimes committed during apartheid. As stated before, one of the strengths of the new South African constitutionalism was its resolution of the issue of transitional justice for crimes committed under apartheid in terms of legal and constitutional measures; in a sense, the Constitution absorbed the problem of reckoning with the past. The constitutionalization of transitional justice had two distinct yet complementary characteristics: a) constitutional *suspension* of a strictly criminal approach for political crimes committed under apartheid; and b) using public confession.

Both post-apartheid constitutions (the 1993 Interim Constitution and the definitive 1996 Constitution) contain measures implemented by the AC allowing the new democratic state to operate in a particular way for political crimes committed under apartheid.

By constitutionally suspending a strictly criminal approach, the post-apartheid constitution set a limit on the state's power to take criminal action. Thus, the new democratic state did not fully exercise the traditional powers associated with sovereignty such as accusing individuals of a crime and, as a result, setting the wheels of justice in motion to ascertain an individual's guilt and order his punishment accordingly. In the system provided by the constitution and implemented by the AC, the state becomes passive and allows individuals to choose the implementation of an alternative procedure; in fact, this happened through a decision to use public confession that would possibly lead to the setting aside of the punishment or the avoidance of trial and punishment. *Testis contra se*, testifying against oneself, was the complementary element to the constitutional suspension of a strictly criminal approach. What we witness is a reversal of the traditional functions of state sovereignty; instead of exercising the power to take penal action, post-apartheid constitutionalism preferred to use a special procedure that was only initiated by individuals who filed a public confession application with the AC. Another traditional element of sovereignty is favoured over the power to punish: the power to set aside a punishment or to refrain from punishing once an individual's criminal and political responsibility has been determined.

The state selectively refrained from manifesting its coercive power of subjecting individuals to a criminal trial; the new constitutional order, with the promise of annulling punishments or no sentences being issued, encouraged individuals to participate in the proceedings before the AC, something set in motion by the individuals themselves.

Post-apartheid constitutionalism provided a possibility for 'redemption' which, of course, was criticized and debated. During its creation phase, post-apartheid sovereignty did not express itself primarily through the state's power to impose justice; instead, it appealed to the individual's choice – with all the ambiguity and contradictions this involved – to decide to be part of the workings of justice. Instead of sovereignty that manifests itself through a monopoly of penal power (punishing the criminal act), the new constitutional order opted for a sovereignty based on the power to refrain from punishing once the crime has been confessed.

The use of public confession sheds light on two additional elements: a) the relationship between confession and truth that implies the greater efficacy of the AC proceedings in reconstructing the facts of the past as compared to a criminal trial's ability to do the same; and b) the symbolic and political dimensions of confession produce effects that directly influence the genesis of the new democratic state.

The constitutional suspension of a strictly criminal approach and public confession should be read as dynamics set in motion in order to correct the inherent weakness of constructing the political body's unity. In fact, if exercising penal action and the punishment that it may lead to always serve the purpose of expelling or concealing the offender's body from society, suspending a strictly criminal approach tends to neutralize this pattern.

Even if modern theories on punishment have gradually given penal sanctions new functions like rehabilitation, confining the offender's body to a place separated from society (the penitentiary) indicates a 'purification' of the political body, in addition to retribution for the damage caused and prevention of future offences being committed. The complementary nature of the suspension of a strictly criminal approach and the public confession demonstrates that in post-apartheid South Africa, consolidating the political body's unity through *inclusion* instead of *exclusion* was of primary importance.

In the final provisions under the heading 'National Unity and Reconciliation', the Interim Constitution expressly states the need to limit the vengeful impulses (including on a judicial level) within a society that was racially segregated for decades. For this reason, the constitutional order was set up in order to reintegrate (or at least not remove by punishment) individuals who committed political crimes under the previous regime.[1] The AC was therefore interwoven with the constitution-making process's primary objective: the political body's unity, without which the Constitution would not have been a reality. Since the political body was extremely diverse (that is, not homogeneous), all inclusive efforts had to be made, including the political decision not to purge individuals who accepted this 'redemptive' option offered by the new constitutional order.

Thus, South Africa chose to reach unity through inclusion as opposed to using 'purification' (by law). In other words, it chose unity through integration instead of unity through subtraction.

The Functioning of the TRC

A proper evaluation of the co-constituent activity of the TRC (and in particular the AC) and the constitutional suspension of a strictly criminal approach for political crimes committed under apartheid must include an analysis of their procedural functioning.[2]

The law instituting the TRC[3] lays down the body's procedural rules and three-committee structure in a detailed manner. The TRC is an organizational body that contains three subcommittees: 1) the Human Rights Violations Committee (HRVC), which collected information from victims about the crimes to which they or their loved ones were subject in order to reconstruct the facts of the past; 2) the Amnesty Committee (AC), the body before which perpetrators publicly confessed in detail the facts of the crimes they had committed in order to potentially receive amnesty from the AC; and 3) the Reparation and Rehabilitation Committee (RRC), which was in charge of recommending a reparations policy and only in urgent cases providing interim relief that the state had set for victims through a closed list of the victims entitled to compensation.[4]

The TRC, as a truth recovery system, had means of gathering, processing and spreading the memory-based and factual information that came from four main sources: 1) the victims' statements made during the HRVC's investigations and hearings; 2) the results of the Investigation Units; 3) the special public hearings and submissions filed at the TRC. Anyone who had a specific interest in providing the Commission with particular information could file notes and documents; 4) the information from applications to and public confessions made before the AC.

The TRC's supporting and integrating functions in relation to the constitution-making process can be seen by analysing the methodology used for managing the factual and historical data that came out of the hearings and investigations. The TRC's co-constituent activity can be seen in a variety of aspects; this section focuses on how historical and factual information as well as narrative and memory-based information about the segregated past contributed to the constitution-making debate. Creating a new community's unity requires knowledge, acceptance, acknowledgment and emancipation from the past, and the rejection of conflicting interpretations of the facts of the past.[5]

The investigation powers granted to the TRC allowed it to gather information regarding crimes as well as data about deep-rooted social dynamics of the apartheid era, thereby officially giving a voice to the black population for the first time.

Gathering, processing and spreading through the media information about the apartheid era was the TRC's first service to the constitution-making process. Even if all the information was a little too quickly defined as the 'truth' about the past,[6] it nevertheless contributed to the gradual creation of a collective memory. Collective memory was not just the fruit of civil society's universities' independent work and the artistic-aesthetic reinterpretation of the facts, but it also came about, above all, through an official state body.

The Human Rights Violation Committee, Investigation Units and Public Special Hearings

The HRVC gathered apartheid victims' statements. Since a large number of South Africans accepted to present publicly the hardship they endured, a limit was put on the number of public hearings. Only the most serious cases that epitomized the regime's conduct were considered for public hearing with radio and television coverage. The victims' public hearings were nevertheless unanimously considered a cathartic event. Individuals who had suffered crimes, violence and injustice had the opportunity for the first time to be officially and publicly heard and acknowledged by the nation.[7] The HRVC moved around South Africa in order to reach rural areas, bringing the Commission to the victims. 'Investigating Human Rights Violations', Chapter 3 of the Commission's statute, exclusively deals with the HRVC's powers. This Committee was given the power to investigate gross human rights violations from 1960 to 1990.[8]

The HRVC was also created to help the Commission in pursuing the general objectives established in s. 3(1). The Committee was therefore an auxiliary body of the Commission, and its main power was to create a team of specialists investigating criminal episodes disclosed by victims. The HRVC also proceeded to gather detailed information about organizations and the apartheid state's apparatus in addition to the individuals responsible for crimes identified by victims.[9]

Victims applied to the HRVC by filling out a submission with their personal details and information about the violations to which they or others had been subject. Each submission, written down by the statement takers, was then examined by TRC staff[10] and the data extracted was entered in a database: the National Data Base (NDB). This information tool was essential to the Commission's work, as it led to a better factual reconstruction of violations committed in different contexts by establishing connections between the persons involved and the events. The NDB also provided a preliminary cross-examination of the reliability of the victims' statements by comparing and cross-referencing the data gathered in South Africa and abroad (where issues arose about the TRC's competence violations).[11]

The NDB was also a very important tool for the AC, which could consult the data contained therein in order to cross-check the truthfulness of the confessions. Once the HRVC concluded the preliminary investigation of an individual case, it decided whether the case would undergo a public hearing and drafted a report to be sent to the RRC.[12] There was an important connection between these two bodies. Once an individual was officially recognized as having victim status by the HRVC, the RRC put their name on a special 'closed list', which was supposed to provide privileged access to compensation.[13]

The Investigation Units were also essential to the TRC's functioning[14] and also distinguish South Africa's Commission from others elsewhere in the world, for example, those in Latin America. Due to the autonomy and powers granted to the Investigation Units by the Commission's statutory rules, they were able to gather further information in addition to information supplied by victims (in the HRVC) and by perpetrators (in the AC). The creation of these units is an important evolution in the truth commission model. Despite complaints that the Investigation Units could have been used more efficiently, they gave the TRC additional factual elements in order to corroborate the statements made during hearings.[15] To fulfil this task, the Commission's statute gave the Investigation Units police powers, such as the right to conduct searches and to demand documents (from private individuals or from state functionaries and offices). A special code of ethics regulated investigatory activities. Each investigator had an 'identity card' in order to verify which institutions, agencies and documents he had contacted or consulted. Some received special authorizations like top secret security clearance, which allowed the investigator access to confidential documents that could possibly have a bearing on delicate international relations related to South Africa's geopolitical role during apartheid. The Investigation Units were divided into one unit for national investigations and four units for regional investigations.

In accordance with the preamble of the TRC's statute, the Commission was appointed with the task of reconstructing the general circumstances, the antecedents and the context of gross human rights violations committed under apartheid. This statement in the statute's preamble is nothing other than a definition of the Commission's work, that is, historical, factual and memory-based reconstructions of the segregated past.[16] One of the main problems was understanding how white citizens, who often defined themselves as 'ordinary, decent and God-fearing', could have ignored the reality of a violent authoritarian regime based on discrimination. In order to address this issue, the Commission organized public proceedings (institutional hearings), during which figures involved in institutions, the judiciary, education, the national health system, the media, religious communities and business were called to testify on how segments of society functioned under apartheid. Most of the people called to testify in public before the TRC pointed out that there was collective responsibility for keeping systematic segregation in place. Public hearings served the purpose of showing the structural nature of apartheid beyond personal responsibility.[17]

The Amnesty Committee

In accordance with Chapter 4 of the TRC's statute, the public confession procedure was held before the AC and the Committee's members had the task of deciding on whether each case met the requirements for receiving amnesty once all criteria were verified as provided by law.[18] The body had many responsibilities and as a result requires a strict legal analysis of the procedure and powers granted to it by law.

First of all, as provided by s. 17(3), the Chairperson and Vice-Chairperson of the AC must be a judge according to South African law. This express statutory reference to specific professional adjudicative experience is due to the fact that the Committee's decisions had direct consequences on the personal liberty of amnesty applicants who were serving a prison sentence when they applied.

It was originally composed of five members and chaired by a judge, but it grew to nineteen commissioners divided into panels of three members to deal more efficiently with the number of applications submitted. Considering that the Committee had to deal with matters relating to criminal law, the AC's composition also included six High Court judges, eight advocates and five attorneys.[19] The transparency of the appointing procedure for AC members was criticized (in fact, no public consultation was held). The position's delicate nature called for legal abilities. It was censured for its markedly adjudicative functioning, and many found fault with the AC for not having members from other areas of expertise (historians, sociologists, etc.) and a gradual shift to an accusatorial type of procedure. This garnered criticism from those who accused the AC of having overly juridicized its procedure.[20] Originally, the AC was also supposed to have an investigative procedure overseeing the investigative phase.

Section 18(1)(2) states that natural persons who intend to apply for amnesty for any act or omission committed for a political objective must do so as prescribed and within twelve months from the cut off date's proclamation (s. 7(3)). This date, which was changed a number of times, was published in the *Government Gazette*. The application form was submitted directly to the TRC and sent to the AC, which had to first prioritize the applications following the criteria of s. 18(2), giving precedence to those who were in prison at the time of applying for amnesty. In agreement with the Minister of Justice and Correctional Service, on 17 May 1996, the AC published the Regulations containing the procedures enacted for informing prisoners of their right to apply for amnesty. This procedure opened the doors to many applications from prisoners sentenced for crimes that the AC would later declare as lacking political motives and, as a result, refused amnesty. Many prisoners convicted for common crimes tried to take advantage of the amnesty process, slowing down the AC's work.[21] According to s. 19, once the AC received an amnesty application, it had the power to ask for further investigations regarding what the applicant confessed, particularly in order to establish whether political motives existed or not.[22] In fact, if no political motive was found, the AC had to deny to amnesty.[23] If instead the crime confessed was committed for a political purpose but did not meet the requirements of s. 1(1), that is, when it did not constitute a gross violation of human rights, the AC might automatically grant amnesty without a public hearing. If the crime confessed did constitute a gross violation of human rights for a political objective, s. 19(4) applied; based on this provision, the AC had to decide to grant or refuse amnesty after a public hearing, during which the amnesty applicant had to publicly repeat the confession made in the written application. In arranging the hearing, the AC notified victims and all the persons interested of the date and location of the hearing.

The statute provides a thorough definition of the confession to be made by the amnesty applicant. The confession had to meet two basic criteria: 1) it had to be 'truthful'; and 2) there could be no denial of guilt. The consistency of the AC's enforcement of its statutory criteria has been fully scrutinized and criticized. Such analysis was made possible by the availability of the AC's decisions and the transcripts of the confessions made before the Committee. For the sake of clarity, references to the official documents published by the TRC online are preceded by the initials AC when referring to the text of an AC decision, or by AM, which precedes the official number given to the amnesty application. These initials and numbers are useful for finding the cases cited in the TRC's database.

The problem of 'truthfulness', the first criterion, is analysed in a subsequent section. For our purposes here, it is important to note that in implementing the notion of 'truth', the AC shifted from an 'objective' perspective to a more 'subjective' one. In almost all its decisions, the Committee mentions whether the criteria of full disclosure were satisfied or not, and it often employs the term 'truthful'.[24] The second compulsory criterion of the confession was that the applicant could not deny guilt. In fact, not acknowledging guilt precluded receiving amnesty, and many amnesty applications were refused precisely for this reason.[25] The juridical analysis of denying guilt is rather complex and controversial. For example, some applicants, even though they admitted the criminal act, stated that they acted out of self-defence; in a more complicated situation, others filed an amnesty application while unfairly serving prison time for political reasons. In these cases the AC could not do anything; if the person confessing insisted on denying guilt, the AC could only advise them to pursue the presidential pardon process in compliance with s. 84(2) of the 1996 Constitution, revealing an obvious gap in the law.

Once the public hearing ended and the decision was made to grant or refuse amnesty, the AC sent the dossier containing all the facts of the case as well as the text of the decision to the TRC, which then informed the applicants, victims or (if the victims were dead) their relatives of the decision (s. 20(5)). The amnesty provided was strictly personal;[26] no member of the same organization of an individual who received amnesty could use this fact in his or her defence. Amnesty, in fact, could only be granted through a personal process for crimes committed and confessed by individuals; if a crime involved more than one person, each accomplice had to make a full public and individual disclosure.

It should also be noted that the AC had decision-making autonomy in relation to the Commission, which mostly acted as a coordinator, though some of the Commission's members officially participated in one of the three Committees.

Temporal and Subject Matter Jurisdiction

The AC's temporal and subject matter jurisdictions are stated in the statute's preamble. As far as temporal competence was concerned, the TRC was appointed with the duty of providing a complete picture of the gross human rights violations committed, within or outside of South Africa, during the period from 1 March 1960 to 10 May 1994. After several postponements, the final date for filing an application was set for 30 September 1997 in order to cope with the extension of the Commission's general mandate period to 10 May 1994. The statute also established the Commission's material jurisdiction, defining all the offences, for any act or omission (even if performing the orders of a superior) that could receive amnesty after the person in question made a confession before the AC: torture, abduction, killing and other severe ill treatment,[27] as well as any attempt, conspiracy, incitement, instigation, command or procurement to commit one of those acts.

When drafting the law instituting the TRC, the South African Parliament chose to define the gross violations of human rights falling under the AC's competence with 'neutral concepts' for offences like murder or kidnapping contained in national criminal law.[28] This decision was made in order to separate the offences – even terminologically – pertaining to the Commission from those falling under national law. This separation sprang from a need to differentiate the special proceedings before the AC from ordinary criminal justice.[29] But what was the line separating ordinary criminal justice from the AC's jurisdiction? That is one of the key issues to understanding the logic of the entire amnesty process. Criminal offences that could be tried for amnesty had to have a 'political objective', that is, qualifying as part of the conflict between the apartheid state and the liberation movements.[30]

The case-by-case application of the normative criteria concerning political objectives was one of the most controversial and intricate areas of the AC decision-making practice. Despite the TRC statute's clear indication of the political requirements needed for amnesty eligibility, the complex phenomenology of political violence compelled the AC to evaluate factual elements disclosed by applicants, creating a compromise between legal requirements and the concrete context of the political struggle. This meant that not all the political elements of the crimes – which the TRC statute required as a condition in order to receive amnesty – were enforced in strict accordance with the wording of the law. In this context, the Committee was prepared to develop a sort of autonomous interpretation of the 'political offence requirements', shaping a broad and pragmatic approach instead of a narrow and strictly legalistic approach.[31]

According to the TRC statute, the AC should have considered the following criteria in evaluating whether political offence requirements were met:

a) the context in which the crimes were committed, if, for example, they took place during a 'political uprising, disturbance or event in reaction to them';
b) the gravity and the proportional relationship between the act committed and the political objectives pursued. Analysis of the AC decision-making practice shows that the principle of proportionality was not consistently implemented. The Committee avoided the practice of measuring the disproportionality between acts and objectives, assuming that the seriousness of the political violence context pushed perpetrators to act far beyond any moral limits;[32]
c) interconnected with the previous element is the issue of whether the victim was a direct political adversary. This requirement was also difficult to evaluate on a consistent basis. In several circumstances, for example, the AC had to decide on cases involving wrong targets or cases in which individuals (women and children) unrelated to the political strategy were wrongfully the victims of a crime. Once again, the Committee tended to assume that the nature of political violence in the apartheid era would have involved not just political targets;[33]
d) the AC more consistently enforced the rule regarding crimes committed for a 'personal gain, out of malice, ill-will or spite against victims'. The existence of these conditions, in several cases, precluded receiving amnesty;[34]
e) additional elements of crime eligibility for amnesty provided by the TRC statute regarded 'orders' and 'affiliation'. In general terms, these elements implied that applicants were entitled to benefit from amnesty if they committed acts following orders or decisions made by the leader in command (whether formal or informal) of political organizations, state institutions, security apparatus or liberation movements in a broad sense. The existence of orders or planned political targets would have made it possible to establish which organization the applicants belonged to and to determine whether the organization was actually an actor in South African political violence. In order to be eligible for amnesty, crimes had to be committed by members of organizations recognized nationally as part of the conflict between the regime's forces and the liberation movements. Section 20(2)(b) further specified the requirements of affiliation. For apartheid apparatus members, amnesty applicants had to be members or employees of state institutions or state security forces; for former freedom fighter applicants, it was more difficult to prove affiliation due to the less organized nature of membership to black liberation movements.[35]

In this way, the drafters of the TRC statute considered these formal parameters as solid elements for fulfilling the AC's general mandate: to separate ordinary acts of violence from political crimes eligible for amnesty. Applications fulfilling these requirements were defined as *bona fide amnesty applications* in which perpetrators were connected with one of the political organizations involved in the conflict and whose actions indeed had a political background that could be separated, broadly speaking, from ordinary crimes.

However, as soon as the AC was confronted with the factual elements of the crimes confessed by applicants during the hearings, the idea of using the formal legal requirements established by law became extremely complicated. It was difficult for formal legal categories to encompass the military strategies and behaviours of the multiple actors involved. Political targets were identified and actions carried out in different ways. In pursuing political objectives, state institutions and security apparatus or black liberation movements acted differently. Even among liberation movement groups, violent actions were planned and ordered in different ways.

In these circumstances, in order to decide whether a crime had a political objective, the Committee had to evaluate applicants' organizational mandate, relevance and significance of the orders. More precisely, s. 20(2)(b), (c) and (d) states that applicants needed to show that they acted 'in the course of the scope of their duties and within the scope of their express or implied authority'.

While, in general, state apparatus perpetrators acted as official members of an organization and mostly on the basis of a personal mandate with instructions that were easier to verify, freedom fighters of less organized political groups perpetrated deeds as mere supporters following general policies. These policies were disseminated through informal means of communication and were implemented independently by affiliated perpetrators. Therefore, in the context of widespread political violence, actions were frequently based on general mandates of 'calling to act' in line with non-formalized instructions or general policies that were rarely laid out in detail. In all of these cases, the AC had a hard time drawing the line between common crimes not eligible for amnesty and politically motivated acts due to a narrow and literal interpretation of the criteria established by law.[36]

A personal mandate was considered to be a determining factor in whether a crime was deemed political and eligible for amnesty. Personal mandate existed when an applicant acted on the clear orders of a known organization.[37] This category included acts committed by both subordinates (of the state apparatus) and cadres of organized black liberation movements.

Much more problematic were the cases in which applicants did not act under clear instructions. In these circumstances, applicants had to demonstrate to the Committee that their organization provided a general 'call to act' and that they performed deeds within the scope of their express or implied political authority. In these circumstances, applicants might have misunderstood targets, erroneously included themselves in the group of people to perform those acts or mistaken what the political objectives their organization intended to achieve were.[38] In these cases, the applicants had to demonstrate to the Committee that the mistake was a reasonable error due to the specific context of the struggle.[39]

The Committee chose to implement a broad, pragmatic and subjective interpretation of s. 20(2)(a). The AC granted amnesties to applicants for acts which they reasonably believed to be in the course and scope of their duties and within the scope of their express or implied authority. In addition to the 'reasonable belief' principle, the Committee also enforced the notion of the 'reasonable mistake', which was an inevitable corollary of the non-formalistic interpretation of 'orders' as a requirement for a crime to be political and thus eligible for amnesty.

Many of the AC's solutions to interpretive problems were a source of dispute. There was the risk with the confessions that applicants manipulated elements regarding political objectives by inventing links or stating that they acted on behalf of an unknown organization. The AC's decisions were complicated by the reticence of political and military leaders to recognize the affiliation of activists, soldiers or service members and of specific orders having been given that led to criminal acts. Given this context, analysis of the AC's decisions reveals some major inconsistencies. As some commentators have pointed out, this is due to the hazy notion of 'political offence'. This was the main reason motivating the Committee's progressive shift towards a broad, pragmatic and merely factual interpretation of the political offence requirements. The line between political and non-political conduct became more and more based on the 'subjective perspective' of the applicants. In the context of widespread political violence, an objective formalization of what is a 'political crime' gives rise to an uncontrollable number of disputes due to the multiplicity of subjective points of view of perpetrators. The broad and pragmatic interpretative approach employed by the AC was defined by critics as too 'generous', but it proved to have some powerful advantages.

On the one hand, only the 'subjective perspective' of the applicants' motivations in committing crimes is able to provide a more comprehensive picture of the multiple facets of the political violence phenomenologies. On the other hand, the fact that the AC was prepared to accept a wide range of strategies adopted by political organizations during the conflict as 'political' – regardless of the unpleasantness of the strategy and of whether formalized orders or decisions from organizations were given – encouraged full disclosure. On the contrary, a narrow and formalistic application of the political offence requirements would have encouraged perpetrators to conceal or manipulate elements in order to comply with requirements, as is often the case in a criminal trial context.

These considerations are what led to the main argument of this book. The real eligibility for amnesty was not really the formal evidence of a politically motivated crime (according to the letter of the TRC statute), but the willingness of the perpetrators to publicly confess the deeds they had committed. Certainly perpetrators had to justify the plausibility of their act as political, give an account of the context in which the deeds were committed and the absence of personal gain, but the core criterion for amnesty was the willingness to undergo the liturgy of the full disclosure.

Furthermore, as we shall see in the following pages, the amnesty procedure may be viewed as a mechanism for delegitimizing political violence and removing it from the new democratic society. The phenomenologies of political violence had to emerge from the voices of the people who perpetrated violent acts on the basis of a subjective motivation of what was 'political'. Once a definition was set as to what could be reasonably and plausibly accepted as 'political', the central factor determining the eligibility for amnesty was the willingness to confess publicly. The Committee's broad, pragmatic approach to the political requirements was intended to induce perpetrators to publicly reveal their deeds, even if it was repulsive to accept that they deserved amnesty. The context of guilt and censure in which perpetrators disclosed the subjective motivations behind committing violent crimes is what created a delegitimizing effect. For this reason, the Committee had to be prepared to accept multiple subjective interpretations of what was perceived as a 'political act'.[40]

Amnesty Hearing Procedure

The proceedings before the AC, which combined investigative and adversarial elements, were marked by an intense preparatory phase. First, applications were received and analysed, including verification of formal requirements (and the request for their correction or completion). The individual application form had to contain personal details and factual information regarding the criminal act the applicant claimed to be responsible for. At this point, an application could be discarded as invalid because it lacked the necessary criteria. Second, preparation for the hearings, which normally required further investigation by the AC's Investigation Units, acquiring documents (including from the HRVC or the NDB) and notifying all the interested parties (in particular the victims or their relatives, but also accomplices, other implicated parties or persons aware of the facts) of the request for amnesty. The AC's basic approach, however, was not to investigate proactively, but rather to act as a receptacle of information submitted by individuals interested in the results of the amnesty application.

The preparatory phase was then followed by an actual public hearing; the AC gradually clarified the rules provided by Act 34, borrowing adjudicative methods from accusatorial proceedings, which generated bitter criticism. Hearings were held only when gross human rights violations had been committed. Otherwise, the AC could decide (in chamber) without a hearing or further evidence (administrative procedure). Sometimes further investigation was requested to clarify any confusion or to verify certain facts and questions, and issues were raised with the applicants before deciding such matters .[41] Basically, the procedure for the public hearing in which confession took place was as follows:

1) After a general presentation of the case by an Evidence Leader (EL),[42] the person confessing had to repeat under oath the self-incriminating statement previously made in writing in the amnesty application. The EL was a central figure in the public hearing. Once nominated, he or she coordinated the work between the AC and the investigative bodies: the EL illustrated the case to those present at the hearing; he was the first to ask questions about the facts of the confession; he or she also illustrated the facts and results of the investigation to the AC members. In addition, the EL also coordinated the hearing, but never had the role of a public prosecutor, since he or she did not have the power to issue an indictment. Where the applicant was legally represented, which was mostly the case in public hearings (legal aid in the form of public defender type lawyers was arranged for people who could not afford their own lawyers) the lawyer would lead the applicant's evidence and then the EL would cross-examine. Victims could also be represented and where they contested the application their legal representatives could also cross-examine the applicants.
2) Witnesses then related the facts supporting the statements of those confessing.
3) Statements were then made by victims (or their relatives) and the witnesses called by them to testify. The autonomy and dignity of victims were respected by allowing them to be free to determine their degree of involvement in the process and their willingness to testify before the Committee. The AC allowed for a large degree of flexibility in the presentation of evidence. All the implicated persons or victims were free to make statements or to put arguments on records.
4) The AC then invited persons aware of the facts to testify.
5) In light of all of this, the AC gave the person confessing the statements in order to review them or fill in any gaps therein.
6) Finally, all those who had made statements over the course of the hearing could be cross-examined. As in an ordinary criminal trial, applicant cross-examination was meant to enhance the reliability of statements made in the amnesty process while also trying to limit the distortions in the applicant's testimony such as inaccuracy, incomplete memory or wilful distortion of the facts.[43] The AC's mandate was to determine contradictions and inconsistencies, as well as to identify fabricated testimony from common criminals trying to present their deeds as politically motivated. The AC could limit the cross-examination in order to protect the victims from heavy questioning (preventing what normally happens in an Anglo-American type of trial). The victims' statements were treated differently from those of the amnesty applicants; for example, they could make informal statements. In a sense, there was a kind of predisposition in favour of the victims. Even if the Committee was not bound to consider the victims' agreement in granting amnesty, their support for or opposition to the AC's decision

played an important role in certain circumstances. In some cases, for example, victims opposed the application and were able to challenge the evidence or version put forward by the applicant; this often led to the AC finding full disclosure had not been made thus resulting in a refusal of the application.[44] It is worth noting that all the protagonists of the hearing could make their statements in one of the eleven official languages. For this reason, the TRC provided an important service of simultaneous interpreting.

7) At the hearing's end, the person confessing (or his or her legal representative) could make final concluding statements in which they formalized the request for amnesty.
8) The AC was then called to issue a written decision and its reasons. The Committee panel was normally made up of three members (on a rotating basis according to the schedule set a month before the hearing); for more complex and controversial cases, there were five members. Decisions were published in the *Government Gazette* and notification was sent to the amnesty applicant, the victims and all other people involved (even through legal representatives if appointed), the Department of Correctional Services, heads of the prisons concerned (if the applicant was in prison), the National Prosecution Authority and the registrar of the court concerned.

Even if the AC's decision had obvious legal effects (for example, for prisoners), it could not be appealed. Only in a few rare cases did victims or applicants, who were not satisfied with the AC's decision, file for a review before the High Court. In two cases, the court judge ordered the AC to reconsider its decision; the AC, nevertheless, reconfirmed its decision.[45]

The Relationship with Criminal Justice: Separation and Complementarity

Defining the relationship between the special proceedings before the AC and criminal justice is rather problematic. This section will review elements determining the relationship between ordinary criminal justice and the amnesty process. In other words, though the TRC suspended a strictly criminal approach, it also maintained several aspects of the criminal justice system. This imbued the South African amnesty process with an element of power, which should be improved and strengthened in future systems of restorative justice. In fact, the experience of the amnesty process in South Africa teaches us that a conditional amnesty system is not effective if not coordinated with the ordinary criminal justice system that exerts punitive power.[46]

Though the AC used 'irregular' procedures as compared to the regular justice system, they were carefully regulated down to the last detail, especially the working procedure and decision-making mechanisms. A clear sign of complementarity between the two systems is demonstrated by the fact that the Committee's decisions were designed to have legal effects and value that would complement judgments made under the criminal justice system. Similarly, an element of complementarity can be deduced from s. 19(5) and (6) of Act 34/95, which basically implies the TRC's primacy over potential pending criminal proceedings for the same crimes being tried for amnesty; in fact, the Commission had the power to order a stay. Complementarity is demonstrated mainly by the fact that most of the people who applied for amnesty were imprisoned after having been convicted by the South African judiciary under apartheid (or during the chaotic transitional phase that began in 1990). The choice to extend the amnesty process to those who had already been convicted for facts falling within the AC's temporal and subject matter jurisdiction meant that coordination between the amnesty process and the criminal justice system was essential. Moreover, the fact that people had been convicted in criminal courts meant that the records of their cases had to be considered as part of the documentation examined during the hearing of the application. In fact, often the police investigation docket was also examined if still available. Since people had been through a criminal process, the paper trial of that process was relevant in determining full disclosure and other relevant facts. Hence the complementarity with the criminal justice system.

The Commission also had powers linked to judicial functions. The most important was the power to subpoena (s. 29 of Act 34/95), with which the TRC could summon all those accused of complicity, persons informed of the facts or witnesses to respond to specific questions. Even if the Committee used this power sparingly, failure to comply with the order to appear before the Commission could lead to a fine or imprisonment for a period not exceeding two years.[47]

In accordance with s. 31 of the TRC Act, the AC's questioning of applicants, victims, witnesses and other persons implicated did not breach the fundamental principle of privilege against self-incrimination. Elements revealed by self-incriminating statements could not be used as evidence in subsequent legal proceedings against the person concerned, with only one exception: committing an offence while giving evidence such as perjury (s. 31(3) of the TRC Act). The privilege against self-incrimination was consistently enforced in relation to all those who testified before the Commission.

The Committee also had to deal with direct or indirect legal elements that came from previous legal trials. In analysing the transcripts of the confessions before the AC, it appears on many occasions that the AC compared the agreement of the statements made by amnesty applicants in previous criminal proceedings with those made before the TRC, noting a substantial change in the attitude of defendants and of the description of the facts of the crimes. In many cases, they claimed that they had lied during the criminal trial, denying the charges. However, the analysis of the confessions demonstrated that the problem of manipulating the truth was not entirely eliminated from the TRC's system. As we shall see, in an attempt to meet the requirements provided by law to receive amnesty, many manipulated and concealed facts about the criminal acts they confessed, especially regarding the crime's political objective and the existence of a direct connection with a political organization.

Complementarity, however, is not the only word to describe the relationship with ordinary criminal justice; there were also elements differentiating the two procedures: the system had to encourage confessions even though it is a special proceeding separate from criminal justice. As already stated, this objective was obtained by creating a division between the TRC and any other judicial body; the evidence gathered by the AC could not be used by other judicial bodies,[48] and civil suits for the damages caused by the crimes confessed were blocked. A decision granting amnesty precluded any future criminal or civil proceeding against the person receiving amnesty.[49] The main distinction, however, lies in the nature of the AC's decision, which was a mere evaluation that the requirements (temporal, material, disclosure) were met, almost as if it were an 'administrative body'.

Another important difference between the AC's decision-making practice and an ordinary judicial decision-making practice is the binding precedent principle. This principle was not applied by the Committee, and this approach was criticized as one of the sources of inconsistency in the AC's decision-making. In reality, it was a type of obligatory choice in order to make a clear distinction from the criminal procedure. In fact, using the binding precedent principle would have made the Committee's decision-making practice similar to criminal proceedings. The AC was suspended between two different 'natures'. Since it could not be an ordinary judicial body, it had to decide on neutralizing the punitive consequences of the crimes committed. Employing or not employing the binding precedent principle created a point of departure between the AC's two natures. The AC was criticized for the lack of clear rules on this matter, because it led to the Committee developing a hybrid decision-making practice in order to meet two needs: on the one hand, in accordance with the principle of equal treatment, consistently applying the *ratio decidendi* adopted in certain circumstances to subsequent cases; on the other hand, not incorporating mechanisms of an ordinary judicial body.[50] For the same reason, the criterion of evidence beyond a reasonable doubt was also not used. Thus, the evaluation of the requirements for amnesty was made on a case-by-case basis according to a criterion of the likelihood of the statements and its comparison with the other information available. Criticism arose whenever the procedure took an approach similar to criminal proceedings.

Generally speaking, the relationship with the criminal justice system was problematic. Such a complicated reward system works only if trials were held in the past that showed the legal system's ability to prosecute.[51] The threat of new trials proved to be a valid incentive for perpetrators to confess crimes. In the end, full disclosure before the AC was a kind of external pressure, even if the amnesty procedure could not be activated without a personal decision to turn oneself in.

The Impact of the Amnesty Process: Questioning Numbers

There is still some confusion about the statistics of the actual number of amnesty applications filed and the number of requests rejected through the administrative procedure. Data sources available today are: 1) the documentation published officially by the TRC on its website (decisions and confession transcripts). Though this is a fundamental source, it is not complete. In addition to classified information this source contains some errors in the documents' numbering; 2) the statistics published in 2003 in vol. 6 of the *Final Report*; 3) the study by AC Secretary Martin Coetzee;[52] and 4) the studies and statistic analysis by scholars like Jeremy Sarkin and Antje du Bois-Pedain.[53]

Jeremy Sarkin, who published the first substantial and quantitative study of the amnesty process, based his analysis on '2341 decisions affecting about 2541 applicants (for 4575 out of the 7116 applicants, no written decisions or audio transcript exist as they were decided administratively)'.[54] According to Sarkin, out of over 7,116 amnesty applications, a total of 1,167 amnesties were granted and 145 were partially successful (that is, for some acts only). Moreover, there were 183 cases of 'Guilt Denied', in other words, those who did not accept responsibility for their crimes over the course of the public hearing, forcing the AC to refuse amnesty.

Some years later, Antje du Bois-Pedain published another careful and comprehensive analysis of the AC's activity, using a different methodological approach that may be defined as a decision-based approach. The numbers proposed by this author were slightly different. She worked strictly on the 1,100 decisions rendered by the Committee. According to this author:

> Despite of the fact that the Committee received over 7000 applications, we can be quite sure that the published decisions deal with all admissible applications the Committee received from potentially qualifying applicants. More than 1100 applications were turned down because they did not meet formal admissibility requirements; and about 4000 to 5000 applications came from common criminals. Further confirmation that the published decisions deal with all applications for *prima facie* politically motivated conduct is provided by a comparison of the number of individual applicants dealt with in the Committee's published decisions (1701) with the number of applicants from different political groupings given in the TRC *Report* (1645).[55]

Despite discrepancies, the amnesty process made an unprecedented amount of information available to national and international public opinion. The impact of the AC's activity could be measured using different parameters:

matters, applicants,[56] decisions, incidents, victims involved, etc. Organizing and managing the entirety of this information was rather complex.

In any event, there is an overarching question that goes beyond controversies about the figures: did the amnesty process deal with a sufficient number of cases of political violence to be considered a representative reflection of the dynamics of the past?

Analysts agree that the number of applications should have been higher, considering the amount of political crime under apartheid and during the transition (even if the TRC publicly claimed that it was surprised at the amount of requests it received and that only with great effort was it able to examine all of them in a reasonable period of time). The number of amnesty applications perhaps justifies downsizing some of the expectations that the TRC created – even internationally. As we shall see, a series of corrections to the procedure would have made the system more effective.

Though there are still important discrepancies in TRC data, reviewing the information regarding the applications and amnesties granted, the following general picture emerges. The first data analysis comes from Jeremy Sarkin's table which, in turn, is based on the information provided by the AC Secretary Martin Coetzee.[57] The IFP always held a clearly hostile attitude towards the TRC. Viewed as a body controlled by the ANC, the IFP feared that it would be an instrument for delegitimizing the Zulu party. There were 110 amnesty applications filed by IFP members, and 49 of the cases regarding gross human rights violations (which would thus receive a public hearing) received amnesty, whereas 41 were refused. Even the ANC seems to have taken an ambiguous position. Only Archbishop Desmond Tutu's threat to resign as TRC Chairman forced the ANC to better explain the TRC's functioning to its members and advise them to ask for amnesty. Consequentially, 1,042 ANC members filed the amnesty application; 568 out of 710 cases of gross human rights violations received amnesty and 111 were refused; there were 213 punishment eliminations out of 332 cases, in which only an administrative procedure was required. The PAC and the Azanian People's Liberation Army (APLA) had the same attitude. Only 176 applications were filed by its members; 149 were for gross violations and 108 were amnesties granted (38 were refused after the public hearing). A total of 99 applications came from members of various far-right groups; only 30 were granted an amnesty and 19 were refused. Members of the South African Defence Force (SADF) presented 885 amnesty applications (18 from members of the Homeland Security Forces). Eighty per cent regarded gross human rights violations; 600 met the criteria for amnesty, 96 were rejected and 48 received partial amnesty.[58]

Antje du Bois-Pedain's detailed study, based on a thorough analysis of only the decisions published by the AC, modifies the data from previous studies, changing the number of applications and subdividing them as follows: ANC 857; IFP 85; PAC (APLA) 116; far-right movements 77; SADF 289.[59] More differences regarding the number of applications can be found in the TRC's statistics published in vol. 6 of the *Final Report*: ANC 998; IFP 109; PAC (APLA) 138; far-right 107; SADF 293. Du Bois-Pedain justifies the discrepancy based on the methodology of reading the Commission's official and unofficial reports and statistics, which often deal with matters and not with applicants.[60] Additional difficulties are due to the impossibility of tracing to which group the confessing individual belonged in some decisions.

Some issues help to contextualize these numbers. First, between 1990 and 1995, a chaotic procedure of indemnity provisions allowed a significant number of potential TRC applicants (especially from the regime's military and police forces) to be protected from legal proceedings. An exact number is not possible, but a reasonable guess is that around 14,000 people received protection from criminal liability for crimes committed during apartheid.[61]

Second, Magnus Malan's acquittal (in the trial where he was a co-defendant along with 19 other people) undoubtedly led to the idea that it was possible to avoid conviction in court.[62] The trial involving De Kock and accomplices and the Motherwell trial (held at the South Eastern Cape Local Division of the High Court) ended with heavy convictions for the defendants and, as a result, counterbalanced the effect of Malan's acquittal, as many applications were made in connection to the crimes of these two trials; this confirms the importance of an effective criminal justice system in making the amnesty procedure appear as a valid alternative.[63]

When the AC first began its work, the amnesty granted to Captain Brian Mitchell[64] for the Trust Feed massacre helped to convince the regime's security force members responsible for serious crimes of the body's impartiality.

The main question, however, is if the amnesty procedure could have had a higher quantitative impact by demonstrating that it was an effective instrument in attracting a higher number of perpetrators. There were many reasons that discouraged potential confessors from using the AC procedure. Fear and diffidence played an important role in dissuading them, partially due to the fact that at first the complex amnesty process was not properly explained and seemed to have a hidden purpose.

The ambiguous role of political parties and organizations was also an influence. After having supported the TRC's creation, they sensed the Commission's autonomy and its tendency to be free from party control. Parties and organizations had a concrete fear that they had created a body that could delegitimize them at any moment.[65] Thus, the political parties and organizations that had contributed to the creation of the TRC often advised members not to request amnesty.

Many members of the regime's security and military forces did not apply for amnesty for fear of not being able to receive it for crimes committed outside of South African territory.[66] Even if s. 20(2) of the Commission's statute provided for amnesty in this situation, in some cases it was refused. Crimes committed as part of the operations against the SWAPO in Namibia or crimes committed in Angola had little to do with the national political conflict, which was a determining factor in meeting the requirement of political motives.[67] The unpredictability of the AC's policy regarding requirements in these cases dissuaded many potential applicants.

The South African amnesty process encountered the fact that it was difficult to proceed against the establishment of political organizations and the criminal state. The AC's narrow interpretation of its own rules partially produced this phenomenon. By giving preference to confessions with specific factual information about crimes (so called focus on incidents) as opposed to asking for information about the chain of command and the general political context in which criminal phenomena were generated, the AC involuntarily contributed to the partial concealment of political responsibility for the crimes reported.[68] As a result, there were few applications made by the political leaders who gave orders to military units or to the militant wings of liberation movements. Only the ANC and APLA acknowledged their guilt before the AC, but they did so using the controversial collective application, which according to the AC's rules did not lead to amnesty. The NP, IFP and Freedom Front, though in different forms, publicly apologized for suffering in the past, but declined specific responsibility for ordering crimes.[69]

Another issue that remained in the dark was the people who collaborated with the regime as spies or informers. To shed some light on this element of political crime, several legal scholars such as Jeremy Sarkin, Jonathan Klaaren and Howard Varney have proposed 'Supervisory Indemnity'. This would mean opening an additional phase of the amnesty process for those who did not commit offences but, as an authority figure in political and military organizations, contributed to them by issuing orders and making political decisions. This second theoretical amnesty would maintain some of the same characteristics of the phase studied here: public confession, no collective applications (accepting personal responsibility), proportionality and lack of personal gain. The presence of political reasons would be implicit.[70]

Thus, a general evaluation of the amnesty process's impact remains an open question with many possible readings. The number of amnesty applications is not proportional to the number of crimes committed for political reasons. Most of the crimes confessed were committed in a relatively recent time period (starting in the second half of the 1980s), whereas there were almost no applications for crimes committed during the previous decades when apartheid was already an outright criminal phenomenology.

If this numerical information is compared with what would have been obtained through the court system, the results appear to be more positive and the South African experience turns out to be a highly innovative model. The cost and the time needed to investigate and hold a similar number of criminal trials are difficult to calculate. Where adjudicative instruments were set up, such as ad hoc criminal courts, with a much larger budget than that of the TRC and more time, the actual number of convictions is actually lower than the amount of cases dealt with by the AC; similarly, the public's view of the activity of these courts in Rwanda and the former Yugoslavia was not positive.[71]

The Full Disclosure of All Relevant Facts and the Idea of 'Truth'

The TRC's mandate clearly states that one of the amnesty procedure's main objectives is establishing 'as complete a picture as possible' about what happened during the era of political violence. The statute contains a complex concept of truth: it ranges from the factual truth of single crimes to the reconstruction of the political and historical context and of the situations that produced these crimes. The reason behind this concept was to provide the community being transformed with an official and 'indisputable' version of the past, which would be one of the unifying elements of the constituent pact.

Thus, within this bilateral relationship of confession-amnesty, truth is a premise for reconciliation and the compensation for abandoning punitive measures. Inevitably, such an ambitious idea was not able to meet all expectations. Almost all scholars who have studied the TRC experience agree that the information gathered over the course of the Commission's activity was considerably important. A number of technical, procedural and political factors weakened the TRC's investigative potential. There are vast grey areas, historical facts were concealed and lies were told. Many of the reasons have already been mentioned: just like the defendant who lies during the criminal trial to hide the 'truth' that would lead to his conviction, the individual confessing before the AC tended to present facts in order to meet the requirements for receiving amnesty. More effective cooperation between external investigative bodies and the TRC and more substantial funding would have led to a more thorough corroboration of the statements made before the AC, forcing those confessing to clarify the ambiguous factual information in their statements.

It would have also been useful if the information coming from the NDB and the victims' statements had been more thoroughly integrated, and if the Investigation Units had been equipped with more financial and technological means.[72] The fact that one lawyer could represent applicants who participated in the same crime also proved to be dysfunctional: the analysis of their confessions clearly shows that they had previously agreed on the factual reconstruction of the events.[73]

The AC's own interpretation of its rules led it to analysing only the factual details of individual episodes (a focus on incidents). Such a precise notion of disclosure often meant not pursuing answers about political organization and chain of command. Yet another complaint was that no members were historians or sociologists. The Committee members had mostly legal training and had less experience with evaluating the plausibility of information concerning the historical context of political or ethnic rivalries or whether the information had been significantly manipulated, as was often the case. The TRC's 'truth' is 'relative'; many new elements of the political conflict were discovered, but they required prudent consideration and contextualization. If the South African TRC model were to be used again elsewhere in the future, technical and procedural changes could be made to improve it.[74]

Nevertheless, analysing the Committee's procedural mechanism – established by law – for performing its 'truth finding' function and mandate is fundamental to understanding the concept of 'truth' pursued and subsequently produced by the AC. The degree of truthfulness of the historical and political information processed by the AC was directly related to the Committee's power to decide if an applicant had actually made a 'full disclosure'. Nothing is more useful than the perpetrators' information for investigating the political violence of South Africa's past.

Section 20(1) of the TRC Act only calls for an applicant's 'full disclosure of all relevant facts' connected to the crime. Based on du Bois-Pedain's quantitative analysis, the full disclosure was a determining factor in the AC's decision-making. About forty per cent of the unsuccessful amnesty applications were due to insufficient information provided by perpetrators, whereas twenty-five per cent were denied for lack of full disclosure.[75]

In some instances, the advocates representing applicants at the hearing discussed how the concept of full disclosure could have more than one meaning.[76] The AC clarified its interpretation of this decisive issue on numerous occasions. First, the full disclosure had to make it possible for the AC to decide if the legal requirements for granting amnesty had been met. Even though a reconstruction of the truth of the past would have required all possible factual, direct, indirect, relative, general or circumstantial elements of criminal phenomena, the AC's primary objective and duty was to evaluate and decide whether a confessed crime was politically motivated or not. For this reason, the Committee needed all the 'relevant facts' of the incidents under consideration. In some decisions, the AC clearly stated that full disclosure meant providing the (relevant) facts 'necessary to enable the Committee to decide whether the requirements set out in s. 20(2)(3) have been met'.[77] The factual elements that the AC needed in order to decide a case were neither specifically defined nor merely subjective. The applicant had to provide specific information regarding the key facts of the crime he or she declared himself or herself responsible for; in other words, all the detailed elements of his or her conduct which would make the Committee able to decide. These elements varied according to the case under consideration, which differed from one another in terms of facts and conduct. As a result, it is not easy to establish a set pattern of the relevant facts that had to be disclosed for an AC decision. The facts could not be determined *a priori*, but were specific and different for each case.

Viewed in this way, it appears that a kind of collaboration or dialogue evolved between the applicant and the Committee. The AC was authorized to make an amnesty decision (its mandate), but the confessing perpetrator had to make it able to do so by disclosing facts. Reticence, obscurity and inconsistency were the very elements that undermined this relationship. Considered to be impediments and problems for decision-making, these elements were evaluated negatively. As such, the Committee demanded transparency and fairness. By interpreting political requirements broadly and pragmatically (for which it was criticized), the Committee demonstrated that it was inclined to grant amnesty. Nevertheless, the applicant could not be reticent about the crucial facts of the crime committed. The applicant was therefore bound to a rather particular 'burden of proof'. The AC itself stated that this onus was neither 'beyond reasonable doubt required in criminal matter' nor 'the onus in a civil matter of proof on a balance of probabilities'.[78] Rather, it was based on 'an honest account of what actually happened',[79] on the fact that the applicant 'is not trying to mislead'. In fact, the AC was willing to accept even the applicant's 'genuine confusion'.[80] More so than evidence based on classical legal criteria, the Committee needed plausible and persuasive information about the facts in the disclosure.[81] Even if on some occasions marginal reticence, downplaying, outright lies and fabricated evasions were provided, the AC was satisfied if the applicant had 'done all he can' or if 'he was honest enough'. The collaborative 'agreement' between the Committee and the applicant was broken when the latter gave the impression of deliberately trying to 'withhold the truth from the Committee'[82] or was 'trying to deceive or mislead the Committee in a calculated manner'.[83] The relationship between the Committee and the applicant, as we shall see in more clarity in the final part of this study, was based on the principle of *do ut des*. The applicant awaits amnesty, but had to put the Committee in the position to provide it. If the applicant does not do so, he is not eligible for amnesty.

The analysis of the AC's decision-making practice regarding full disclosure reveals how the idea of truth about the past enacted by the AC was quite specific. In fact, the notion of truth about the facts provided by the applicant is a 'reasonably probable truth'. Truth is therefore established by 'reasonable approximation'. The issue then becomes how this idea of truth contributes to revealing the dynamics of the past.

The reconstruction of the overall image of political violence was therefore influenced by multiple factors: first, by the benchmark set by the AC in considering a disclosure satisfactory, even with some inconsistencies or gaps; second, the 'truth' about the past was determined by two main factors: 1) to which organizations active in political violence the applicants belonged; 2) how many members of individual organizations agreed to present themselves before the Committee, that is, which organizations urged their members to confess crimes and political strategies. With regard to the latter, we have seen how organizations took on different positions. The organizations that fought in the past did not contribute equally in terms of the number of members who appealed to the TRC and in terms of the information disclosed. The image of the past is therefore brighter in some parts and darker in others. This result is directly related to the quantity and quality of the information provided by individual actors and organizations – each comprising a piece of the complex puzzle of the picture of South African political violence.

That said, there are a number of strong points to note. First, the amount of information revealed over the course of the AC hearings was comparatively higher than the information obtained in criminal trials.[84] Both the number of applicants and the 'honest and collaborative attitude requested' were key factors in producing an unprecedented amount of information. This result was also due to the freeform nature of applicants' statements before the AC. The hearing transcripts contain a vast amount of information that over time will become part of a more in depth historical investigation.

An additional significant aspect of the amnesty process is that it neutralized the possible phenomena of denialism, which has evolved in other historical and geographic contexts, despite there being criminal trials, and with it social and political consequences. In a system where the facts of the past are determined through a criminal trial that uses an indictment that the defendant must fight in order to escape conviction, it is entirely plausible that the defendant would deny the facts contested. In a system like the South African amnesty process, this situation does not arise, or at least only arises to a much more limited extent. Despite several objective problems of the proceeding's functioning, one factor is nevertheless decisive on this point. The applicants in this case embraced the opposite position, even if with potential inconsistencies. They voluntarily admitted having committed a crime, even just by sending the amnesty application form. The initiative for doing so came from the perpetrators themselves, that is, from the protagonists of the past's political violence and dramatic events. The various segments of public opinion could no longer deny what happened in the past, since the perpetrators themselves had admitted publicly to what took place. This fact neutralized potential debates among white South Africans who had benefited from the segregationist system. It also had an effect on the black population. Horrible crimes were also committed by the black liberation movements, although in response to apartheid and the fight against inequality. Every form of political violence is by nature complex and ambivalent. The South African amnesty process was perhaps the best attempt at conveying to the public an image of the past that was less ideologized by the 'winners'. Its stabilizing effect in social terms is extremely important for a country trying to rebuild the foundations of a new democracy. In light of this, the type of 'truth' produced by the amnesty process is different for yet another reason. It makes a departure from positivist or objective criteria becoming part of the political terrain as a 'constituent truth', that is, it makes a public discourse about the past useful for the constitution-making process.

Constitutional Suspension of a Strictly Criminal Approach for Political Crimes Committed under Apartheid

This section will analyse the constitutional suspension of a strictly criminal approach and its constituent role.[85] The model of transitional justice in South Africa is based on a system of 'conditional amnesty'. It can reasonably be said that the post-apartheid Constitution, in which the TRC system is rooted, constitutionalized a novel legal practice. The material and temporal requirements, in addition to the terms for filing the amnesty application, show the transitory nature of the process. At least from a formal legal standpoint, the premise is that all those who decide not to accept the state's 'redemptive' offer or who, despite confessing, are not granted amnesty may face the criminal justice system. Offering this possibility, the new state suspends the exercise of punitive measures during that period of time for crimes committed for political reasons with the proviso that the application for amnesty is in fact granted: hence the idea of suspension or the state's self-limitation on exercising one of its most important public powers.

Formalizing the suspension of a strictly criminal approach corrected a problem that permeated the transition from its inception. An analysis of the Indemnity Acts demonstrated that the lack of will and the inability of political power to resolve problems deriving from political conflicts were a fundamental issue of the constitutional transition. The TRC system was thus an intervention to stop the chaos, arbitrariness and utilitarianism that had been used to confront the problem at the beginning of the transition, attempting to convert the state's weakness and inability into a strong point.[86]

The constitutional suspension of a strictly criminal approach is implied by the new state's decision to waive the use of punitive measures for retributive reasons, which are exemplified in the power to indict, prosecute, convict and sentence and in which punishment is the price for the damage caused. Thus, the new constitutional order offered a temporary opportunity for renouncing the formalization of the apartheid regime's political defeat through punitive actions.

Abandoning the winner-loser opposition – historically widespread – and the former's retaliation/reward over the latter through punishment enforced by the court left room for a new powerful tool whose symbolic value is just as problematic: confession. Exercising punitive power is not denied *a priori* but is simply postponed; in fact, the explicit premise is that it will be used for those who did not accept and comply with the 'redemptive' proposal. In creating this route, constituent actors did not set out to automatically eliminate every possible judicial action regarding political crimes committed under apartheid. Theoretically, even during the TRC's activity, these offences would have been prosecutable. Nevertheless, since there was the possibility to apply for amnesty, standard justice could be suspended until the end of the AC procedure.

This suspension is also confirmed by the fact that whenever the AC received an amnesty application from an individual in a criminal trial, it could order a stay for the duration of the amnesty procedure (public hearing and confession) and thus evaluate the requirements for granting amnesty.

The constituent pact (which will be discussed in further detail below) is based on the exchange of confession for the state's temporary waiving of exercising one of its most important public powers. Aside from the reasons already mentioned related to the negotiated nature of the political transition, other practical considerations should also be noted. The South African trial, basically an Anglo-American model, had some problematic characteristics: first, the expensive costs for a high number of criminal trials; second, the difficulty of establishing the 'truth' of individual episodes in a wider political and historical context.[87] Moreover, the adversarial nature of an accusatorial system, a procedure that embodies the conflict and declares a victor, seems only to perpetuate the conflict in the public sphere and in the courtroom.[88]

Creating a system encouraging public confession satisfies different needs that do not necessarily coincide with the social requirements that standard criminal justice is called on to deal with (in particular, the impulse of victims to demand that the state inflict a punishment that is equal to the pain they unfairly underwent). Yet another problematic element was that crimes committed by liberation movements were treated the same way as those committed by the regime's institutions. Though on many occasions it has been stressed that, ethically, crimes committed as a part of the struggle for freedom are not similar to those committed by the regime, from a formal legal point of view, they nevertheless constituted gross human rights violations and hence required the same amnesty procedure.

The symbolic and political significance of deciding to formally put these crimes on the same level unleashed bitter debate, especially from the members of the liberation movements, who criticized the decision made in Parliament. The need to include crimes committed by individuals who were not part of the apartheid state in the amnesty process was a result of a fundamental characteristic of the conflict that took place under apartheid. This conflict not only manifested itself as the apartheid state against the black people, but there was also a dynamic of inter-civilian conflict between supporters of the different political groupings inside the country. A collateral effect of apartheid politics, violence was also practised by people who were not directly related to the racist state, hence the disputed decision that gross human rights violations committed by members of non-racial liberation movement groups or organizations also had to be confessed publicly.[89]

The constituent actors were thus aware that the constitution-making process required profound work on a social, political and historical level; by constitutionally limiting the schizophrenic vision of the past (which a criminal approach would have fed) and demystifying ideological manipulations of past events, the constitution-making process could open the road to a new path as a process that would build towards the future while simultaneously freeing itself from the past.

Individual Volition as a Premise for the Suspension of a Strictly Criminal Approach

Suspending a strictly criminal approach was not a unilateral decision. The state's temporary waiving of prosecuting political crimes of the apartheid era had to be completed by a voluntary, spontaneous and independent acceptance of the confession-amnesty exchange procedure.[90]

Even if, as previously observed, the 'promise of amnesty' creates considerable external pressure, entering the amnesty procedure, whatever its consequences may be, is a decision to be taken by the individual. Undergoing public confession is thus an act determined by the individual's free will. Though the TRC had the power to subpoena, it did not have the power to indict; those who decided to acknowledge guilt for political crimes did so with the awareness of assuming personal responsibility publicly for specific facts. Many obviously 'hid' by not accepting the offer made by the new democratic community in formation. Nevertheless, those who decided to ask for amnesty by incriminating themselves did so autonomously. Even though authoritative TRC members often tried to convince perpetrators to accept the offer of confession for amnesty, the final decision was up to the perpetrators; if they declined, the TRC could do nothing. This simple observation leads to an additional point. Retributive justice systems based on a criminal trial tend to create a passive relationship: the accused cannot do anything other than be subject to the political powers related to exercising 'prosecutorial' and then if convicted punitive action. In fact, independently choosing to start criminal proceedings against oneself is only marginal and hypothetical.

The TRC system is based on the opposite idea. Individuals choose whether to initiate the amnesty procedure. In fact, one of the fundamental characteristics of the TRC model created by the new constitutional rules is in fact this difference between a justice system that makes the individual passive and a system that requires the individual's voluntary act in order to start.

Post-TRC: Suspension or Definitive Cancellation of Criminal Justice for Political Crimes under Apartheid?

The 'clauses' of the constituent pact on transitional justice seem unquestionable: once the TRC terminated its work, those who had not applied for or who did not receive amnesty would be subject to a criminal trial. The limitation of the victims' constitutional right for justice is acceptable only if temporary and valid if in conjunction with a public confession. The issue of settling the past, however, was still far from being resolved; the government's political line was clearly ambiguous at the end of the TRC's mandate, showing the difficulty that handling the problem of transitional justice continues to generate. There are different political and legal dynamics that intersect in a disorderly manner.

In May 2002, President Thabo Mbeki, in accordance with s. 84(2)(j) of the 1996 Constitution, pardoned thirty-three ANC members who were refused amnesty by the AC due to their decision to file a collective application. At the same time, cases of political violence under apartheid were prepared for trial, several of which were denied amnesty by the AC.

In 1999, at the Office of the National Director of Public Prosecution (NDPP), a special investigation unit was set up, the Special National Project Unit, appointed with preparing proceedings for crimes without amnesty coverage. Initially part of the Directorate of Special Operations, the Unit had its offices at the National Prosecuting Authority in Pretoria; one of its first official acts was obtaining the documents gathered by the Transvaal Attorney-General (which had concluded the trials involving De Kock and accomplices). In March 2003, the Unit was restructured and was called the Priority Crimes Litigation Unit (PCLU) under the direction of the Special Director of Public Prosecutions.[91] The result of these trials is anything but positive. The punitive action exercised by the state did not produce convictions, and the new acquittals contributed to agitated public debate regarding opposing options: a) amending Act 34/95 by extending its effectiveness; b) passing a new amnesty law (the constitutional legitimacy of such a law was harshly criticized by authoritative scholars);[92] c) using the President's pardon (nevertheless considered by the Constitutional Court and scholars as power that is not unlimited or absolute);[93] and d) continuing to exercise punitive action. In the shadows looms the government's strategy of tacitly neutralizing judicial actions as long as the pressure of public opinion supported such a policy.

In accordance with s. 179(5)(a) of the 1996 South African Constitution, in December 2005 new prosecution guidelines were made public through the Prosecution Policy. In this context, the NDPP became the state body responsible for deciding whether or not to investigate and prosecute offences falling under the former TRC's jurisdiction. The rigidity of the criteria contained in the Prosecution Policy raised serious doubts about the will of the South African government to proceed with post-TRC prosecutions, despite the fact that some criminal trials were underway.[94]

The first and most important post-TRC trial was the case against Dr. Wouter Basson, the head of the chemical and biological warfare project during apartheid. He was charged with the murders of anti-apartheid activists (there is some suspicion as to whether the aforementioned weapons were studied in order to be used against the black population)[95]. On 11 April 2002, after two years of proceedings, hundreds of witnesses and at the enormous cost to the State the High Court of Pretoria acquitted the defendant of the 67 charges. The reaction to this was divided between those who stressed the uselessness of these trials, which simply drained the state's resources, and those who, on the contrary, accused the post-apartheid judiciary of still conspiring with the former oligarchy, criticizing the fact that the prosecutors still appeared reticent to examine the segregated past.[96] Two Ciskei soldiers (V.A. Mkosana and M.T. Gonya) were tried after the AC denied them amnesty for the death of twenty-nine ANC members and the wounding of 300. On 7 September 1992, the defendants opened fire on protesters in Bisho. They were acquitted by the court since there was no evidence that such an order was given to the two soldiers, who instead acted out of self-defence in the face of protesters threatening them.[97]

Another important case was the trial against Michael Luff for having caused the death of an ANC activist (W. Dyasi) in 1985. The AC refused amnesty due to a lack of full disclosure and political motives. During the criminal proceedings, the court decided that the evidence was not enough to prove Luff's guilt beyond a reasonable doubt.

Two other trials need to be mentioned. In the first case the defendants were P. Gumengu and A. Tyani (two former Transkei Security Branch operatives) for the murder of S. Zokwe in 1988 (who have been found guilty by the Eastern Cape High Court in 2005). In the second case the defendants were G. Nieuwoudt, J. Koole and J.M. Van Zyl for the murder of three people in the famous PEBCO case. In 2009, the National Prosecution Authority provisionally withdrew the case due to the ongoing review of the amnesty decision and the death of one of the accused (G. Nieuwoudt).[98] In these cases, the AC previously denied all the defendants amnesty. Information has leaked from the National Director of Public Prosecutions that out of the 459 investigations underway, eight could soon turn into criminal proceedings.

The prosecution of Adriaan Vlok (Minister of Law and Order under apartheid), Johann van der Merwe and four other South African police officials for attempting to assassinate Frank Chikane (an important activist and secretary-general of the South African Council of Churches) in 1989 made a strong emotional impact on South African public opinion. The case ended with the defendants' entering in to a plea bargain and conviction; however, it took place in an atmosphere that was in many ways reminiscent of the AC hearings. The concepts of reconciliation and pacification figured throughout the long trial; during informal exchanges between the victim and the accused and during cross examination, the defendants repeatedly asked for 'forgiveness' for the crimes committed.[99]

There are conflicting opinions about which criminal policy to apply. Human rights associations, former TRC members (especially Desmond Tutu) and segments of public opinion are emphatically against the idea of new amnesties. The government, however, seems to believe that ending discussion of the past with a new amnesty programme could increase the support of strong economic sectors that were close to the regime, thus making the country more governable.

It is my opinion that definitively cancelling criminal justice for political crimes of the past would constitute the failure of the TRC model and inevitably weaken the constituent pact.

The Problems of Using a Criminal Approach during Regime Transitions

Constitutional suspension of a strictly criminal approach in South Africa should be placed within the larger context of regime-state to democratic-state transformation. In other words, suspending a strictly criminal approach must be explained in relation to the constitution-making process that led the country from an authoritarian to a democratic system.

Multiple problems are connected to the extraordinary moment between the regime's end and the new system's birth. The two issues that are important for this study are the legal problem of confronting crimes committed in the past and the methods used for coming to terms with the past.

The first methodological division has repeatedly resurfaced internationally: criminal punishment or renouncing an adjudicative reaction. This division breaks down into deciding whether to use criminal trials for coming to terms with the past or, on the contrary, using instruments that are an alternative to strictly adjudicative instruments.[100] In my opinion, this dichotomy is too limiting because it excludes a series of intermediate alternatives between the two extremes of to punish and not to punish.[101] If the new democratic order decides to exercise punitive action, two additional choices have to be made, one political and the other legal and philosophical.[102] As the case of South Africa demonstrates, both choices have a clear constitutional value: applying a policy of retributive criminal justice or an alternative policy to criminal trials produces profoundly different consequences in the political body being formed, determining different constitutional systems and social orders.

The political choice is between the option to use or not use criminal justice for the old regime. This choice is not merely hypothetical, but refers to actual historical situations; for example, all the European political transitions at the end of the Second World War and the problems resulting from the legal proceedings undertaken in different countries for the crimes committed during the War.[103]

In general, coming to terms with the past using a retributive approach means facing political choices. Historical and factual analysis of the latest political transitions in Latin America, Africa and Central and Eastern Europe show that this approach is not always possible due to political reasons. Nevertheless, once an adjudicative system has been opted for, other legal issues have to be taken into consideration. In other words, once the feasibility and political appropriateness of using criminal justice for the past regime's crimes have been established, the legal rules to be used for taking such action must be defined.

This problem, which criminal law scholarship has studied in considerable depth, is directly based on the theory of state continuity. In theory, the legal rules in force prior to the state's transformation in a non-democratic regime could be used for legal proceedings against crimes committed under the regime (possibly modifying statutory limitations *ex post facto*) or to set new norms that permit retroactive punishment of the criminal state's actions. To give an example, we can look at the work of the German law scholar Gustav Radbruch. In the aftermath of the Second World War, he launched the debate on the problem of state continuity in relation to Germany's atonement. Radbruch's formula of 1946 is still used today as a point of departure for identifying the norms applicable for judging crimes committed under an illiberal regime. According to Radbruch, the first problem was identifying the moment in which the legal system was no longer democratic. In Radbruch's opinion, a legal system begins to lose its democratic nature (and therefore substantive validity), becoming 'non-law' when its statutory law becomes 'intolerable'. The theoretical problem that Radbruch tried to resolve is establishing the moment when the activity of the institutions of a particular system can be put 'between brackets', isolating an entire period of activity, including legal activity, from the rest of a legal system that seeks to uphold a historical and legal continuity. So, first there is the problem of identifying a norm or body of norms prior to the degeneration of the legal system due to 'intolerable statutory laws', in order to prosecute the crimes. If these norms do not exist, the new democratic state must use retroactive laws to punish conduct that, from a positivist point of view, was not considered an offence by the legal system 'between brackets'. This legal, political and philosophical issue was dramatically dealt with in all European countries when denazification and defascistization began at the end of the Second World War. The problem that law scholars like Radbruch confronted was the validity of laws passed by the Nazi regime. This legal problem existed in most European countries. The most obvious example related to the rules regarding the notion of 'collaboration', which allowed many states to try and eliminate war criminals; however, this also led to a large number of contradictions. Bearing in mind that the laws of a non-democratic legal system can be considered formally legitimate, what would be the correct legal approach for sanctioning a criminal state without violating one of the fundamental principles of law, that is, the non-retroactivity of criminal law?

The other problem that Radbruch attempted to solve was whether the 'between brackets' acts are to be considered simply a 'hole' in the state's history or whether the legislative and administrative work of the authoritarian state should in some way be incorporated into the new democratic system. The issues investigated by Radbruch were concrete issues at the end of the Second World War, in particular, the conflict between the law (produced respecting formal legislative procedures) of a criminal state and the notion of justice (with a strong natural law bent).[104]

Instruments for extending the statutory limitations or using the concept that particular crimes are not subject to those limitations (as is the case for crimes against humanity) are two methods that have both been experimented with. In Europe, the idea of no statute of limitations appeared during the second phase of the post-fascist and post-Nazi transitions. In fact, starting in the 1960s, the legal ploy of not being subject to statutory limitations, leaving the doors open to a *remise en question judiciaire* of the past, became the core feature of a bitter legal and political debate. All the latest legal developments due to the expansion of international criminal law go in the same direction. With the experiences of the two ad hoc international criminal tribunals (for the former Yugoslavia and Rwanda), the approval of the International Criminal Court (ICC) and its Statute, the core of a valid international criminal code, the court-based methodology used for coming to terms with the past has changed considerably. Scholars agree that in the future these elements could resolve some of the legal contradictions that began to appear after the Second World War.

The bottom line of this political and legal issue does not change over time. Starting with the transitions after the Second World War, criminal law and an adjudicative approach are globally considered as fundamental instruments for coming to terms with the past. From this perspective, law and (criminal) sentences involve enormous normative decisions. If using positive law produced prior to the illiberal or authoritarian state is used as a means of prosecuting the crimes committed under the regime, then, as Radbruch suggested, identifying the exact moment in which a state stopped being democratic (and became a promoter of criminal conduct) is of the utmost importance. Thus, the norms created prior to and violated by the authoritarian state must be defined. Doing so would make it possible to identify the positive law valid for convicting the authoritarian state without violating the principle of non-retroactivity. This same measure would also make it possible to invalidate the statutory law produced by the illiberal state that permitted certain conduct to be legal. If instead new laws are created *ex post* for acting against the criminal state, the principle of non-retroactivity would be violated and it would provoke a dangerous slippage towards notions of natural law.

This was basically the range of choices facing the new democratic orders in Europe at the end of the Second World War when the decision was made to pursue a retributive approach to deal with Nazi or fascist crimes.

Once using the criminal trial methodology has been chosen, there is the problem of identifying the criminal laws to implement the adjudicative model. Europe has witnessed valid historical and legal experiments in which we can verify the evolution of these dynamics; in particular, the broad use of retroactive laws or *ex post* changes to statutory limitations for certain crimes shows that the law (applied in violation with fundamental principles of legality) was called to serve an essential social and political function in Europe after the Second World War.[105] Exercising punitive action, though in violation of the fundamental principles of law, was considered one of the important instruments for coming to terms with the past.

The alternative to a retributive approach for dealing with the crimes of an authoritarian regime should also be analysed. In fact, there are two alternatives to be explored: on the one hand, there is what international law scholars define as impunity, that is, the inability or unwillingness of a state emerging from an authoritarian state to punish the crimes of the latter; on the other hand, there are alternative or complementary instruments to criminal justice, the most important of which are the truth commission models.[106]

Some international law scholars in favour of a strictly adjudicative approach claim that truth commission models are nothing more than a form of impunity and are thus incompatible with the precepts of international public and criminal law. In reality, the elements creating impunity are quite different: 1) prohibition against holding criminal trials for crimes committed in relation to the former regime; 2) the approval of general amnesty measures (blanket amnesty); 3) immediate statutory limitations for crimes of the past; and 4) silence and legal and political oblivion.

The South African amnesty process cannot be considered a system producing impunity, since it never applied blanket amnesty, ensuring some important tenets of accountability, and it formally prohibited the disregarding of the crimes committed.[107] As a body appointed with applying the constitutional suspension of a strictly criminal approach, the TRC appears not to fall within the polarization between punishing and not punishing. It escapes being classified within this dichotomy and demonstrates that there are transitional justice methods that are an alternative to those used after the Second World War.

Post-conflict Justice in Europe between Hypertrophy of History and Law

At the end of the Second World War, many European countries followed similar routes of transitional justice. In fact, if we analysed the historical moment in which a new political order decided to bring justice to the crimes of the former regime, there were no alternative models or visions to adjudicative action and reinforcing the adversary's political and military defeat with a criminal sentence. Nevertheless, pacification, reconciliation, healing fractures and social polarization, state reconstruction and collective mourning were challenges that all countries faced when emerging from the wreckage of war.

The trauma of war, genocide and Nazi-fascist crimes weighed heavily on the post-War transitions in Europe. The 'constituent pacts' of the new

European democracies were based on the defeat of the totalitarianism and authoritarianism of the first half of the twentieth century. They were also founded on the right to reconstruct a collective memory of the responsibility for the crimes committed under the former regimes.

These elements have fed so much historical and political debate that scholars have coined expressions such as 'memory syndrome' or 'obsession with the past'.[108] One of the particular qualities of the European transitions, as many scholars have noted, is the overlapping of law and memory. Adjudicative methodologies and the processes for collectively reconstructing the past blended together, producing a very complex constituent dynamic.[109]

As historical, legal and political science studies show, in both post-War European transitions and in the more recent Latin American, African and Central and Eastern European transitions, the constitution-making process is not just the moment in which the new state is created, but it is also when important social elements solidify, such as emerging political myths or the reconfiguration of the national identity that – through the construction of a collective memory of the past – reconstructs the social bond for future coexistence.[110] Historians and psychologists seem to agree on one basic idea: memory is a product of 'selection – invention – manipulation – suppression'. What is interesting to note here is that facts of the past, more or less selected through conscious processes, become a kind of social bond. This bond becomes an actual 'pact' or 'agreement' about the past that is then passed on to new generations. Creating a shared collective memory of the past serves the purpose of legitimizing present political setups. Attention is thus given to analysing the political and cultural forces that might influence the process of selecting and defining memory. These dynamics are actually old and characterized many societies in the past, including ancient ones. In this framework, the shared interpretation through memory and facts of past events appears to be of fundamental importance to the stability of the new political, social and constitutional order.

'Controversial memory' or 'memory syndrome' in republican France after the Vichy experience and its colonial past, especially regarding Algeria,[111] exemplifies all of this. France's reconstruction of the past through memory and facts outlines the political and legal issues that all of Europe had to provide answers for.[112]

The most important issue, however, is to understand the deep-rooted reasons that sparked these mechanisms. After the Second World War, a criminal approach for dealing with those responsible for Nazi-fascist crimes was used internationally (at Nuremberg) and nationally, with trials held with varying degrees of legitimacy and respect of rights across Europe.[113] This page of history of violent purges and waves of judicial action immediately after has been forgotten or silenced, but its study shows just how often retributive methods were used as a type of 'cleansing'.[114] Nevertheless, though the European stance towards the Nazi-fascist past was informed by a criminal approach, encouraged by the cathartic events of Nuremberg, its outcome was rather controversial. In fact, the exacerbations of political conflict and social polarization, too many defendants for the regular court system to handle, and the economic and political impracticality of not coming to terms with the past (linked to the need to set the pacification process up quickly in order to start economic reconstruction) demonstrated that using a criminal approach for confronting the conflict's symptoms was not practical. Amnesty laws began to loom on the horizon all over Europe as political transitions consolidated. The wound of ideologies that had brought about Nazi-fascist regimes had upset the social fabric. Collaboration and complicity in inhuman war crimes involved a rather high number of potential defendants, including civilians and not just the police and military.[115] The adjudicative solution could not technically, functionally and substantially satisfy the victims' needs for justice for such a high number of perpetrators. The element of time should not be overlooked: widespread use of criminal proceedings, especially if they are compliant with basic rights and principles, would have required too much time for the political and economic priorities of the states repairing the fractures created by totalitarian ideologies and the War. It was in this context that parliaments began to pass amnesty laws. Forgetting certain aspects of the War and the definition of a precise memory of the past, which always accompanies amnesty measures, began to settle due to the contradictory use of a strictly criminal approach.[116] Purges, which began rigorously, would never be completed.

However, this process did not lack important social consequences. In fact, the following decades in Europe saw cyclical irrational *refoulements* of the memory of the facts of the Second World War in which an adjudicative approach is present, either directly or indirectly. Court rooms have been repeatedly used as the setting to discuss the history and memory of the past. Because of legal concepts such as no statutory limitations for crimes against humanity, many war criminals who had escaped being purged (even taking on important institutional roles in the new democratic system) were put on trial. In a sense, it was necessary to continue the process of legally taking charge of the Nazi-fascist past, which had begun with the legal purging process but was never concluded. French proceedings such as the Touvuer, Barbie, Lenguay and Papon trials, the Priebke trial in Italy or the proceedings against Eichmann in Jerusalem marked the return of confronting the past with a criminal approach.[117] This profound (perhaps even irrational) need to rely on the presumed rationality, objectivity and intrinsic power of the law (even for its official qualities) in order to reconfirm the interpretation of the past did not stop with the new round of trials.

Other more complex signs of this dynamic have appeared in Europe during the last decades of the twentieth century. In particular, the dissemination of Holocaust denial claims attacked the core of the social and constitutional pact of remembrance (with its ethical scope and formalization in post-War constitutions), a foundation stone of the new democratic states. There is a proliferation of studies denying or minimizing the Holocaust that question the actual numbers of deaths caused by the Final Solution, the methods used and the historical and memory-based image of the resistance to it.

As a response to this destabilizing phenomenon that violates the pact of remembrance, the legal systems of Austria, Spain, Germany, France, Switzerland and Portugal (as recommended by the European Union) provided penal sanctions for the crime of denial.[118] Denying the Holocaust has become a crime in many European countries, resulting in criminal proceedings and convictions. The memory of the War, extermination and totalitarianism is beginning to be considered as a new asset that deserves legal protection. Courts are called on simply to verify if a particular idea denies or minimizes the Holocaust, and their decisions have the effect of legally solidifying a particular version of historical facts. The overlapping of a 'trial truth' and 'historical truth' is quite apparent. An irrational fear appears to be spreading: historical investigation alone does not seem to support the collective memory. Law authorities are being called upon and adjudicative mechanisms are being set up to defend it.

Memory, history and justice systems seem to be inevitably involved in this constantly changing attitude towards past wars, genocide and resistance.[119] Mourning, memory, repentance and guilt are themes that consistently appear in public speeches on politics, history and memory.

Thus, it appears that the reason for the constant re-emergence of judicial disputes about the past is to be found in a precise political and legal approach, the origin of which lies in the use of criminal justice during post-Second World War political transitions. In fact, this approach dominated social spaces, including memory. In other words, running alongside historical investigation and memory through testimony, literature and film, the use of a criminal approach also created a form of memory, in which the judge and the historian overlap.[120]

Additional points about the European approach towards the past should be made. First, there is the idea that the reconstruction (based on facts and memory) of the past has a foundational or constituent value for a state created after the collapse of a regime. Second, the process of coming to terms with the past seems to be checked by two opposing forces: hypertrophy of history and hypertrophy of law. In the process of reconstructing the past in Europe during the second half of the twentieth century, it seems that the adjudicative and historical approaches both grew chaotically in cycles. On the one hand, information and historical research continued to accumulate, as did the legal material interpreting the facts of the past. In many circumstances, when the pact of remembrance was at risk, the (apparent) power of the law and the authority of the court were called upon. In moments like these, the adjudicative method grew hypertrophically in comparison with other social mechanisms used to analyse the past. A possible explanation of this phenomenon can be found in the court decisions. Aside from the imperative force of these decisions due to their connection to a public power, they have the power to simplify the complexity of the facts. Limited to a simple true-or-false check, the court decision creates assurance with its illusion of controlling and stabilizing complex and unstable elements. Courts have often been authorized to rule on what was historically true; during this hermeneutic operation, elements are produced that become part of the heritage of memory, underlying the political balance of the present that will be handed over to future generations.

In all of this, there appears to be a specificity of the mechanisms for dealing with the past which clashes with South Africa's constitutional choice to limit or neutralize a strictly criminal approach for crimes committed for political reasons.

Notes on Post-conflict Justice and Political Transitions Outside of Europe

The end of the twentieth century saw many political transitions from military regimes to democracies in Latin America and the breakup of the Soviet Union.[121] In particular, we can observe some similarities in terms of form and substance between the post-apartheid constitutional transition and transitions in Latin America.

As has been noted by historians, countries like Chile, Argentina and El Salvador saw negotiated transitions between military oligarchies who led South American authoritarian regimes and democratic powers, just as South Africa experienced a long phase of negotiation and compromise.

Both the transitions in Latin America and South Africa experimented with creating mechanisms of post-conflict justice which were quite similar in many ways: the truth and reconciliation commissions. In all these transitions, a strictly criminal approach for coming to terms with the past was not possible politically.[122]

The South African TRC was not the first experiment with this type of transitional justice, but it was a development of previous models. Even though the first application of this type of post-conflict justice was used in Uganda (1986),[123] the truth commission models were consolidated by the Latin American commissions. The commissions in Bolivia (1982), Argentina (1983), Uruguay (1985), El Salvador (1993), Chile (1990) and Guatemala (1994) opened the doors to the development of this type of alternative justice.[124] Though of secondary importance, the commissions in Haiti (1993) and the Philippines (1986)[125] were additional signals of the development of alternative post-conflict systems. Another important example was the German commission instituted in 1992 during the unification process in order to deal with crimes committed under the German Democratic Republic. Even though this commission was more like a parliamentary investigative committee, it had the benefit of producing a large amount of information that fed the public debate on the past of the communist regime. It had a notable impact on producing the collective memory of the communist past.[126] It is also worth mentioning the so called mixed configurations, which saw the institution of commissions alongside strictly adjudicative systems of resolving conflicts, such as the commissions in East Timor and Sierra Leone.[127] Additionally, there have been recent developments in this type of transitional justice that have integrated newly-instituted commissions, for example in Morocco and Burundi, and in Cyprus they have been working for a long time on defining the transition system.

However, the South African model is radically different from other truth commission models for two reasons: for the powers granted to the TRC (in terms of investigative independence and powers, especially the power to grant amnesty) and the constituent role that it acquired.

If we reflect on the issue of amnesty, we can observe how the South African model is substantially different from all others that have been instituted. In South Africa, it was decided on a constitutional level to use a procedure of granting amnesty on a strictly personal basis and only after verifying the prerequisites set down by the law (as such, it was not a blanket amnesty). The Latin American commissions were not bound by amnesty measures independently decided by parliament. Nevertheless, the wide parameters of these amnesty laws produce the effect of impunity regarding the crimes committed by previous regimes. Hence, it was in order to satisfy the need of a 'public truth' that ad hoc bodies were adopted, that is, the commissions appointed with the task of officially determining the elements of 'truth' about the past. The official quality of these bodies is very important. Since the commissions are bodies created by the state, the conclusions of their investigations, published and made public knowledge by reports, created a truth theoretically imbued with a stronger representative power than the truth produced by other social actors.

The South African model is thus much more juridically complex. Functioning as a body connecting the ordinary justice system with the special transitional justice system in addition to having decision-making powers, the TRC established itself as a highly innovative solution. The Commission, as opposed to all other models, was appointed with the task of putting specific political and constitutional decisions to work, such as counterbalancing avenging forces and any other social dynamic that could feed the centrifugal forces that were historically part of the social fabric and exacerbated by a segregationist ideology.

In conclusion, Europe and South Africa thus seem to offer two opposing types of post-conflict justice, while the other truth commission models form a grey intermediate area between the two. In Europe, a dynamic of constant juridification of the past and memory was created, with the consequences discussed. In South Africa, the idea of suspending a strictly criminal approach based on the exchange of confession for amnesty was an attempt at making a model to constitutionally create the new social body out of one that was deeply divided. Thus, in juxtaposition with the European model of purging and expelling (including by adjudicative means), the South African model adopted an approach of inclusion through confession.

Notes

1. Chapter 4 analyses the Interim Constitution's last provisions, which were included in the definitive Constitution.
2. See J. Klaaren. 1998. 'The Truth and Reconciliation Commission, the South African Judiciary, and Constitutionalism', *African Studies* 57: 197–208, p. 203; M. Coetzee. 2003. 'An Overview of the TRC Amnesty Process', in C. Villa-Vicencio and E. Doxtader (eds), *The Provocations of Amnesty, Memory, Justice and Impunity*. Claremont: David Philip, pp. 181–95.
3. Promotion of National Unity and Reconciliation Act 34/1995.
4. This issue generated much controversy. See C. Jenkins. 2000. 'The Dilemmas of Reparation and Reconstruction in South Africa', *South Africa Journal of Human Rights* 16: 415–85; C.J. Colvin. 2000. *We Are Still Struggling: Story-Telling, Reparation and Reconciliation after the TRC*. Cape Town: Centre for the Study of Violence and Reconciliation; K. Koppe. 2003. *Wiedergutmachung für die Opfer von Menschenrechtsverletzungen in Südafrika*. Berlin: Berliner Wissenschafts-Verlag; B. Hamber. 1998. 'Repairing the Irreparable: Dealing with Double-Binds of Making Reparation for Crimes of the Past', *Comparisons and Transitions, 14–16 September 1998*. London: University of London.
5. See E. Doxtader. 2003. 'Easy to Forget or Never (Again) Hard to Remember? History, Memory and the 'Publicity' of Amnesty', in Villa-Vicencio and Doxtader (eds), *The Provocations of Amnesty*, pp. 121–56; A Lollini. 2002. 'Reconstructing the Past between Trials and History: The TRC Experience as "Remembrance Space"', in *Quest: An African Journal of Philosophy* 16(1–2): 61–69. In the same journal issue, see also Cassin (pp. 14–18) and Villa-Vicencio, 'Learning to Live Together with Bad Memories' (pp. 37–49); and A. Lollini. 1999. 'La construction d'une mémoire collective en Afrique du Sud. La Commission vérité et réconciliation: "hypertrophie de la sentence" ou hypertrophie de l'histoire', *Astrée. Revue de Droit Pénal et Droits de l'homme* 8: 25–30.
6. The TRC's results in terms of historical reconstruction have been carefully analysed and criticized. A. Jeffery. 2000. *The Truth about the Truth Commission*. Johannesburg: Institute of Race Relations. Jeffery emphatically criticizes the TRC's activities, demonstrating the limits of the AC's procedure, which seem to have created a manipulated view of the past. If some of the procedure's malfunctions actually limited the possibility of factually reconstructing the past (part of the TRC's mandate), the author's criticisms seem to be more of an ideological nature and cannot be shared where she claims that the apartheid justice system (mostly acting in accordance with the regime) contributed more to providing information regarding human rights violations than the TRC did. On this matter, I share the opinion of J. Sarkin. 2004. *Carrots and Sticks: The TRC and the South African Amnesty Process*. Antwerp: Intersentia, pp. 259–60.
7. See A. Krog. 1998. *Country of My Skull. Guilt, Sorrow, and the Limits of Forgiveness in the New South Africa*. New York: Random House.
8. See s. 14(1)(a) of Act 34/95. See also S. Levinson. 2000. 'Trials, Commissions, and Investigating Committee: the Elusive Search for Norms of Due Process', in R.I. Rotberg and D. Thompson (eds), *Truth v. Justice. The Morality of Truth Commissions*. Princeton: Princeton University Press, pp. 211–34.
9. See s. 14(1)(b) of Act 34/95.

10. L. Buur. 1999. 'Monumental History: Visibility and Invisibility in the Work of the TRC', *TRC: Commissioning the Past Conference, Johannesburg, 11–14 June 1999*. Johannesburg: University of Witwatersrand. This study sheds light on the role of the statement takers. In particular, it stresses: a) the importance of the interpersonal relationship between the Commission's personnel, representing the state, and apartheid victims; b) the importance of allowing victims to narrate the violence they experienced and the quasi-psychiatric qualities of this activity; c) the fundamental role of the statement takers in interpreting and transcribing the facts revealed by victims in a database.
11. For more information about the functioning of the NDB (defined as an Information Management System), see the *TRC Final Report*, vol. 1, pp. 322–63.
12. See s. 15(1) and (2) of Act 34/95.
13. Reparations were a fundamental issue. The policy followed by Thabo Mbeki's government, which was in some ways ambiguous, revolved around two concerns: a) first, the RRC did not have its own financial resources on which it could draw to provide compensation for the victims. That was a state function under the state's monopoly on managing funding; b) originally, as stated in the Commission's rules, there was supposed to be a closed list of victims who were to be the first to receive reparations. The closed list was composed of persons recognized with victim status by the RRC for two reasons: if the victim had collaborated with the HRVC or if they were identified clearly as a victim at the end of proceedings before the AC. What is important to stress here is the type of reparations provided by the rules by the reasoning behind a systemic need for reparations. The idea of creating a closed list of victims entitled to reparations stems from the TRC's participatory setup. The perpetrators' participation is fundamental, just as the victims' participation is essential to acquiring factual information for corroborating the perpetrators' confessions and for symbolic reasons. In other words, creating a common collective space for social reconstruction requires the participation of all the actors (victims and perpetrators). See L. Fernandez. 1996. 'Possibilities and Limitations of Reparations for the Victims of Human Rights Violations in South Africa', in M.R. Rwelamira and G. Werle (eds), *Confronting Past Injustices. Approaches to Amnesty, Punishment, Reparation and Restitution in South Africa and Germany*. Durban: Butterworths. This meant that the victims also had to assume their responsibilities as new citizens. If some international conventions on international crimes call upon the duty of the state that follows a criminal regime to prosecute, the TRC substitutes it with a duty to recognize reparations. Due to economic difficulties, the government hesitated at length before paying the reparations promised. In Mbeki's opinion, the black population as a whole, and not just the names on the closed list, should be recognized as victims of apartheid, hence favouring the idea that individual reparations should not be made and instead using the funds for general development programmes (see W. Orr. 2000. 'Reparation Delayed Is Healing Retarded', in C. Villa-Vicencio and W. Verwoerd (eds), *Looking Back, Reaching Forward*. Cape Town: University of Cape Town, pp. 240 *et seq*).
14. See *TRC Final Report*, 'Management and Operational Report. Investigation Unit', vol. 1, pp. 326–43.
15. See S. Garkawe. 2003. 'The South African Truth and Reconciliation Commission: A Suitable Model to Enhance the Role and Rights of the Victims of Gross Violations of Human Rights?', *Melbourne University Law Review* 27: 334 *et seq*.
16. See *TRC Final Report*, 'The Mandate', vol. 1 and 4, pp. 48–102.
17. See D.B. Ntsebeza. 2000. 'The Uses of Truth Commissions: Lessons for the World', in Rotberg and Thompson (eds), *Truth v. Justice*, pp. 158–69; *TRC Final Report*, 'Institutional and Special Hearings', vol. 4, pp. 1–316. The judicial system was found to be responsible, as it had diligently applied segregationist laws. See D. Dyzenhaus. 1998. *Truth, Reconciliation and the Apartheid Legal Order*. Cape Town: Juta; 'The

Truth and Reconciliation Commission, and the Bench, Legal Practitioners and Legal Academics', 15–106.

18. See *TRC Final Report*, 'Legal Basis of the Amnesty Process', vol. 4. The AC was instituted by Chapter 4 of Act 34/95 (Art. 17(3)). The last public hearings ended in December 2000. The AC continued its work until its official termination on 31 May 2001.
19. See *Judges' Remuneration and Conditions of Employment Act 1989*, Act 88 of 1989. According to the rules governing the AC, appointments of members 'were made exclusively from the ranks of legal professions: that is, its members were judges, advocates and attorneys' (see *TRC Final Report*, vol. 6, ch. 5, 85, s. 13).
20. Many analysts agree on this point in Villa-Vicencio and Doxtader (eds), *The Provocations of Amnesty*, especially M. Fullard and N. Rousseau, 'Truth, Evidence and History', pp. 195–216; according to P. Pigou, 'Degrees of Truth' (pp. 217–36), a larger presence of historians and anthropologists would have produced a broader understanding of the facts confessed and a more effective corroboration of them. According to Coetzee, 'An Overview of the Amnesty Process' (pp. 181–94), many viewed the AC as an adjudicative body. The AC responded to this criticism, stating: 'in the view of the Committee, this argument entailed the danger of assuming findings of fact prior to evidence having been heard. It also felt that the presence of non-lawyers could have increased fears of those persons who were concerned that they might not receive a fair and impartial hearing' (*TRC Final Report*, vol. 6, ch. 5, 85, s. 12)
21. The preliminary screening of the 'improper applications' (filed by persons serving prison sentences for clearly non-political crimes) that flooded the amnesty process is examined in detail by A. du Bois-Pedain. 2007. *Transitional Amnesty in South Africa.* Oxford: Oxford University Press, pp. 36–40.
22. Analysts agree that one of the weaknesses of the AC's procedure was undersized facilities for investigation. The human resources and logistics that the Department of Correctional Services, the National Prosecuting Authority and the courts made available to the South African Police Services generally proved to be insufficient for the breadth of the investigative work.
23. See s. 19(3)(b)(i),(ii) and (iii) of Act 34/95.
24. See AC 034/2001 and AC 068/2001. The legal criteria shaping the notion of 'full disclosure' are in s. 4(c) and 20(1)(c) of Act 34/95.
25. One of the most famous examples included the murderers of Steven Biko (G.J. Nieuwoudt (AM 3920/96); H. Snyman (AM 3918/96); D.P. Siebert (AM 3915/96); J.J.O. Beneke (AM 6367/97); R. Max (AM 3521/96)). Amnesty was refused for denial of guilt in the cases of P. Gumengu (AM 3610/96) and F.B. Nombanga (AM 6364/97) (for the murder of Craig Duli (AC/2000/036)). Another very controversial case dealt with the dramatic Boipatong attack of 17 June 1992, which led to the death of 45 people. Though he confessed, Mqambeleni Buthelezi (AM 6128/97) was refused amnesty for denial of guilt (AC 2000/209). The AC faced the problem of applicants denying guilt in the case of a shooting outside Shell House on 28 March 1994 (AC/2000/142). Many members of the ANC – G.J. Kruser (AM 5542/97), B.M. Zuma (AM 5544/97), M. Singaram (AM 5545/97), J.M. Molefe (AM 5546/97), B.E. Khumalo (AM 5547/97), C.T. Beea (AM 5548/97), S.M. Moolman (AM 5549/97), M.V. Llale (AM 5550/97), N. Potsane (AM 7159/97), M.S. Mangena (AM 5275/97) and S.P. Simelane (AM 5552/97) – stated that they acted in self-defence or defence of property, but the AC decided, in this case, that their conduct was objectively unlawful.
26. See s. 20(7)(b) of Act 34/95.
27. See s. 1(ix)(a)(b) of Act 34/95.

28. The term 'neutral concept' referring to 'Torture and Abduction, Killing and Severe Ill Treatment' is used in the *TRC Final Report*, vol. 1, p. 70.
29. Some doubts have been raised about the subject matter jurisdiction established by law being too limited. The criminal offences contemplated are those compromising the physical wellbeing of individuals. For example, the TRC could not investigate the effects of social and economic marginalization caused by apartheid. This restriction in subject matter jurisdiction is the reason why the TRC and its *Final Report* largely ignored apartheid's social and economic damage. The AC was not equipped with the legal instruments to investigate the effects of denying 'social citizenship'; see F. Barchiesi. 1999. *Socio-Economic Exploitation, Meaning Contestation, and the TRC Foundation for a Discourse of Social Citizenship in Post-Apartheid South Africa.* Johannesburg: University of Witwatersrand; and N. Nattrass. 1994. 'Controversies about Capitalism and Apartheid in South Africa: An Economic Perspective', *Journal of Southern African Studies* 17: 654; N. Nattrass. 1999. 'The Truth and Reconciliation Commission on Business and Apartheid: A Critical Evaluation', *African Affairs* 98: 373.
30. See s. 20(2)(3)(a)(g) of Act 34/95. See K. Greenawalt. 2000. 'Amnesty's Justice', in Rotberg and Thompson (eds), *Truth v. Justice*, pp. 189–210.
31. One of the most thorough and sensitive analyses of the AC decision-making practice regarding political offence requirements can be found in du Bois-Pedain, *Transitional Amnesty in South Africa*, pp. 97–138.
32. The proportionality principle between the gravity of the acts and the political aim was almost ignored in AC decision-making (see Sarkin, *Carrots and Sticks*, p. 311; du Bois-Pedain, *Transitional Amnesty in South Africa*, pp. 122–28). When the AC explicitly addressed the question of proportionality, it was reluctant to apply a formalistic interpretation of the principle. In the case of the murder of J. Mabotha (AC/2000/084) by E. de Kock (AM 66/96), D.J. Brits (AM 3745/96), K. Klopper (AM 3762/96), D.L. Snyman (AM 3766/96), N.J. Vermeulen (AM 4358/96) and L.W.J. Flores (AM 4361/96), the principle of proportionality was implemented indirectly. The evidence leader stated that the 'conduct was not proportionate with the objective they intended to achieve', speculating that there was a lack of full disclosure. In significant cases, the principle of proportionality was not an element that urged the Committee to refuse amnesty. See, for example, the case in which two right-wing AWB supporters killed a black man simply driving past them on the day of the first democratic elections. The only aim was to instil fear and chaos (AC/1998/032). The AC was prepared to recognize proportionality even in the killing of Jeanette Schoon's daughter, deciding it was an innocent 'collateral effect' of the letter bomb sent by the security police (AC/2000/082). The Committee did not consider the eleven people killed indiscriminately by APLA cadres in the St James Church Massacre to be disproportionate.
33. Sergeant A. Cloete (AM 5726/97) was refused amnesty for the killing of thirteen people in Kwa Makutha (KWZ Natal) during the attack on the residence of political activists where, instead, the victims had no connection to them. Most of the victims were innocent woman and children. The lack of proportionality between means and objective precluded Cloete from receiving amnesty (AC/2000/224). The interpretation of the existence of these requirements is sometimes contradictory; in R. McBride's application (AM 7032/97 and others) the wrong target (victim) receives the opposite interpretation. The case dealt with the bombings of nightclubs thought to be patronized by security force members in which three innocent people were killed as a 'collateral effect' of the attack (AC/2001/128). A very controversial case was the decision to refuse amnesty for the famous Motherwell bombing (killing three police officers and an 'askari'); the protagonists were E. de Kock, D.L. Snyman, N.J.

van Rensburg, G.J. Lotz, J. Kok, W. du Toit, N.J. Vermeulen, M.D. Ras and G.J. Nieuwoudt. The applicants Nieuwoudt, Lotz and du Toit were convicted of homicide before the TRC opened its doors; they were refused amnesty as the victims could not be considered political objectives and the criterion of proportionality had not been met (AC/1999/0345). In their High Court appeal, they complained that the AC did not take into account a number of factual elements that would have led to the opposite conclusion. The AC claimed instead that the murders were carried out only to eliminate potential witnesses of previous secret operations without a political objective. The High Court later ordered the revision of the AC's decision. In the meantime, the Committee had already finished its term and the Minister of Justice was forced to reconvene the AC with an ad hoc extension of its functions.

34. See A. Bhargava. 2002. 'Defining Political Crimes: A Case Study of the South African Truth and Reconciliation Commission', *Columbia Law Review*, 1304 *et seq.* Cruelty and sadism were elements that often caused the AC to refuse amnesty; members of the Ciskei Police K.E. Thoba, J. Makoma and W.R. Thompson (AC/1997/25) were refused amnesty because they used acid to torture a woman suspected of being a dissident. Cruelty was in some circumstances evaluated as an element that determined whether an act was non-politically motivated.
35. The decision to recognize the South African Prisoners Organisation for Human Rights with the status of organization with political objectives was criticized. Some members (who were also responsible for violent acts) received amnesty like K. Tsotetsi (AM 7974/97). Paradoxically, the organization's mission expressly stated that it was not a politically affiliated entity that focused on prisoner issues. The AC was convinced that this organization was political due to a very broad definition of 'political' that was subject to much scrutiny. On the contrary, J.P. du Plessis (AM 151/96) was refused amnesty for the acts committed on behalf of the *Nasionale Sosialistiese Partisane*, which had only four members. The fact that the organizations had to be publicly recognized created significant problems: see also the case of *Toekomsgesprekt* and its members D.B. Snyders (AM 74/96), J.P. Kruger (AM 2734/96) and M.C. Ras (AM 2735/96). Despite of the fact that it was a secret right-wing organization, attempting not to be publicly known, the Committee was satisfied that it was 'political' (AC/2000/121).
36. See, for example, the J.T Benzien case, in which a police member tortured black activists to gain information. The applicant's superior was generally aware of the interrogation techniques (which were forms of torture) used by Benzien, who received amnesty (AC/1999/027). A similar AC reasoning was used in the cases of torture by the ANC of affiliates suspected of being informers (AC/2000/149). In the case regarding the death of activist Stanza Bopape while in custody, the AC stated that a narrow literal interpretation of s. 20(2)(b) would result in almost all acts committed by policeman being considered unlawful according to criminal law, because these acts were beyond 'the scope of his duties'. On the contrary, according to the AC, these acts proved to be clearly politically motivated and eligible for amnesty when considered from a more concrete perspective of South African political violence (AC/2000/059). The issues of 'orders' and cases related are analysed in J. Sarkin, *Carrots and Sticks*, pp. 299–302.
37. See the cases of the Witbank police station and Ellis Park Station bombings (AC/2000/055), in which the AC accepted that the applicants were ANC members acting under clear instructions.
38. See, for example, the killing of a local politician by ANC Youth League activists (AC/1997/020).
39. On this type of case and AC-related amnesty decisions, see the analysis of du Bois-Pedain, *Transitional Amnesty in South Africa*, pp. 113–21.

40. On this specific issue, see the analysis of du Bois-Pedain, *Transitional Amnesty in South Africa*, pp. 293–99.
41. The administrative procedure was used for 77% of the amnesty applications. This procedure was employed for cases that did not involve torture or murder, such as illegal possession of weapons, bombing attempts not resulting in injury, theft or damage.
42. See I. Lax. 2004a. 'Amnesty, Reparation and the Object of Reconciliation in the Context of South Africa's TRC', in C. Villa-Vicencio and E. Doxtader (eds), *To Repair the Irreparable: Reparation and Reconstruction in South Africa*, Cape Town: David Philip.
43. See the careful analysis of du Bois-Pedain, *Transitional Amnesty in South Africa*, pp. 191–94.
44. Legally speaking, the AC was not bound to the victim's agreement. In practice, however, it led to different consequences: relatives of the ANC supporter Emmanuel Bhengu who was killed by IFP supporter V.T. Manqele (AM 4037/96) agreed that the confessor should receive amnesty, despite doubts about the crime's political objective; the AC was positively influenced by the attitude of the victim's family. The same attitude can be seen in AC/2001/048, in which the victim's family was in favour of amnesty being granted to applicants S. Hendricks (AM 6146/97), V.R. November (AM 7988/97) and M.A. Salie (AM 6146/97). In another case, ANC activists I.N. Ndzamela (AM 5051/97) and P. Mayaphi (AM 5247/97), who were convicted of murder for an attack on the Wild Coast Casino (in April 1986), made open apologies during the hearing. The victim's family forgave both applicants and the Committee made a decision to grant amnesty at the end of the hearing. On the contrary, in other cases, the victims strongly opposed granting amnesty, at times leading to long cross-examinations (for example, the victims tortured by H.J.P Botha, M. Greyling, K. Durr and F.S. Bothma). In this case (AC/2000/120), the Committee granted amnesty. Sometimes victims managed to influence the decision in their favour when there were doubts about all the requirements for amnesty, as in the famous Bisho massacre case of 1992 (AC/2000/122). Victims vigorously cross-examined the two applicants (V.A. Mkosana (AM 4458/96) and M.T. Gonya (AM 7882/97)) and found inconsistencies and contradictions which led the Committee to deny amnesty. Victims were against amnesty in other cases, such as the Heidelberg Tavern attack case (AC/1998/026) and the case regarding Chris Hani's assassination, in which the activist's family opposed amnesty for C. Derby-Lewis and J. Walus. Despite the strong opposition of victims and relatives, the Committee granted amnesty in the first case, but it did not do so in the second (AC/1999/172).
45. See the cases mentioned in note 33 of this chapter.
46. On this matter in general, see M. Freeman. 2006. *Truth Commissions and Procedural Fairness*. Cambridge: Cambridge University Press.
47. The power to subpoena was mostly used during the investigative phase and during the HRVC's hearings. Often, at the hearing's conclusion, the evidence gathered regarding the persons invited to testify was officially communicated to them and, as a result, they could file an application for amnesty. Some scholars view this practice as a violation of the right to silence. In the case of Magnus Malan or Winnie Mandela, even though they agreed to appear before the HRVC, they refused to file an amnesty application (and thus to continue with a full disclosure). By contrast, former President P.W. Botha was subpoenaed before the AC but refused to appear, responding only with a written reply. Since Botha refused the offer, he underwent a criminal trial before the High Court. Botha's conviction was overturned on appeal due to a legal technicality. Robert McBride and Greta Applegreen were the first members of the liberation movement to be subpoenaed. They were summoned to

answer questions about the involvement of the ANC's armed unit in bomb attacks (Magoo's Bar and the Why Not Bar bombings). The news unleashed violent debate; as a result, the HRVC made another controversial decision: to use the procedure provided by s. 29 (Act 34/95) and hold the hearing behind closed doors (see Sarkin, *Carrots and Sticks*, pp. 78–86; T.A. Borer. 2003. 'A Taxonomy of Victims and Perpetrators: Human Rights and Reconciliation in South Africa', *Human Rights Quarterly* 25(4):1088 *et seq*).

48. See s. 31(3) of Act 34/95
49. See s. 20(7)(a) and (b) of Act 34/95.
50. Applicant Derby-Lewis filed an appeal with the High Court for not having received amnesty for killing Chris Hani; the applicant claimed that on other occasions the AC had interpreted Act 34/95 differently. The High Court (in *Derby-Lewis v. TRC* (2001)(3) SALR 1033–1056 (C)) ruled that the AC was an administrative body which, though it had some quasi-judiciary powers, should not use a binding precedent system equal to *stare decisis*. The AC was nevertheless bound to apply decision-making and interpretive criteria according to its rules without discrimination, just as the Constitution requires of all administrative bodies. The AC itself stated that its only obligation in terms of decision making was the constitutional obligation of a fair administrative action (*TRC Final Report*, vol. 6, § 38). For an analysis on this delicate issue and for an overview of the cases in which the AC referred to previous decisions, see Sarkin, *Carrots and Sticks*, pp. 181–91.
51. Before the institution of the TRC, an important trial was held against former minister Magnus Malan, whom public opinion regarded as one of the most zealous supporters of the apartheid system. For a number of reasons, the trial ended with Malan's acquittal. The judgment caused anger and frustration (see H. Varney and J. Sarkin. 1997. 'Failing to Pierce the Hit Squad Veil: An Analysis of the Malan Trial', *South African Journal of Criminal Justice* 10: 141–61; J. Sarkin. 2003. 'To Prosecute or Not to Prosecute? Constitutional and Legal Issues Concerning Criminal Trials', in Villa-Vicencio and Doxtader (eds), *The Provocations of Amnesty*, pp. 249–61). As we shall see, taking penal action against political crimes of the apartheid era was particularly difficult, even after the TRC: Dr Wouter Basson's trial ended with an acquittal. Basson was charged with having developed a biological weapons programme against the black population during apartheid. Even if there was substantial evidence against him, in court his guilt was not proven to be beyond reasonable doubt. See D.W. Shriver Jr. 2003. 'Truth Commissions and Judicial Trials. Complementary or Antagonistic Servants of Public Justice?', in Villa-Vicencio and Doxtader (eds), *The Provocations of Amnesty*, pp. 61–91. Malan's acquittal was followed by the important case of Eugene de Kock (see E. de Kock (AM 0066/96)), the bloodthirsty leader of the special armed unit known as the Death Squad, which had systematically eliminated anti-apartheid activists. De Kock, prior to appearing before the AC to confess the crimes he had committed, had been convicted by the court for many of these deaths. As he admitted a number of times before the AC, he had constantly tried to conceal the truth during the criminal trial. Before the Commission, however, his attitude radically changed. If he wanted to receive amnesty, he had to tell the most 'truth' possible. The AC possessed information gathered during the investigations and criminal trial; thus, it was able to corroborate de Kock's confessions and verify their reliability. If there were any doubts about the confession's truthfulness, amnesty would not be granted. De Kock confessed and received amnesty for some of the crimes he committed. However, political objectives were not found for all the criminal episodes; in some situations, he executed orders with undue cruelty, while in others he committed crimes without a political purpose or for personal interests. As a result, de Kock did not receive amnesty for all the crimes confessed, and he had to serve the life sentences previously decided. The TRC's report shows, however, that de

Kock's case and the information therein revealed led to other security force members having to appear before the AC. See *TRC Final Report*, vol. 6, § 15–16, 184 stating: 'There is no doubt that, without the prosecution of Colonel Eugene de Kock, the Commission would have received far less amnesty applications. In October 1996, De Kock, (...) was found guilty on 89 charges and sentenced to two life terms plus 212 years imprisonment. De Kock was one of the first to submit an application for amnesty to the Amnesty Committee. Indeed the number of applicants in De Kock related incidents accounts for 48 per cent of all Security Branch applications.' See also J. Pauw. 1997. *Into the Heart of Darkness: Confessions of Apartheid Assassins*. Johannesburg: Jonathan Ball.

52. See M. Coetzee, 'An Overview of the TRC Amnesty Process', in Villa-Vicencio and Doxtader (eds), *The Provocation of Amnesty*, pp. 193–94.
53. See Sarkin, *Carrots and Sticks*, pp. 107 *et seq* (especially the table on p. 126) and the detailed study by A. du Bois-Pedain. 2004. 'Was Amnesty a Lottery? An Empirical Study of the Decision of the TRC's Committee on Amnesty', *South African Law Journal* 121(4): 785–828; du Bois-Pedain, *Transitional Amnesty in South Africa*, pp. 60–96.
54. See Sarkin, *Carrots and Sticks*, p. 106.
55. Du Bois-Pedain, *Transitional Amnesty in South Africa*, p. 63.
56. Complicity applications, for example, presented several problems. First, some applicants claimed to have confessed only because accomplices had filed an application. An even more serious problem was evaluating the truthfulness of the statements made in cases of co-authorship; the murder of Stanza Bopape is an exemplary case. Ten policemen requested amnesty for having killed Bopape after torturing him in prison (A.P. van Niekerk (AM 4353/96), H.A.B. Mostert (AM 4403/96), J.H. Engelbrecht (AM 4402/96), C.A. Zeelie (AM 3751/96), J.L. du Preez (AM 4404/96), G.N. Erasmus (AM 4134/96), P.L. du Toit (AM 4131/96), J.V. van der Merwe (AM 4157/96), S.J. Visser (AM 5000/97) and L. van Leggerenberg (AM 5010/97)). Relying on the same legal representative, they filed applications, obviously agreeing on the 'truth' beforehand. Making the confessing accomplices not use the same legal representative would have prevented the 'fabrication' of a previously agreed upon version of the facts (Pigou, 'Degrees of Truth', pp. 227 *et seq*).
57. See Sarkin, *Carrots and Sticks*, p. 126.
58. Jeremy Sarkin's information regarding the number of SADF applications is the one that varies the most from the statistical studies cited. In fact, the *Final Report* mentions only 293 applications and Pedain 289.
59. Du Bois-Pedain, *Transitional Amnesty in South Africa*, pp. 68 *et seq*; du Bois-Pedain, 'Was Amnesty a Lottery?'.
60. Du Bois-Pedain, *Transitional Amnesty in South Africa*, p. 63, note 25.
61. The measures for eliminating punishment and the immunity granted up until 1995 had a negative effect on the AC procedure on a number of occasions such as: M.J. Hlope (AM 1779/96), T.P. Tshika (AM 5962/97), B.F. Msibi (AM 5617/97) and E.T. Mokati (AM 5897/97). These cases are quoted and analysed in Sarkin, *Carrots and Sticks*, pp. 194–98.
62. See *State v. Msane and 19 Others* (*Durban and Coast Local Division of Supreme Court* CC1/96). The judgement arrived six weeks before the application deadline when most potential applicants had to decide whether to apply to the TRC. The acquittal was a dissuasive factor. Some complain that the weakness of the court system prior to the AC's institution, in addition to the loss of reliability in the criminal justice system following Malan's acquittal, contributed to the low number of applications. The threat of punitive measures is a valid incentive for pursuing alternative routes like the AC. The situation was aggravated by the lack of cooperation between the courts and the TRC. Tense relations between bodies (which were at times com-

petitive) weakened the TRC's investigative ability (Sarkin, *Carrots and Sticks*, pp. 127 *et seq*; J. Quinn and M. Freeman. 2003. 'Lessons Learned: Practical Lessons Gleaned from Inside the Truth Commissions of Guatemala and South Africa', *Human Rights Quarterly* 25(4): 1117 *et seq*).

63. During the transition, it was rare that the judiciary would take punitive measures against the regime's institutions with which it had shared power for decades. Only two important investigations were conducted regarding large-scale crimes committed during apartheid: in Pretoria (under the authority of the Transvaal attorney-general) and Durban (under the Natal attorney-general). The first case was rather successful and led to de Kock and his accomplices being tried and convicted for crimes committed by the South African police and *Vlakplaas* units. In the second case, the heads of the investigating court were not helpful and sabotaged the preliminary investigations for the Malan trial (which, in fact, ended with an acquittal), refusing to cooperate with the investigations of crimes committed by the KwaZulu Police; the political reasons are as obvious as the damage caused. If the Pretoria investigations led to the conviction of de Kock and to many amnesty applications, the Durban investigations only encouraged the perception of impunity.
64. See AM 2586/96.
65. See J. Klaaren and H. Varney. 2003. 'A Second Bite at the Amnesty Cherry. Constitutional and Policy Issues around Legislation for a Second Amnesty', in Villa-Vicencio and Doxtader (eds), *The Provocations of Amnesty*, pp. 265–93.
66. See *TRC Final Report*, vol. 6, p. 185.
67. Extraterritoriality is a complex legal issue involving international law and relations between states (extradition). The crimes committed by D.G. Stopfoth and M.L. Veenendaal in Namibia as operations sabotaging the transition went through the court system. The two, held as prisoners in Namibia, escaped to South Africa and filed an application with the AC; Namibia asked for extradition. The Supreme Court of Appeal had to decide the issue. If amnesty was granted, they could not be extradited. The judgment answered negatively, orienting the AC's policy regarding similar cases. Extraterritorial crimes cannot be granted amnesty if they do not have a specific connection with the political conflict in South Africa in the context of reconciliation. Crimes committed during operations in Namibia, Angola and Mozambique had a hard time meeting this requirement. Another example is the case of the bombing of the ANC office in London. Amnesty was granted, even if the AC did not clearly explain whether it was directly connected with the national political conflict. Applicants applied for and obtained amnesty for the assassination of Ruth First in Maputo in 1982 and for Janette and Katryn Schoon in Angola in 1984. Even though the victim was an important anti-apartheid activist, the AC was still hesitant as to whether this was the reason for granting amnesty in this case of extraterritoriality. Though amnesties were granted also for crimes committed within the liberation movement in camps in Angola and Zambia (sixteen for the ANC), amnesty was not granted to J.F. Vesters (AM 7991/97) for crimes connected to SADF actions in Angola (due to no political motives). See the analysis on this issue of Sarkin, *Carrots and Sticks*, pp. 335 *et seq*.
68. See Fullard and Rousseau, 'Truth, Evidence and History', pp. 195–216; Pigou, 'Degrees of Truth', pp. 217–36.
69. For an overview of these public positions, see Sarkin, *Carrots and Sticks*, pp. 357–61.
70. See Klaaren and Varney, 'A Second Bite at the Amnesty Cherry', pp. 272–74 and 282–84; Sarkin, *Carrots and Sticks*, pp. 277–78.
71. See A. Lollini. 2004c. 'L'istituzione delle giurisdizioni Gacaca: giustizia post-genocidio e processo costituente in Ruanda', *Rivista di diritto pubblico comparato ed europeo* 3.

72. The assassination of Ms Ntombi Khubeka (an ANC activist) is a good example. The victim vanished in 1987. All trace of her was lost until eight members of the Security Branch of Durban filed an amnesty application for having caused her death. In their public confessions, they stated that the victim died of a heart attack during questioning. In this case, TRC investigators did additional research which led to the discovery of the victim's body. The corpse was examined by medical specialists, who showed that a bullet was still present in the skull. Thus, the victim in reality had been executed. The eight were denied amnesty for lack of full disclosure and they risked going to court. If the AC had similar support for all cases, the degree of factual 'truth' would have been higher. In similar circumstances, security force members claimed in their confessions that activists who underwent 'questioning' (torture) died from a heart attack. Even in the aforementioned Stanza Bopape case, a heart attack was the reason given for the activist's death. However, as stated in the confession, the victim's body was thrown in a river inhabited by crocodiles. Recovering the body and verifying the confession's truthfulness would have been impossible. All cases in which victims' bodies were not found, and thus where the statements could not be corroborated, should be viewed with suspicion; however, these confessions did clear up what had happened to people who had disappeared over the years.
73. The work of Fullard and Rousseau, 'Truth, Evidence and History', pp. 195–216, clearly shows that this element was overlooked by many and that it could easily be corrected in the future.
74. Important scholars claim that an effective instrument for making the confessions as truthful as possible would be an amnesty that could be revoked if subsequent proceedings clearly showed that the person confessing had lied or concealed or manipulated the facts (see Klaaren and Varney, 'A Second Bite at the Amnesty Cherry', pp. 269–70).
75. See du Bois-Pedain, *Transitional Amnesty in South Africa*, pp. 95 *et seq*.
76. See the arguments made by Gorge Bizos in the Civil Cooperation Bureau (CCB) case (AC/2001/232) defending a 'wide interpretation' of full disclosure and the arguments made by Du Plessis and Booysen in the Pebco Three case, who called for a 'restrictive approach'. See the analysis of this issue in du Bois-Pedain, *Transitional Amnesty in South Africa*, pp. 143–51.
77. See AC/2001/248. This AC interpretation is carefully analysed by du Bois-Pedain, *Transitional Amnesty in South Africa*, pp. 152 *et seq*.
78. See case AC/2001/270.
79. See case AC/1999/230.
80. See case AC/2000/215.
81. In case AC/2001/248, the AC, despite the fact that the disclosure was 'truthful', clarified that the amnesty process was not an adversarial process, establishing that different versions of the facts may coexist. In the decisions on A. Shoke (AM 8014/97), H. Matshididi (AM8007/97), L. Dumakuke (AM7679/97), and J.I. Dube (AM 5310/97) regarding the Ellis Park Rugby Stadium bombing incident, the AC took note of inconsistencies and contradictions, but none of these elements invalidated the truthfulness of the confession (as such, amnesty was granted; see AC/2001/161). A controversial issue, however, was how to apply the criteria of truthfulness uniformly, especially when the statements could not be corroborated; for example, no corroboration is possible for confirming that an applicant acted following the orders (which includes the requirement of political motives) given by individuals no longer alive at the time of the hearing (as was the case for the Heidelberg Tavern attack and the bombing of the NBS Building in Witbank). The AC often examined the delicate psychological issue of repressed memories (something that is often the case for torturers) as in cases AC/2000/084 and AC/1999/350. There are

numerous cases, however, in which amnesty was denied for lack of full disclosure; for example, for all those involved in the Pebco Three case: H.B du Plessis (AM 4384/96), J.M. van Zyl (AM 5637/97), G. Nieuwoudt (AM 3920/96), G.J. Lotz (AM 3921/96), G.C. Beeslaar (AM 5640/97) and J. Koole (AM 3748/96). This case is significant as it was the first example of refused amnesty followed by a criminal trial; in fact, van Zyl and Nieuwoudt were arrested on 11 February 2004.

82. See case AC/1997/045.
83. These considerations are also to be found in du Bois-Pedain, *Transitional Amnesty in South Africa,* pp. 162–63. In some circumstances, the applicants deliberately manipulated the facts of the crimes confessed so as to meet the requirements for receiving amnesty. This is one of the main reasons for denying amnesty for lack of full disclosure and political motives: an obvious case is B.S. Khumalo (PAC member, AM 5415/97); and the case of A. Mokofane (AM 1474/96). The case of E.N. Mavuso (AM 7921/97) is rather interesting: the IFP member asked for amnesty for the murder of M. Mcetywa in 1993 in Pongola. Over the course of the hearing, it emerged that at the time and the location in which the crime occurred, there was no political violence between the IFP and the ANC. The crime was actually related to the fighting between rival groups for control of a part of the pubic transport business (minibus "taxis"): amnesty was refused. Masking regular crimes with political motives happened frequently and created one of the AC's main problems. N. Danster (AM 40/96), M.E. Khundulu (AM50/96) and L. Kwakwari (AM 4296/96) murdered Mr and Mrs Palaie in Cradock, farmers in close contact with the local police. Amnesty was refused for the murder of Mrs Palaie (on the ground of no political motive). The assassins, however, later received the presidential pardon from Mbeki in May 2002.
84. Du Bois-Pedain agrees on this point: *Transitional Amnesty in South Africa,* p. 215.
85. Its constitutional dimension will be analysed in Chapter 4.
86. See the section entitled 'The First Phase: Removal of Obstacles' in Chapter 1 for an analysis of the Indemnity Acts passed at the beginning of the transition.
87. See *TRC Final Report*, vol. 1, p. 6.
88. A very interesting study on this matter is M.J. Damaška. 1986. *The Face of Justice and State Authority.* New Haven: Yale University Press. A. Garapon. 1997. *Bien Juger. Essai sur le rituel judiciaire.* Paris: Odile Jacob. D. Salas. 1992. *Du procès penal.* Paris: Presses Universitaires de France. The AC in the *Final Report* claims: 'the striking difference between an amnesty application and a criminal trial lies in the fact that, in criminal trials, the accused invariably try to exonerate themselves, while at the amnesty hearing they incriminate themselves (…). Not only did amnesty applicants who had earlier been accused admit to having presented perjured evidence to the trial court, but similar admissions were often made by amnesty applicants who had appeared as prosecution witness at criminal trials.' See *TRC Final Report*, vol. 6, 50, § 62. See also R. Claasen. 1996. 'Principles of Restorative Justice', *Conciliation Quarterly* 15(3): 6 *et seq*; L. Walgrave. 2002. *Restorative Justice and the Law.* Portland: Willan Publishing; E.G.M. Weitekamp and H.J. Kerner (eds). 2002. *Restorative Justice. Theoretical Foundation.* Portland: Willan Publishing.
89. As confirmation, the IFP was the primary non-State perpetrator responsible for 33% of the violations brought before the TRC.
90. Voluntariness is often a characterizing feature of so called restorative justice systems: see D.W. van Ness. 2002. 'The Shape of Things to Come: A Framework for Thinking about a Restorative Justice System', in Weitekamp and Kerner (eds), *Restorative Justice. Theoretical Foundation*, p. 4.
91. Anton Ackerman was the head of the Unit; the Unit was also appointed with another duty which, in the future, could become rather delicate: the coordination of the national prosecution of crimes with the Prosecutor Office of the International Criminal Court, which could constitute an additional variable in the complex issue of South African transitional justice. See Sarkin, *Carrots and Sticks,* pp. 375 *et seq.*

92. See Klaaren and Varney, 'A Second Bite at the Amnesty Cherry', pp. 265–93; J. Klaaren. 1999. 'A Second Organisational Amnesty?', *TRC: Commissioning the Past Conference, Johannesburg, 14 June 1999*. Johannesburg: University of Witwatersrand.
93. In the Constitutional Court decision *President of the Republic of South Africa and Another v. Hugo* (1997) (4) SA 1 (CC), President Mandela granted prison remission (s. 82(1)(k) of the 1993 Constitution) to a female prisoner based on the fact that she was solely responsible for a twelve-year-old child and that imprisonment would endanger the child's life. The Court declared the presidential measure to be unconstitutional. The remission granted by Mandela violated the equality clause of other prisoners in similar situations. The precedent was thus a strong deterrent; President Mbeki was aware that his power to pardon could be brought before the Constitutional Court by anyone in the valid interest according to the principle of direct access: the victims or other individuals excluded by the measure could call upon unfair discrimination. It was the Constitutional Court, in s. 115 of its decision approving the Constitution's compliance with the 34 CPs (CCI (1996) (4) Sa 774 (CC)), that stated the supremacy of the Constitution over the presidential power of pardon. Even if it derives from royal prerogatives typical of the common law, it can now be exercised only within the limits of the Constitution; all presidential conduct may be subject to judicial review. Scholarship confirms that the president's right to pardon is legitimate if two requirements are met: a) as an instrument to correct adjudicative mistakes; b) as an act with a public interest.
94. Analysis of the details of the 2005 Prosecution Policy can be found in du Bois-Pedain, *Transitional Amnesty in South Africa*, p. 57.
95. See *State v. Basson* (2001) (1) SACR 235(T). See also M. Burger and C. Gould. 2002. *Secrets and Lies: Wouter Basson and South Africa's Chemical and Biological Warfare Programme*. Cape Town: Zebra Press.
96. The *Basson* case was a long and controversial case involving several charges, which were brought before the the Supreme Court of Appeal of Bloemfontein and the High Court of Pretoria for which Basson was acquitted.
97. See *State v. Mkosana and Another* (2003) JDR 0018 (B).
98. http://www.algoafm.co.za/newsarticle.asp?newsid=150105.
99. 'Vlok Pleads Guilty', *South African Mail & Guardian*, 17 August 2007.
100. See J. Elster. 2004. *Closing the Books. Transitional Justice in Historical Perspective*. Cambridge: Cambridge University Press.
101. See J.M. Osiel. 2000. 'Why Prosecute? Critics of Punishment for Mass Atrocities', *Human Rights Quarterly* 22: 125; C.J. Niebur Eisnaugle. 2003. 'An International "Truth Commission": Utilizing Restorative Justice as an Alternative to Retribution', *Vanderbilt Journal of Transnational Law* 36: 209–34; R. Aldana-Pindell. 2003. 'Vindication of Justiciable Victims' Rights to Truth and Justice for State-Sponsored Crimes', *Vanderbilt Journal of Transnational Law* 35: 1399 *et seq*; A.M. Gross. 2004. 'The Constitution, Reconciliation, and Transitional Justice', *Stanford Journal of International Law* 40: 47–99; A.M. Gentili and A. Lollini. 2000. 'L'esperienza delle Commissioni per la Verità e la Riconciliazione: il caso sudafricano in una prospettiva giuridico – politica', in G. Illuminati, L. Stortoni and M. Virgilio (eds), *Crimini internazionali tra diritto e giustizia: dai Tribunali internazionali alle Commissioni verità e riconciliazioni*. Turin: Giappichelli, pp. 163–216.
102. See G. Vassalli. 2001. *La formula di Radbruch e diritto penale. Note sulla punizione dei "delitti di Stato" nella Germania post-nazista e nella Germania post-comunista*. Milan: Giuffrè.
103. On European political transitions and the problem of justice for crimes committed during the War, see K.D. Henke and H. Woller. 1991. *Politische Säuberung in Europa. Die Abrechnung mit Faschismus und Kollaboration nach dem zweitem*

Weltkrieg. Munich: Oldenbourg. See also the second part of Vassalli, *La formula di Radbruch*, pp. 209–319.

104. For all these issues, see the posthumous work G. Radbruch. 1957. *Der Menche im Recht. Ausgewählte und Aufsätze über Grundfragen des Rechts*. Göttingen: Vandenhoeck & Ruprecht; and Vassalli, *La formula du Radbruch* (see note 1 on p. 4). Radbruch's thoughts have been collected and expanded on by F. Saliger. 1995. *Radbruchsche Formel und Rechtsstaat*. Heidelberg: Müller Juristisches Verlag; K. Adomeit. 1999. 'Gustav Radbruch zum 50. Todestag', *Neue Juristische Wochenschrift*, 34–65; A. Kaufmann. 2000. 'Gustav Radbruch und die Radbruchsche Formel. Brief an meinen Enkel FinnBaumann', *Rechtshistorisches Journal*, 604 *et seq*.
105. See A. Demandt. 1990. *Macht und Recht. Grosse Prozesse in der Geschichte*, Munich: Verlag C.H. Beck; and the important study in O. Kirkhheimer. 1961. *Political Justice. The Use of Legal Procedure for Political Ends*. Princeton: Princeton University Press.
106. For a general overview, see S. Ratner and J. Abrams. 1997. 'Non-Prosecutorial Options' in *Accountability for Human Rights Atrocities in International Law. Beyond the Nuremberg Legacy*. Oxford: Clarendon Press, pp. 193–215; L. Huyse and E. van Dael. 2001. *Justice après des graves violations de droits de l'homme. Le choix entre l'amnistie, la commission de la vérité et les poursuites pénales*. Leuven: University of Leuven. See also the three volumes of N.J. Kritz (ed.). 1995. *Transitional Justice: How Emerging Democracies Reckon with Former Regimes*. Washington, DC: United States Institute of Peace Press; A. Lollini. 2003. 'Le processus de judiciarisation de la résolution des conflits: les alternatives', in E. Fronza and S. Manacorda (eds), *La justice pénale internationale dans les décisions des TPY ad hoc*. Milan: Giuffrè, pp. 312–27; C. Cunneen. 2002. 'Restorative Justice and the Politics of Decolonisation', in Weitekamp and Kerner, *Restorative Justice. Theoretical Foundation*, pp. 32–49.
107. On this issue, see also du Bois-Pedain, *Transitional Amnesty in South Africa*, pp. 293 *et seq*.
108. See the studies by the French historian H. Rousso. 1987. *Le Syndrome de Vichy, de 1944 à nos jours*. Paris: Seuil; H. Rousso. 1994. *Un passé qui ne passe pas*. Paris: Fayard; H. Rousso. 1998. *La hantise du passé*, Paris: Textuel.
109. See F. Domb. 1994. 'Treatment of War Crimes in Peace Settlements. Prosecution or Amnesty?', *Israel Yearbook on Human Rights* 24: 253–67. S.R. Ratner. 1995. 'Judging the Past: State Practice and the Law of Accountability', in Kritz (ed.), *Transitional Justice*. Debate became widespread in Germany regarding the double transition; see S. Kattago. 2001. *Ambiguous Memory. The Nazi Past and German National Identity*. London: Praeger; J.A. McAdams. 2001. *Judging the Past in Unified Germany*. Cambridge: Cambridge University Press. On the intersection of memory and law, historical and legal methods, and the use of legal notions such as 'treason', 'guilt' and 'complicity' in contemporary history studies, see A. Wieviorka. 1998. 'Justice, histoire et mémoire. De Nuremberg à Jérusalem', *Droit et Société* 38: 59–67; K. Jaspers. 1990. *La culpabilité allemande*. Paris: Minuit. More recently, see also H. Jones, K. Östberg and N. Randeraad (eds). 2007. *Contemporary History on Trial*. Manchester: Manchester University Press.
110. On the concept of 'collective memory' and its effects on the dynamics and processes of political transitions, see M. Halbwachs. 1950. *La mémoire collective*. Paris: Albin Michel; M. Halbwachs. 1925. *Les cadres sociaux de la mémoire*. Paris: Albin Michel. More recent studies on the implications of 'collective memory selection' can be found in A. Finkielkraut. 1989. *La mémoire vaine. Du crime contre l'humanité*. Paris: Gallimard; T. Todorov. 1998. *Les abus de la mémoire*. Paris: Arlèa; T. Todorov. 2000. *Mémoire du mal. Tentation du bien. Enquête sur le siècle*. Paris: Robert Laffont; P. Ricoeur. 2000. *La mémoire, l'histoire, l'oubli*. Paris: Seuil. For an

interesting overview, see Y.H. Yerushalmi et al. 1988. *Les usages de l'oubli*. Paris: Seuil (including the famous studies by Loraux on the Athenian amnesty in the fifth century, whereby amnesty measures were provided for crimes committed during the thirty-year dictatorship at the end of the Peloponnesian War, including provisions forbidding public remembrance of the distress caused by the tyranny. For further information, see N. Loraux. 1997. *La cité divisée*, Paris: Payot & Rivages). On the importance of memory in Jewish history as fundamental element of the people's identity, see Y.H. Yerushalmi. 1982. *Zakhor. Jewish History and Jewish Memory*. Seattle: University of Washington Press. This survey leads to the idea that the processes of constructing collective memory about the past directly influence the processes of creating the legal, political and ethical principles that are the material constitution of a new community (see also B. Cassin. 2001. 'Politiques de la mémoire. Des traitements de la haine', *Multitudes* 3(6): 177–96. Retrieved 31 March 2008 from http://multitudes.samizdat.net/Politiques-de-la-memoire; F. Lussana. 2000. 'Memoria e memorie nel dibattito storiografico', *Studi Storici* 4: 1047–81.

111. The difficult and unresolved relationship between France and Algeria has translated into cyclical *remises en discussion* of the past 'events in Algeria'. See D. Nicolaidis (ed.). 1994. *Oublier nos crimes. L'amnésie nationale: une spécificité française?*. Paris: Autrement.

112. As Rousso has noted, the overlapping of memory and law has been part of many phases of French history during the second half of the twentieth century. The first phase (1944–54), shared by all European states, sees the conclusion of the Second World War and the confrontation of the problems of latent civil war, purging (which culminated in amnesty) and mourning; during the second phase (1954–71), the memory of the Vichy experience seems less controversial, aside from sporadic denials. The third phase (1971–74) is witness to renewed debate on the memory of the past and the post-War political myths were subject to discussion. In the opinion of the French historian, there is also a fourth phase, in which the issue of memory becomes an obsession, goaded by the claims for redefining the memory of the War by Jewish social segments. See Rousso, *Le Syndrome de Vichy*, pp. 19–20.

113. For a survey of national trials in Belgium, Germany, France and the Netherlands, see L. Huyse. 1996b. 'Justice after Transition: On the Choices Successor Elites Make in Dealing with the Past', in A.J. Jongman (ed.), *Contemporary Genocides: Causes, Cases, Consequences*. Leiden: PIOOM, pp. 187–214. For Italy, see H. Woller. 1997. *Conti con il fascismo. L'epurazione in Italia 1943-1948*. Bologna: Il Mulino; R. Canosa. 1999. *Storia dell'epurazione in Italia. Le sanzioni contro il fascismo 1943-1948*. Milan: Baldini & Castoldi. For Germany, see Kattago, *Ambiguous Memory*; and McAdams, *Judging the Past*. For France, see P. Novick. 1985. *L'épuration française*. Paris: Ballan. In general, see Elster, *Closing the Books*, pp. 77 *et seq*. For a complete overview of the legal phenomena in Europe at the end of the Second World War and after the collapse of communist regimes, in Latin America, Africa and Asia, see Kritz, *Transitional Justice*.

114. A quantitative analysis, although not thorough, provides insight into the scope of European adjudicative purges at the end of the Second World War. The information that follows was taken from Vassalli, *La formula du Radbruch*, pp. 212–24. In Germany, starting in 1945, there were 105,000 criminal investigations and 6488 defendants were convicted. Twelve were sentenced to death and 163 were imprisoned for life. The period of 1947–49 saw the *Euthanasienprozesse*, which led to seven death sentences. In France, purges and criminal proceedings for collaborating were rather violent. With the ordinance of 28 August 1944 regarding war crimes and the ordinance of 28 November 1944 regarding the punishment for the crime of collaboration, many criminal proceedings ended with death sentences. Speaking of '*l'épuration, politique professionnelle, idéologique*', Rousso points out that: '*l'épuration a mécontenté tout le monde, car elle n'a pu trouver un compromis satisfai-*

sant entre la justice traditionnelle, réclamée par les plus modérés (mais aussi par les plus menacés politiquement) et la nécessité d'en finir avec le fascisme et ses hérauts. Le dilemme n'était pas seulement moral, le droit contre la revanche légitime, la mémoire courte contre la rancune tenace, il était politique, les communistes étant les plus intransigeants. Il a conditionné en grande partie le souvenir ultérieur de l'Occupation: le nouveau conflit s'est substitué au premier, presque aussi virulent car purement interne et amplifié par une presse libre et déchaînée; il a engendré à son tour des mythes négatifs, comme les 100000 exécutions sommaires (en réalité dix fois moins), ou la menace de soviets rouges' (see Rousso, *La syndrome de Vichy*, pp. 35–36; and Novick, *L'épuration française*). As for Italy, though the wave of purges had the same characteristics as other European countries, the amnesties of 1946 greatly discouraged the process of coming to terms with the past (see Woller, *Conti con il fascismo*; and Canosa, *Storia dell'epurazione in Italia*). Criminal punishment for the offence of collaboration was also rather violent in the Nertherlands and Austria. In the Nertherlands,120,000 arrests were made by the end of the War, 154 of which led to death sentences; 49,000 trials were held by the court. In Austria, between 1949 and 1955, 136,000 went to trial and 13,000 were convicted (including 43 capital punishment convictions, 30 of which resulted in executions). Vassalli's study shows how the purging with criminal justice methods also appeared in all the Northern and Eastern European countries (Vassalli, *La formula du Radbruch*, pp. 238 *et seq*).

115. For example, the studies of historians such as Daniel Jonah Goldhagen have recently looked into the direct involvement of German civilians in supporting military actions and the Holocaust. See D.J. Goldhagen. 1997. *I volenterosi carnefici di Hitler. I tedeschi comuni e l'Olocausto*. Milan: Mondadori.
116. See Elster, *Closing the Books*, pp. 80 *et seq*.
117. For the proceedings against Paul Touvier, see F. Bederida. 1996. *Touvier le dossier de l'accusation*. Paris: Seuil; L. Greilsamer and D. Schnaidermann. 1994. *Un certain Monsieur Paul*. Paris: Fayard. As for Klaus Barbie's trial, in order to verify the extent to which it involved French public opinion, see J. Verges. 1988. *Je défends Barbie*. Paris: Jean Picollec; A. Finkielkraut. 1989. *La mémoire vaine. Du crime contre l'humanité*. Paris: Gallimard. For Papon's trial see J.M. Dumay. 1998. *Le procés de Maurice Papon*, Paris: Fayard; J.J. Gandini. 1999. *Le procès Papon. Histoire d'une ignominie au service de l'Etat*. Paris: Libro. On Priebke's trial, see R. Bentivegna. 1996. *Operazione via Rasella. Verità e menzogna: i protagonisti del racconto*. Rome: Editori Riuniti.
118. See the comparative criminal law study by E. Fronza. 1999. 'Profili penalistici del negazionismo', *Rivista italiana di diritto e procedura penale* 42(3): 1034–74, which analyses the revision of the Austrian constitution of 26 February 1992, which opened the way for punishing the denial and justificiation of genocide and other crimes against humanity; Art. 607 of the Spanish Criminal Code, which provides that dissemination of ideas denying or justifying genocide is punishable; the analogous Art. 240 of the Portuguese Criminal Code; French law 90-602 of 13 July 1990 (Loi Gayssot) (for further information, see J.P. Feldman. 1998. 'Peut-on dire impunément n'importe quoi sur la shoah?', *Revue Trimestrielle des Droits de l'Homme*); Art. 130 of the German Criminal Code and the new formulation of Art. 261 bis of the Swiss Criminal Code. The European Union expressly urged Member States to punish denial claims in adopting a joint action (Joint Action of 15 July 1996 adopted by the Council on the basis of Article K.3 of the Treaty on European Union, concerning action to combat racism and xenophobia, *Official Journal of the European Communities*, 24 July 1996). See V. Igounet. 2000. *Histoire du négationnisme en France*. Paris: Seuil; D. Daeninckx and V. Staraselski. 1998. *Au nom de la loi*. Paris: Parole d'Aube; M. Troper. 1999. 'Droit et négationnisme', *Les Annales* 54(6): 1239–56.

119. The memory-based and historical image of the resistance is often discussed with legal parameters and concepts, such as treason, collaboration and complicity. For example, in France the newspaper *Libération* organized a roundtable (published 9 July 1997) during the course of which important historians and journalists (including Henry Rousso, François Béderida, Dominique Veillon, Laurent Douzou, Maurice Agulhon, Jean-Pierre Vernant, Daniel Cordier and Jean-Pierre Azéma) discussed the idea of treason and collaboration of a couple who symbolized the French resistance: the Aubracs.
120. The differences and similarities between the methods used by judges and historians have been analysed in depth from a historical perspective by C. Ginzburg. 1991. *Il giudice e lo storico. Considerazioni a margine del processo Sofri*. Turin: Einaudi; and from a legal perspective by P. Calamandrei. 1939. 'Il giudice e lo storico', *Rivista di diritto processuale civile* 17: 105–28. Ginzburg and Calamandrei both think that the judge and the historian use a somewhat similar methodology for interpreting facts. Both analyse documents, evaluating their value as evidence. Ginzburg points out, however, that though the judge and historian start out similarly, they differ greatly in their final judgement on the facts. A judge can decide that there is no need to proceed to judgement, for example, if the facts are obviously false or legally inconsistent; the historian, on the other hand, may continue their investigation, reaching valid historical conclusions from these kinds of elements. Ginzburg continues his thoughts with the concept of proof from an historical perspective, arguing against the claim that history is a simple interpretation or representation, since proof, rationally speaking, must be the basis of the historical method in its struggle towards the truth; see C. Ginzburg. 2000. *Rapporti di forza: storia, retorica, prova*. Milan: Feltrinelli (especially Chapter 1). The same issues are dealt with in P. Ricoeur. 2000. *La mémoire, l'histoire, l'oubli*. Paris: Seuil (in particular, the section entitled 'l'historien et le juge', pp. 413–36), which states that: '*les rôles respectifs de l'historien et du juge, désignés par leur intention de vérité et de justice, les invitent à occuper la position du tiers au regard des places occupées dans l'espace public par les protagonistes de l'action sociale. Or un voeu d'impartialité s'attache à cette position du tiers*' (p. 413). After demonstrating the similarities, the French philosopher shows where the two methods part ways: '*perspicacité à déceler contradictions, incohérences, invraisemblances; même attention accordée aux silences, aux omissions volontaires ou involontaires; même familiarité avec les ressources de falsification du langage en termes d'erreur, de mensonge, d'auto intoxication, d'illusion. A cet égard, le juge et l'historien sont tous deux passés experts dans la mise à jour des faux et, en ce sens, maîtres l'un et l'autre dans le maniement du soupçon*' (p. 417). The underlying difference thus regards the conclusion of the factual reconstruction: '*la sentence marque par son caractère définitif la différence la plus évidente entre l'approche juridique et l'approche historiographique des mêmes faits: la chose jugée peut être contestée par l'opinion publique mais non rejugée (…). Le juge doit juger – c'est sa fonction. Il doit conclure, il doit trancher. Il doit remettre à une juste distance le coupable et la victime selon une typologie binaire*' (pp. 420–21). Ricoeur adds: '*tout cela l'historien ne le fait pas, ne peut pas, ne veut pas le faire; s'il le tente, au risque de s'ériger tout seul au tribunal de l'histoire (…). Son audacieux jugement est proposé à la critique de la corporation historienne et à celle du public éclairé, son oeuvre offerte à un processus illimité de révisions qui fait de l'écriture de l'histoire une perpétuelle réécriture*' (p. 421).
121. See de Vergottini, *Le transizioni costituzionali*; L. Mezzetti. 2003. *Teoria e prassi delle transizioni costituzionali e del consolidamento democratico*. Padua: CEDAM, p. 275. On Latin American transitions, see L. Mezzetti. 2000. *Le democrazie incerte. Transizioni costituzionali e consolidamento della democrazia in Europa orientale, Africa, America Latina, Asia*. Turin: Giappichelli; L. Mezzetti. 2000. 'Transizioni Costituzionali e consolidamento democratico in America Latina agli albori del XXI

secolo', *Diritto pubblico comparato ed europeo*, pp. 29–48; G. Rolla. 2001. 'Luci ed ombre dell'esperienza delle transizioni pactdas', *Diritto pubblico comparato ed europeo* 3: 1084–96. On the connection between political transition and the constitution-making process, see B. Gaddes. 1996. 'Initiation of New Democratic Institutions in Eastern Europe and Latin America', in A. Lijphart and C.H. Waisman (eds), *Institutional Design in New Democracies. Eastern Europe and Latin America*. Boulder: Westview Press; M. Carducci. 1999. *Il costituzionalismo "parallelo" delle nuove democrazie. Africa e America Latina*. Milan: Giuffrè; S. Bartole and P. Grilli di Cortona (eds). 1998. *Transizioni e consolidamento democratico nell'Europa centro-orientale*. Turin: Giappichelli.

122. See G.L. Smith. 2001. 'Immune to Truth? Latin American Truth Commissions and U.S. Support for Abusive Crimes', *Columbia Human Rights Law Review* 33(1): 241–73; C. Tomuschat. 1999. 'Human Rights and National Truth Commissions', in P. Baehr, C. Flinterman and M. Senders (eds), *Innovation and Inspiration: Fifty Years of the Universal Declaration of Human Rights*. Amsterdam: Royal Netherlands Academy of Arts and Sciences, pp. 151–60. E. Cuya. 1996. 'Las Comisiones de la Verdad en América Latina', Ko'aga Roñe'eta 3. Retrieved 31 March 2008 from http://www.derechos.org/koaga/iii/1/cuya.html; J. Zalaquet. 1992. 'Balancing Ethical Imperatives and Political Constraints: The Dilemma of New Democracies Confronting Past Human Rights Violations', *Hastings Law Journal* 43(6): 1425–38.

123. See D. Cassel. 1993. 'International Truth Commissions and Justice', *The Aspen Institute Quarterly* 5(3): 77–90; Tomuschat, 'Human Rights and National Truth Commissions'; P. Hayner. 1998. 'The Contribution of Truth Commissions', in B. Duner (ed.), *An End to Torture. Strategies for Its Eradication*, London: Zed Books, pp. 203–21; P. Hayner. 1994. 'Fifteen Truth Commissions – 1974 to 1994: A Comparative Study', *Human Rights Quarterly* 16(4): 597–655; R. Siegel. 1998. 'Transitional Justice: A Decade of Debate and Experience', *Human Rights Quarterly* 20: 433 *et seq*; M. Smiley. 2000. 'Democratic Justice in Transition', *Michigan Law Review* 99: 1332–47; see also C.M. Bassiouni (ed.). 2001. *Post-conflict Justice*. Ardsley: Transnational Publishers.

124. See M. Ensalco. 1994. 'Truth Commissions for Chile and El Salvador: A Report and Assessment', *Human Rights Quarterly* 16: 656–75; T. Burgenthal. 1994. 'The United Nations Truth Commission for El Salvador', *Vanderbilt Journal of Transnational Law* 27(3): 497-544; M. Kaye. 1997. 'The Role of Truth Commissions in the Search for Justice, Reconciliation and Democratisation: The Salvadorian and Honduran Cases', *Journal of Latin American Studies* 29(3): 693, 716; P. Ayllwin and J. Zalaquett. 1995. 'Commission of Truth & Reconciliation: Chile', in A. Boraine and J. Levy (eds), *The Healing of a Nation?*. Cape Town: Justice in Transition, pp. 38–43 and 44–55. See also the dated but interesting Kritz, *Transitional Justice*.

125. See R.A. Chapman and P. Ball. 2001. 'The Truth of Truth Commissions: Comparative Lessons from Haiti, South Africa, and Guatemala', *Human Rights Quarterly* 23(1): 1–43.

126. See M.R. Rwelamira and G. Werle. 1996. *Confronting Past Injustices. Approaches to Amnesty, Punishment, Reparation in South Africa and Germany*. Durban: Butterworths; Kattago, *Ambiguous Memory*; and McAdams, *Judging the Past*.

127. See K. Ambos and O. Mohamed (eds). 2003. *New Approaches in International Criminal Justice: Kosovo, East Timor, Sierra Leone & Cambodia*. Freiburg: Max Planck Institute for Foreign and International Criminal Law; S. Linton. 2001. 'Cambodia, East Timor and Sierra Leone: Experiments in International Justice', *Criminal Law Forum* 12: 185–202; C. Romano. 2002. 'Mixed Jurisdictions for East Timor, Kosovo, Sierra Leone and Cambodia: The Coming of Age of Internationalized Criminal Bodies?', *Yearbook of International Law and Jurisprudence*, vol. 2; H. Strohmeyer. 2000. 'Building a New Judiciary for East Timor. Challenges of a

Fledgling Nation', *Criminal Law Forum* 11: 259 *et seq.* On Sierra Leone, see J.M. Chataigner. 2001. 'L'ONU et la Sierra Leone: d'une crise à l'autre (mai 1997–mai 2000)', *Afrique Contemporaine* 198: 29–50; and A.J.M. McDonald. 2000. 'Sierra Leone's Uneasy Peace: The Amnesties Granted in the Lomé Peace Agreement and the United Nation's Dilemma', *Humanitäres Völkerrecht* 13: 11–26; S. Beresford and A.S. Muller. 2001. 'The Special Court for Sierra Leone: An Initial Comment', *Leiden Journal of International Law* 3(14): 635–52; J.L. Poole. 2001. 'Post-Conflict in Sierra Leone', in Bassiouni, *Post-conflict Justice*, pp. 563–92.

4

Confession as a Strictly Constituent Act

Introduction

One of the elements that distinguishes the procedure employed by the AC was the use of a 'verbal act against oneself'. Defined in the Committee's statute as a 'full disclosure of all relevant facts', this self-accusatory statement has characteristics that can be traced back to the practice of confession; however, it also has its own particular features.

First, the subject of the self-accusatory declaration: the statute in fact states that the disclosure must cover the 'context' and the facts leading to the crime.[1] Juridically speaking, the AC was interested in the general, historical and social context in which the crimes were committed (even if, as we have seen, this objective was not always pursued) and every factual detail useful for determining personal responsibility for the crime.

The centrality of the self-incriminating verbal statement made in public is undoubtedly the distinguishing characteristic of the TRC model. There are two fundamental issues. First, what was the reason for using a practice (the confession) that in the historical past had caused violence and ambiguity, both in terms of law and theology?[2] Second, what were the symbolic, linguistic, political and legal attributes of the self-incriminating statement that the TRC tried to exploit? By answering these two questions, we will analyse the logic of the functioning of the TRC and how it was at the centre of the political dynamics of the new post-apartheid constitutional order.

The TRC and the Constitution-making Process

Before answering these questions, the specific connections between the TRC's activity, the constitution-making process and the new Constitution should be analysed. This analysis will allow us to demonstrate that the TRC exercised a constituent function.

The TRC, as an instrument implementing constituent decisions formally set down in the 1993 Constitution, operated only during the creation phase of the new constitutional order, where the conditions for effectively exercising constituent power were laid down. This observation, in terms of political philosophy, immediately points to the concept of the social contract. This concept is normally considered a theoretical phenomenon, as an external philosophical necessity prior to constructing the institutions of the state producing the positive norms (from a Kelsenian perspective) or 'civil law' (from a Hobbesian perspective). Thus, during the contractual phase, the unity of the political body 'represented' by the sovereign is formed. As we shall see, this formative moment in which the new unitary political body (the new community) and the new post-apartheid sovereign simultaneously manifest themselves seems to take place before the TRC. Due to the verbal act stated before the AC (the confession), the social contract took on a historical form, articulated according to a specific legal syntax.

Before analysing these specific elements, it is important to evaluate the links connecting the TRC's activity with the constitution-making process: 1) the strictly temporal link; 2) the link based on legal and formal elements; 3) the link based on material elements.

The Strictly Temporal Link

From a temporal point of view, the process of adopting the post-apartheid constitutional text partly coincided with the Commission's creation. As mentioned before, the discussion on the form of transitional justice took place during the MPNP multiparty negotiations, which adopted the Interim Constitution and the Constitutional Principles. The decision to suspend exercising punitive action against political crimes under apartheid had a strong impact on the positive outcome of the negotiations.

From a temporal point of view, the origin of constituent decisions regarding punitive measures for past political crimes coincided with all the other constituent decisions made by the MPNP. Any veto to suspending a strictly criminal approach would have compromised the entire constitution-making procedure.

The temporal link between the TRC and the constitution-making process is confirmed by the dates in which various decisions were made. The final measures of the Interim Constitution, which paved the way for conditional amnesty, were produced in 1993 during the MPNP; the discussion on how to implement these constitutional measures formally began in 1994 and culminated in 1995 with the newly-elected Parliament passing the Promotion of National Unity and Reconciliation Act 34/95.[3] The Commission formally began its work on 16 December 1995 and became fully operational by January 1996 (prior to the adoption of the definitive Constitution).[4] In conclusion, the period from the TRC's creation until the body began to actually work (1994–96) coincides precisely with the final phase of the process of adopting the new Constitution.

The Formal and Legal Link

The formal and legal link between the TRC and the constitution-making process can be seen in the fact that the TRC's creation had its constitutional basis in the final measures of the 1993 Constitution.[5]

The entire text of these measures under the title 'National Unity and Reconciliation' was transferred to s. 22 of the Transitional Arrangement (Schedule 6) of the 1996 Constitution, creating continuity between the interim and final texts.[6] Therefore, both Constitutions provided for the adoption of an ad hoc mechanism that would implement amnesty proceedings for political crimes, based on prohibiting retribution and seeking the truth, thereby giving the TRC a specific constitutional foundation. There was much debate about the preceptive or merely political value of these provisions and their compatibility with other constitutional norms.[7]

The Constitutional Court's decision of the *AZAPO* case[8] resolved both issues, ruling that the final provisions, which lay the foundations of the TRC, were to all intents and purposes part of the Constitution. Hence, it established that Act 34/1995 was completely constitutional. The families of the three political dissidents, victims of the apartheid regime, and the members of AZAPO used the procedure to directly access the Constitutional Court in the interests of justice and raised the issue of the constitutional legitimacy of the amnesty procedure, since it violated s. 22 of the Interim Constitution.[9] It was argued before the Court that the provision in question was part of a body of rules lying 'outside' the Constitution, so was not equal to the rest of the constitutional text. It was also argued that it was a violation of international public law norms obliging states to prosecute the perpetrators of crimes during the criminal regime and those who ordered that the crimes be committed.[10]

In the decision written by Justice Mahomed,[11] the Court confirmed that granting amnesty was an instrument created for dealing with the special nature of the peace process. As it was the primary political objective of the new constitutional order in formation, the peace process called for the temporary limitation of other constitutional rights. In this context, limiting individual rights that are normally highly protected is allowed, considering the collective objective of ending a serious state of internal conflict. Individual interests implied by the right to justice yield to the needs of the collective peace process, which was to be pursued through the implementation of the final constitutional provisions regarding amnesty.

The relationship between the post-apartheid constitution and international criminal and public law is a complex and debated issue. In the aforementioned Constitutional Court decision, even if many commentators said that this issue was dealt with by the Court in a deeply unsatisfactory way, the judges claim that international law is not automatically applicable to South African law; a law passed by Parliament that implements the international rules is always required (s. 231 of the 1993 Constitution). It is then Parliament's responsibility to verify the compatibility of the new Constitution with all international legal obligations (including those ratified under the regime's constitutions). The new Constitution therefore clearly prevails over international treaty law. When adopting international law, according to s. 35, Parliament must verify that it is applicable. International law can be implemented only after an evaluation of its 'applicability' and thus of its compatibility with the Constitution.

The Court did not consider the political and military context of the conflict between the apartheid regime and the liberation movements as falling under the situations contemplated by the 1949 Geneva Conventions (and additional Protocols), which the applicants had cited as the basis for the state's obligation to prosecute the crimes committed during apartheid. In fact, the Court evaluated only the applicability of the Geneva Conventions to the conflict of apartheid, adhering only to the arguments put forward by the applicants; as such, it avoided a broader evaluation of the compatibility of the amnesty provision with the whole branch of international law regarding this matter. The Court did not view the 'war' context of apartheid as being compatible with the types of war provided by the Geneva Convention and ruled that the amnesty procedure was constitutional.

This interpretation did not fail to generate fierce debate. Though there is not the space here to analyse the obligatory nature of certain norms of international customary law and international treaties (which would appear to impose an obligation to prosecute perpetrators of crimes under international law), the fact that only the Geneva Convention rules were considered, rather than the whole body of international treaty law on crimes, can easily be criticized. According to that branch of law, crimes against humanity (which include apartheid based on the 1973 Convention) would impose the duty to prosecute on the state.[12] However, the amnesty rules overcame this formal legal obstacle by not granting de facto amnesties for apartheid crimes but only for punishable offences, acknowledged by the regime's criminal law, committed during apartheid.

The Court's last argument regards the type of amnesty applied; the South African amnesty process is not a blanket amnesty. The obligation of the TRC to verify the individual prerequisites for receiving amnesty prevents a general and undifferentiated amnesty from operating, a type of amnesty that received criticism abroad.[13]

The political and legal issue behind the decision to reject the unconstitutionality of the amnesty process (thus confirming the existence of a deep constitutional link between the TRC and the post-apartheid Constitutions) was rather delicate. The Court only confirmed that the constitutional suspension of a strictly criminal approach is one of the crucial elements of South Africa's new *constituent pact* for interracial peace and the start of a new democracy.[14] The Court's decision thus reconfirms that the amnesty process is one of the fundamental parts of the constitution-making process.

The Material Link

This section discusses the last series of arguments demonstrating the link that is perhaps the most important between the TRC and the constitution-making process: the substantive-material link.[15] Once again, in this case there are two elements that demonstrate this link: a) the methods, principles and values that guided the constitutional transition; b) constitutionalization of the concept of *ubuntu.*

The material link between the TRC and the constitution-making process can be seen in the methods and principles that characterized the constitutional transition. First of all, we must analyse how the TRC was actually created in order to enforce the final provisions of the Postamble (which was one of the 'clauses' of the constituent pact of pacification whereby the old adversaries mutually recognized and legitimated one another).

The actors of the constitution-making process made the decision, with varying degrees of conviction, to include their respective adversaries from the apartheid years in the new political body. Making this fundamental political step a reality required a mutual decision to waive some partisan claims. No one could believe they would obtain everything they desired; important concessions had to be made between the former adversaries, who were now partners in the process of constructing the unitary political body. Justice for past crimes was obviously one of the many components of this pact: the provisions of the National Unity and Reconciliation Postamble represented the constitutionalization of this pact, and the TRC was one of the instruments to make it concretely effective.

As we shall see, due to the transitional justice system put to work by the AC, members of the white oligarchy protected themselves from criminal liability, but not from having to publicly respond for crimes committed in the past. By waiving the right to criminal prosecution of the perpetrators of crimes, the black population secured the transition's success, the transfer of political power (relying on a progressive redistribution of economic power) and the perpetrators' confession of guilt for crimes in the past. The TRC is therefore intimately connected with the political transition, being one of the driving forces behind the effectiveness of the constituent pact.

The second element that indicates the substantive link between what animated the constitution-making process and the TRC lies in the concept of *ubuntu*, which was widely used during the constitutional negotiations. The term is used in the final provisions of the Interim Constitution as well as in the definitive Constitution (the Postamble, which is the basis for the Commission); it literally means 'humanity'. Normally employed in the expression *umuntu ngumuntu ngabantu*, it implies the principle based upon which individuals are people only through other persons, thus clearly emphasizing the concept of community. Therefore, the deep meanings of the term *ubuntu* are the relationship between individuals – not barriers or exclusion – and the necessity of building a community.[16]

By using a native language term, the post-apartheid Constitution incorporates a concept that recognizes the importance of community, reconciliation, forgiveness and social peace, that is, the interruption of the 'state of nature' of civil war and the delegitimation of political violence. The latter is grounded in refusing to accept the existence of political adversaries and even goes so far as to authorize their physical removal. By contrast, the 'democratic game' accepts the existence of differences and polarizations that may be recomposed, voiced and peacefully arranged within the shared political and institutional space. *Ubuntu*, even if at times it has a demagogic connotation, summarizes and represents the spirit of the transition and the construction of the new post-apartheid order. What is important to note here is that the concept of *ubuntu* accompanies the constitutional provisions, leading to conditional amnesty for political crimes. The concept is therefore a logical, ethical and legal precondition of the Commission,[17] which was set up as an instrument to implement this constitutional principle.

This term not only had a political meaning, but it also had a connotation in terms of constitutional law, since it was interpreted by the Constitutional Court. In the court decision *S. v. Makewanyane and Another*, in which the Court declared capital punishment to be unconstitutional under the new constitutional order, the concept *ubuntu* is used repeatedly. The constitutional judges declared that the principles and the values implied by it composed the fundamental structure of the Constitution. The concept of *ubuntu* was therefore used as a supporting argument to declare capital punishment unconstitutional, annulling s. 277 of the Criminal Procedure Act 51/1977. In this judgment, two judges (P.N. Langa and T.H. Madala) expressly mentioned the concept of *ubuntu* as a sturdy basis for declaring the death penalty to be unconstitutional. If the decision's rationale is based on the complete incompatibility of capital punishment with many of the rights laid down by the Bill of Rights, such as the right to life (s. 11), the respect of human dignity (s. 10) and the right not to be treated in an inhuman or degrading way (s. 12(1)(e)), the two judges confirmed that the concept of *ubuntu* and the ethical and philosophical idea contained in it forbade every form of cruelty towards human beings.[18] The concept of *ubuntu* in Justice Langa's interpretation takes on the explicit meaning of the importance of the community, therefore emphasizing once again the centrality of constructing the unity of the political body.[19]

This analysis indicates how this notion translates into a variety of values that guided the political transition and informed the new Constitution. The Constitutional Court acknowledged its fundamental importance by using it as an argument for declaring capital punishment unconstitutional.[20] The TRC was one of the bodies appointed to implement this constitutional principle, and we can thus sense how the Commission had a substantive and material link to the principles embodied by *ubuntu* with which the new democratic order radically differentiated itself from the previous regime.

Confession as a Strictly Constituent Act

The fundamental link between the activity of the TRC (especially that of the AC) and the creation of the new democratic state emerges more clearly from a careful analysis of confession.

The self-incriminating verbal statement (of crimes committed for political purposes) is stated publicly before the AC. The new 'democratic sovereignty' acknowledges through the AC (which is one of its bodies) certain legal consequences (such as the elimination of punishment) in exchange for these statements. The apparent simplicity of this verbal statement actually contains extraordinarily powerful symbolic and political properties.

First of all, a seemingly tautological question must be answered: is full disclosure a confession? This question leads to another: what is a confession? The answer to this question makes it possible to confirm the conjecture that confession is a speech act with a constituent value.[21]

Full Disclosure

Historically, the practice of confession has taken forms that have continually changed over the centuries depending on their use for legal trial, religious or liturgical reasons. The self-incriminating locution with which the speaker acknowledges the violation of a legal, religious or ethical rule is the constant feature in all types of confessions. The rhetorical and probative power of self-incrimination is that, rationally speaking, no one admits to punishable violations of rules or norms. Falsely accusing oneself of a crime is conceivable only if there is the prospect of an advantage being obtained.[22]

Many historians have demonstrated that a confession can be produced using two different methods:

1) in its classical form, confession is the result (the answer) of an accusation formulated by a political, religious or police authority. Confessors can either resist the power and violence used to make them confess or capitulate and approve the allegation made against them. As such, they are asked to confirm and make their own a statement formulated by

others. This type of confession in its most violent form is typically used in inquisitorial circumstances;

2) the confession may also be produced without any apparent external power acting upon confessors in order to make them admit their guilt in the violation of a particular rule. In this case, the confessor reveals a legally, religiously or morally reprehensible conduct which no one was aware of prior to the confessor declaring its existence by accusing him or herself of it.[23]

Starting with this division, we can first say that the full disclosure before the AC clearly has the general characteristics of a confession. In fact, the self-incriminating locution would have automatically compromised the speaker if amnesty were not provided (for example, confirmation of conviction for those who filed the application while serving previously sentenced prison time). Furthermore, statements of denying guilt were not allowed; in fact, the act of denying guilt automatically led to the refusal of amnesty, confirming the confessional nature of the statements made before the AC.[24]

The analysis of the origin (induced or spontaneous) of this form of self-incrimination is much more problematic. In fact, though it is true that the TRC had no power to indict, the offer of amnesty could be interpreted as a rather underhand form of external pressure. If the claim can be made that the promise of amnesty is a valid motive for inducing confession, it should also be noted that the full disclosure also has elements of spontaneity. In fact, the majority of crimes confessed before the AC regarded crimes of which the Commission and the general public were not aware. For this reason, the claim can also be made that the self-incriminating statement came about in many cases due to the spontaneous initiative of the confessor, even if in an external context that could induce confession (social pressure expressing a negative opinion about past violence and the hope of obtaining the elimination of the punishment).

The issue of induced or spontaneous confession is thus directly connected to the formulation of an accusation. In the TRC model, there is no figure appointed with the task of formulating an indictment (the prosecutor). On the one hand, no one is accused of anything; on the other hand, there is no external figure that exerts physical and moral pressure on the individual so that he or she confesses. Even though from an analysis of the hearings it is clear that the amnesty applicant is subject to numerous questions (from the commissioners or representatives of the victims), the agonistic element that normally leads to a confession is mitigated. By the same token, we cannot say that the disclosure before the AC is the result of an internal impulse of the conscience of an individual who decides to accuse himself or herself of a crime. The contingent interest of the confession leading to the cancellation of the effects of the crime (the punishment) is therefore quite strong.

The practice of confession employed by the TRC is hybrid, suspended between different historical forms and rationales. Its hybrid form, as we shall see, has dialogic, linguistic and symbolic effects in relation to the criminal policy objectives that were to be pursued through the TRC.

The Attributes of the Confession

We have seen that disclosure before the AC is a self-incriminating statement that does not faithfully follow the historical forms of the confession (in fact, it be could argued that it is a linguistically innovative form), but that it does share their basic characteristics; however, its effects, properties and attributes on a linguistic, symbolic, political and legal level should also be examined.

The attributes of the self-incriminating public statement are divided into four distinct levels:

1) confession as an act of 'capitulation' and renunciation of self-defence. In this case, the confession is a verbal act that puts an end to the conflict by symbolizing the confessor's decision to no longer pursue the conflict or a 'defence to the bitter end';
2) self-incrimination in relation to a problem of 'truth' in terms of the history and memory of the past;
3) the confession as a mechanism activated to construct or preserve a community's unity;
4) according to a legal philosophy approach, it is claimed that the confession is a speech act that translates into empirical and concrete terms, giving rise to the social contract from a Hobbesian perspective.

Confession as an Act of Capitulation

As briefly stated before in reference to the forms of confession, confirming (or stating) having acted in a particular way and accepting that such an action, as a violation of rules or laws, has legal, religious or ethical consequences, also means: a) renouncing defending oneself. In particular, for confessions made in response to an accusation, denying the facts or offering different versions means engaging in a duel (that may be verbal or even physical) with the person who is making the accusation; b) surrendering oneself to the sanction (whatever it may be) decided by the authority before which the confession is made, implicitly pleading for leniency. Configured in this way, the confession represents an 'act of capitulation' by which the confessor acknowledges that he or she committed a reprehensible act (and that the values defended by the rule violated deserved protection). The confessor basically recognizes that the rule should not have been broken.[25]

Yan Thomas's studies in the history of law confirm that confession is an 'act of capitulation'. He distinguishes at least three archetypal forms of confession in Roman law: confession in a civil trial, in a criminal trial and under Roman military law.[26]

Confession in a civil trial consisted of admitting responsibility for not complying with an obligation that a creditor brought before a judge for enforcement. The civil trial confession was in no way connected to the concept of offence and had no probative value. Its value was merely procedural; recognition of the debt extinguished the issue of the dispute and the conflict ended, making a trial unnecessary. When the verbal statement 'you are my debtor' was made, the defendant confirmed this, producing a homologous statement. 'Peace' was established between the parties (in relation to a conflict of interpretation of a contract's terms) in which the debtor recognized the existence of the debt and undertook to compensate for it.

According to Thomas, the confession in a criminal trial under Roman law was different from a civil trial. The defendant's confession in this case functioned as a strategic ploy with which the defendant tried to obtain a benefit: pardon (with either the sanction's cancellation or reduction). The coercive power of the prosecutor plays a decisive role; the threat of punishment and the hope for a lenient outcome exert pressure on the defendant. The mercantile logic of the confession – whereby the confessor indirectly gives him or herself up to the court's mercy by asking to be pardoned – creates an ambiguous relationship that can be an advantage for the defendant by strengthening his or her original weak position. If the defendant confesses, not eliminating the punishment would seem to be a great injustice. Acknowledging responsibility for the offences he or she is accused of, the confessor obliges the counterparty to form a reciprocal relationship that produces the 'pardon paradox', introducing a kind of automatic relationship between confession and being pardoned.

In civil law, confession is linked to procedural pragmatism (and to abandoning defence within a judiciary space); however, the analysis of confession in criminal law sheds light on interesting symbolic attributes. The asymmetry and imbalance of power between the accused and the accuser is affected by the confession; the confession in fact tries to add a new variable within this relationship, thereby rebalancing the values at play. A confession puts the accuser in check (having to respond automatically to the defendant's move), though he or she in return receives his or her adversary's unconditional surrender.

In Roman military law, though, the self-incriminating speech act demonstrates powerful symbolic properties. According to Thomas, a victorious Roman general cannot define himself officially as such (receiving the triumph that it entails) if he does not obtain a declaration of defeat from his adversary (defined as a confession). The defeated party's recognition of the victory is of capital importance to the victor. The relationship between the two speakers is rather delicate; the victor's right to triumph also gives him the power of life and death over the defeated. The latter therefore has reason to define him as the defeated because granting the winner the status of victor means that the victor may exercise his right to decide on the life of the defeated. The mutual interest is evident; by authorizing the victory, the defeated acts in such a way that the victor exerts his right connected to victory in order to save the defeated person's life. However, the victor's right to be considered as such is in the hands of the defeated; the latter exchanges his consent to the victory with his life. The confession ends the war, formally determining the victor's new identity, and the defeated party's life is saved.

Confession as an 'act of capitulation' happens in any situation where there is an agonistic dialogic form. In fact, this is the case for inquisitorial trials in which a confession was extorted from the accused ratifying the inquisitor's allegations. Those who could not resist 'capitulated'.[27] Confessing meant accepting the accusatory paradigm presented by the inquisitor. The confessor in this case entered into an 'agreement'.[28] With the confession, a *verbal homology* is created between the person formulating the accusation and the person forced to confess.[29] This dialogic relationship between the confessor and the person who receives the confession is full of ambiguity. In fact, it is a bilateral contractual relationship.[30] By ratifying a confession and publicly abjuring the conduct, the confessor saved his life; only relapses would have been punished with capital punishment (because they did not respect the pact of submission implied by a previous act of capitulation).

Confession as an 'act of capitulation' emerges from this analysis, as does another extremely important attribute: homology. Homology means that there are versions of the facts (which normally are conflicting) provided by the accuser and the accused that are of equal value; the conflict of interpretation therefore ceases to exist. The two speakers end up 'saying the same thing'. There is no longer a physical, symbolic or interpretive conflict about the facts. The confession of defeat, recognition of the adversary's victory and ratification of the interpretations of events (normally enclosed in a paradigm) annul the conflict. Without an act of capitulation, the conflict would continue and would create a martyr: a person who dies but whose ideas do not, and who does not recognize the power and authority of the person demanding his or her capitulation (confession). As a result, the criminal trial risks creating a martyr figure. The martyr is convicted, despite claiming innocence and denying the facts of which he or she is accused. The martyr never acknowledges defeat, sometimes denying even the authority of the judge sentencing him or her. Martyr figures, even if they die, demonstrate that the authority sentencing them is mere force. From a political point of view, the martyr figure can trigger denialism that, in criminal trials with a vast historical context, such as those for crimes under authoritarian or illiberal regimes, can lead to instability in the new state's social fabric and political relations.

Within the Christian sacraments, confession has traces of this dialogic form. Though the sacramental practice is very difficult to describe since it has constantly changed over the centuries due to different political and theological needs, a few observations can be made. From the introduction by the Fourth Lateran Council (1215) of the sacrament of auricular confession to the change in the obligation of confessing sins once a year[31] to frequent confession,[32] the sacrament has covered different functions. From *cura animarum*[33] to a mechanism used for pedagogically imposing proper conduct according to Catholic doctrine,[34] to a mechanism for social and political control to oppose the spread of heresy in the sixteenth century, to an act that, by capitulating before God (an act administered by a priest), was the rite symbolizing the new bond of faith between the confessor, God and the community.

During the sacrament of confession, an extremely important rite takes places whereby the sinner becomes part of the community again. If baptism is the sacrament that authorizes entry into the community (creating a bond between the individual and the group), the confession of sins symbolizes the new bond previously broken by the sin committed. In this way, the sacrament of confession is a rite of re-entry into the community of believers, an act of belonging to the *Ecclesia* and a renewal of subjecting oneself to the power of the Church.

The agonistic element, coupled with that of capitulation, though weakened, is evident in the priest's *questionnement* during the sacrament of confession. The sinner is asked to answer questions and to capitulate before the evidence that man is inevitably a sinner, an immanent truth that only has to be certified.[35] Confessing was and still is the means of formalizing an individual's surrender to the power of the rules shared or imposed by a community.

Confession: The Constitution and Preservation of a Community's Unity

As many historians have helped us to understand, the practice of public confession has been used in different periods and different cultural, legal and religious contexts. Some examples are *exomologhēsis* of the early Christian communities, the rite of public confession used by the Puritans called *admonition* or the importance of public confession in monastic communities (of which there are clear traces in the monastic rules and codes). All of these examples of self-incriminating statements made publicly before a community are cited in order to flesh out the political and social attributes of this type of statement.

Michel Foucault studied the ritual of *exomologhēsis* as a sacramental and legal practice of the first Christian communities. *Exomologhēsis* was the act through which Christians recognized themselves as sinners and penitents before their community. A person who acknowledged this status simultaneously made an express request to the bishop to enter a period of penance, which could also have been very long (up to ten years). To attain the status of penitent, the individual had to publicly reveal the sins he or she committed. Foucault emphasizes how *exomologhēsis* is a form of *self-exposure* before the community. Paolo Prodi's studies underline the gradual fusion between theological-sacramental concepts and practices and the legal categories of Roman law. His studies on *exomologhēsis* show the gradual juridicization of this sacramental practice. *Exomologhēsis* is interesting because it shows the relationship between violating a rule (the sin), the resulting exclusion from the community (punishment), the confessor's request to re-enter the community by publicly recognizing the violation committed and undergoing a period of penance (in order to 'remove' the sin's effects, almost as if it were infectious).[36]

From the perspective of the history of legal thought, the practice of admonition among Puritans is even more interesting. According to some scholars, the institution of plea bargaining was fine-tuned by Puritan judges, who modified the formal and functional characteristics of the Puritan rite of admonition. According to this theory, it was the high crime rate in early nineteenth-century Boston (due to the chaotic and complex process of economic, political and institutional renewal in the state of Massachusetts) and the pedagogical need to spread new behaviours and habits in a social fabric including Irish and Italian immigrants which forced judges to change the rigid adversarial criminal proceedings. Using the rite of admonition (also based on self-incrimination before the community), the Puritan judges began to solicit the defendant's plea of guilt in exchange for a less harsh punishment.[37]

Looking at medieval monastic rules (in particular, the rules on penance and public expiation of those who had been excommunicated) shows other important elements. There are interesting references to the practice of public confession (before the monastic community) in the Rules of St. Bernard, St. Isidore and in the Spanish Rules. For a 'sinning brother', it was better to proceed with a public confession (capitulation) before the community than to go through the dispute system before the authorities of the monastic order. Once again, publicly admitting the negative value of the act committed (generally included in the concept of sin) indicates the individual's capitulation before the community. The individual's realm is considered relative to that of the community in order to preserve its unity (and thus its survival).[38]

The analysis of these forms of public self-incrimination demonstrates that public confession has always produced an important dialogic and symbolic relationship between the individual and a particular community. Admitting to violating legal, religious or ethical rules before one's own community ensures that: 1) the individual completely recognizes the importance of those rules; and 2) the public confession, which requires some kind of contrition, is actually a formal request to continue to be a part of the community. The archetypal sanction normally accompanying the violation of the community's fundamental rules is expulsion from the group: from ostracism (or expulsion from the community), to the more modern concealment of the criminal's body (prison) to its elimination (the death penalty).

Important conclusions can be made from this analysis. Each time a public admission of responsibility is employed, the goal is actually to preserve, constitute or impose the unity of the community. If the sin or crime represents a break in the trust binding the individual to the group due to the violation of rules, the public self-accusation embodies the 'rite' through which the criminal or sinner formally asks to be reintegrated into the community. The crimes or sins are in fact the symbol of the disintegration of the community's unity. Disintegration manifests itself through the breaking of a pact or the violation of rules or customs. Refusing to respect rules and values shared by a community symbolizes the break of the social bond. Historical studies have shown how public self-accusation is one of the most widespread rituals for abjuring betrayal and asking for reintegration (creating a new social contract).

These considerations shed new light on the functioning of the TRC. It increasingly appears to be an instrument for the constitution of a new social unity based on the sharing of new democratic values and the unconditional capitulation of those who have committed political crimes.[39] Public self-accusation, a pillar of TRC justice, is, at least from a symbolic point of view, the instrument to be used to reach those goals. Public confession thus becomes a 'contractual' act in which the new community in the process of being formed accepts all those who agree to the offer of inclusion embodied by the TRC once they publicly expose the violent act (and its intrinsic negative value). A shift was made from a society based on segregation, differentiation and segmentation of the *corps politique* to a new community founded on unity and mechanisms for integrating adversaries. Therefore, if there is confession, then there is a community (bound together by values and rules) that has a form of 'sovereignty' (being able to exert force and pressure on an individual so that he or she accepts its superiority).[40] Thus, there is a force operating behind the TRC and the AC, the body that actually administered the confession-amnesty exchange. As stated earlier, there is no confession without a force that acts through political, religious or community institutions. In the field of law and politics, this force has a name: sovereignty. Here it is not necessary to name specific state bodies that have the legitimacy to operate due to the principles of representation and popular sovereignty. For our purposes here, the fact that South Africa employed a specific act called confession administered by the AC means that there was also a force imposing this particular act of capitulation. This force was nothing other than the new 'democratic sovereignty' of the post-apartheid era that was created by the new unitary political body. As an example, we can say that the applicants publicly confessing before the AC were actually doing so before the community; more specifically, they surrendered before the power of the new post-segregationist democratic sovereignty, which forced the confessors to abjure political violence. This act was an indirect acknowledgement of obedience to the new democratic values professed by the new democratic sovereignty. Political crimes, the precondition for eligibility for amnesty, intrinsically negated the principle of democracy. The new democratic sovereign had to assert itself by first delegitimating political violence. This took place through an act of capitulation and submission, that is, the act of confession before the AC. In exchange, the new 'democratic sovereign' granted amnesty.[41]

Amnesty as a Non-automatic Provision: Counterbalancing the Right to Pardon

As we have seen, the AC for the most part rigorously followed its statutory rules, verifying the prerequisites required by law for granting amnesty on a case-by-case basis.[42] The result was a considerable number of decisions to refuse amnesty; this fact can be interpreted in different ways. First, it shows that the AC operated rather independently. Though most of the applications were barred from proceeding further after the administrative procedure, a high percentage of the cases subject to public hearing received amnesty. This does not change the basic functioning of the mechanism: the provisions for eliminating punishment were by no means automatic, thereby counterbalancing one of the possible effects seen in the use of self-accusation in the Roman criminal trial, that is, obliging the interlocutor of the confessional relationship to perform an act of kindness.

The amnesty process was therefore designed so as not to create a 'right/obligation to pardon'. Confession, in fact, could be a risky procedure for the 'new democratic sovereign' who accepts it; if the sovereign obtains the adversary's capitulation, it is 'forced' to respond with leniency. This is the implicit contractual foundation.

The functional form of South African amnesty deserves further discussion. It appears that South African amnesty was not really an amnesty, but measures eliminating punishment or sentencing altogether – measures that are more similar to a pardon. In fact, even if the South African amnesty law contained in the text of the statute was passed by Parliament (an element to be found in the amnesty form), it operated in a completely different way as compared to the way in which amnesty laws adopted by other constitutional systems normally operate. The AC issued specific and individual measures; because these measures did not automatically lead to amnesty, they share the exceptional nature of pardoning measures. Although it was not the President of the Republic of South Africa who directly granted the measure but a preorganized body (the AC), it is true that the decision to waive punishment did not eliminate the enforceability of criminal law, the unlawfulness of the fact, the traces and memory of the crime, and the ascertainment personal criminal responsibility, which is normally the case for the institution of amnesty.[43] The measures granted by the AC were strictly *ad personam* and exceptional. Amnesty is normally a general measure that benefits individuals, including those whose identity may not be known, for behaviour no longer considered by the state to be unlawful. Pardoning is a measure of remission or commutation of a punishment (while keeping the unlawfulness of the fact intact), but it is also normally a general measure. The South African amnesty, however, operated strictly *ad personam*, as a mechanism for waiving punishment. The identity of the beneficiaries and the facts of the crimes are thus known and made public. In all these cases, regular proceedings were held, whereas the confession during the public hearings ended up determining the individual responsible for crimes in cases that had not gone to court. Thus, the only thing that was eliminated was the penalty. The memory of the crime and the unlawfulness of the fact continue to mark the 'pardoned' person. The elements that traditionally characterize the institution of pardoning, that is, the retention of the unlawfulness of the deed and the individual nature of the measure, seem to predominate over the elements of the institution of amnesty.[44] These considerations show even more clearly how the amnesty process played with something extremely important from a legal, political and symbolic point of view, which regarded the legitimation of the constitutional order being instituted.

The new democratic sovereignty, through the utterances of the AC, found in the pardoning measures one of the most important attributes of sovereignty itself, which is useful for manifesting its presence while differentiating itself from the previous regime; nevertheless, it did not yield to an automatic relationship of confession-pardon. It reinforced its sovereign nature by keeping its right to decide when to administer 'salvation' from punishment, despite working with a framework of criteria created to limit arbitrary decisions.

Confession and Truth

I have already mentioned Quintilian's declamation.[45] Self-incrimination is an act with political, symbolic and rhetorical power. Except for rationally incomprehensible cases, no one accuses him or herself of reprehensible actions if they did not 'truly' take place. It does not matter if in reality this is all a mere rhetorical strategy. When the only witness of the crime is the person who committed it, the confession is the only act that symbolically represents 'the truth'. Even if there is evidence, the truth of the facts remains weak without a confession. Modern trial systems are familiar with the ambiguity and the risks (in terms of violence) that this syllogism conceals. The right to silence and the principle of the judge's free evaluation of the self-incriminating statements (as is the case for some European codes of criminal procedure) are strongholds of modern systems as compared to the indiscriminate use of confessions in trials over the past centuries.[46] Nevertheless, the link between self-incrimination and truth continues to be very problematic in trial systems that use confession as a source of evidence.

Instead, in the TRC system, once the punishment has been eliminated, self-accusation takes on a different shape. In South Africa, the intent was that the protagonists of the 'apartheid war' formally state the 'truth' that everyone was already aware of, as opposed to a judge certifying with a judgement the reconstruction of events that everyone witnessed. In order to do so, the only choice was to ask for the protagonists' involvement. They were the ones who could certify a preformulated accusatory paradigm: apartheid produced crimes just as the resistance movement, in the name of the struggle against segregation, caused suffering. This 'truth', however, had to be 'accepted' within the logic of a contract. The acceptance had to come from the mouths of the protagonists and not the judge's pen. In exchange, the need for expiation was dropped.

In short, everyone, victims and tormentors alike, had to capitulate before the new democratic principles: uprooting the conflict, refusing an approach of systematically excluding adversaries from the *corps politique,* as well as refusing violence (whatever its origin, even on behalf of the resistance). Everyone must participate in constructing a 'collective truth' by saying 'the same thing' and creating homology between visions of the past.

Even if historians or meticulous analysts of the activity of the TRC have often stressed that the 'truth' of the amnesty process is partial and that confessors often manipulated facts in their self-accusation in order to have their punishment eliminated, the primary effect of the confession was nevertheless produced. More than the truth about the past, what was really at play here was the capitulation of all those who carried out political violence – the true enemy of democracy – before the new constitutional order. By formally rejecting political violence, the individual implicitly asked for citizenship in the new democratic constitutional order.

Notes

1. From a procedural point of view, the reasons that led to this practice are interesting. As is known, the Anglo-American trial tradition includes the concept of plea of guilty (plea bargaining), which contains a form of self-incrimination. See A.S. Saltzburg. 1984. 'Self-Incrimination and Confessions', in *American Criminal Procedure. Cases and Commentary*. St. Paul: West Publishing, pp. 65–82; P.M. Bekker. 1996. 'Plea Bargaining in the United States of America and South Africa', *The Comparative and International Journal of Southern Africa* 29(1): 168–222. The South African procedural model, which is accusatory, includes the procedure of plea bargaining (see G.A. Barton. 1981. 'Standards for the Acceptance of a Plea Guilty – A Comparative Evaluation of Section 112(1)(b) of Act 51 of 1977 (Part I)', *South African Journal of Criminal Law and Criminology* 5: 212–23; G.A. Barton. 1982a. 'Standards for the Acceptance of a Plea Guilty – A Comparative Evaluation of Section 112(1)(b) of Act 51 of 1977 (Part II)', *South African Journal of Criminal Law and Criminology* 6: 46–61; G.A. Barton. 1982b. 'Standards for the Acceptance of a Plea Guilty – A Comparative Evaluation of Section 112(1)(b) of Act 51 of 1977 (Part III)', *South African. Journal of Criminal Law and Criminology* 6: 158–67; and R.W. Nugent. 1999. 'Self-Incrimination in Perspective', *The South African Law Journal* 116: 501–

22; C.T. Clarke. 1999. 'Message in a Bottle for Unknowing Defenders: Strategic Plea Negotiations Persist in South African Criminal Courts', *The Comparative and International Law Journal of Southern Africa* 32: 141–68). Therefore, it is plausible to argue that the practice of 'full disclosure' as formulated in the AC procedure was borrowed from or was in some way a development of a procedural concept that already existed within the South African legal system. Whether plea bargaining has its roots in the concept of 'confession' is still subject to discussion. See M.M. Feeley. 1979. 'Perspective on Plea Bargaining', *Law & Society Review* 13: 199 *et seq*; M.M. Feeley. 1982. 'Plea Bargaining and Structure of the Criminal Process', *Justice System Journal* 7: 338 *et seq*. On the general issue of confession in British common law, see P. Mirfield. 1985. *Confessions*. London: Sweet & Maxwell. The full disclosure before the AC possesses characteristics that differentiate it from plea bargaining.

2. On a theological approach to analysing the TRC model, see A. du Toit. 1998. *Confession and Reconciliation. A Challenge to the Churches in South Africa*. Pretoria: Research Institute for Theology and Religion; J.W. de Grounchy. 1993. 'Guilt, Amnesty and National Reconstruction', *Journal of Theology for Southern Africa*, 3–14; and D. Smit. 1995. 'The TRC – Tentative Religious and Theological Perspectives', *Journal of Theology for Southern Africa*, 3–17.
3. For an analysis of how amnesty had already been a delicate issue during CODESA, see J. Sarkin. 2004. *Carrots and Sticks: The TRC and the South African Amnesty Process*. Antwerp: Intersentia, pp. 41–49.
4. See K. Christie. 2000. *The South African Truth and Reconciliation Commission*. London: Macmillan, especially Chapter 3 'Negotiation the Truth in Times of Transition' (pp. 65 *et seq*).
5. For the text of these measures see p. 79 in the first part of this book. See also X. Philippe. 2004. 'Commission Vérité et réconciliation et droit constitutionnel', in B. Cassin, O. Cayla and J.P. Salazar (eds), *Vérité, réconciliation, réparation*. Paris: Le Seuil, pp. 119–241; J. Klaaren. 1998. 'The TRC, the South African Judiciary and Constitutionalism', *African Studies* 57: 197–209; J. Klaaren and H. Varney. 2003. 'A Second Bite at the Amnesty Cherry. Constitutional and Policy Issues around Legislation for a Second Amnesty', in C. Villa-Vicencio and E. Doxtader (eds), *The Provocations of Amnesty, Memory, Justice and Impunity*. Claremont: David Philip, pp. 265–93; J. Sarkin. 2003. 'To Prosecute or Not to Prosecute? Constitutional and Legal Issues Concerning Criminal Trials', in C. Villa-Vicencio and E. Doxtader (eds), *The Provocations of Amnesty: Memory, Justice and Impunity*. Claremont: David Philip, pp. 237–64.
6. This states: 'Notwithstanding the other provisions of the new Constitution and despite the repeal of the previous Constitution, all the provisions relating to amnesty contained in the previous Constitution under the heading "National Unity and Reconciliation" are deemed to be part of the new Constitution for the purposes of the Promotion of National Unity and Reconciliation Act, 1995 (Act 34 of 1995), as amended, including for the purposes of its validity.'
7. See C.J. Botha. 1994. 'Interpretation of the Constitution', *South African Public Law* 9: 257–63; and J. de Ville. 2000. *Constitutional and Statutory Interpretation*. Cape Town: Interdoc Consultants.
8. See Case CCT 17/96, *The Azanian People's Organisation (AZAPO), Nontsikelelo Margaret Biko, Churchill Mhlleli Mxenge, Chris Ribeiro v. State*. Many studies and commentaries on this court decision have been published. See D. Moellendorf. 1997. 'Amnesty, Truth and Justice: AZAPO', *South African Journal on Human Rights* 13(2): 283–91; C. Braude and D. Spitz. 1997. 'Memory and the Spectre of International Justice: A Comment on AZAPO', *South African Journal on Human Rights* 13(2): 259–69; J. Sarkin. 1996. 'The Trials and Tribulations of South Africa's Truth and Reconciliation Commission', *South African Journal on Human Rights* 12: 617–41. See also *TRC Final Report*, 'Legal Challenges', vol. 1, Chapter 7, pp. 174–

200; and A. Lollini. 1998. 'Human Rights and Past Wrongs: The Constitutional Concepts of Truth and Reconciliation Commission in South Africa', in V. Piergigli and I. Taddia (eds), *International Conference on African Constitutions*. Turin: Giappichelli, pp. 97–106.

9. See s. 20(7) of Act 34/95; s. 22 of the 1993 Constitution defines the 'right to justice' by stating: 'Every person shall have the right to have justiciable disputes settled by a court of law or, where appropriate, another independent and impartial forum.'
10. Mr. Soggot, the applicants' attorney, structured the argument of the amnesty procedure's unconstitutionality around breaches of the 1949 Geneva Conventions: 'art. 49 of the first Geneva Convention for the Amelioration of the Condition of the Wounded and Sick in Armed Forces in the Field, art. 50 of the second Geneva Convention for the Amelioration of the Condition of Wounded, Sick and Shipwrecked Members of Armed Forces at Sea, art. 129 of the third Geneva Convention relative to the Treatment of Prisoners of War and art. 146 of the fourth Geneva Convention relative to the Protection of Civilian Persons in Time of War.' See § 25 (CCT 17/96) delivered by Justice Mahomed. The issue is nevertheless very complex in terms of international law. See R.C. Slye. 2002. 'The Legitimacy of Amnesties under International Law and General Principles of Anglo-American Law: Is a Legitimate Amnesty Possible?', *Virginia Journal of International Law*, 174–247.
11. See CCT 17/96.
12. Apartheid was defined as a crime against humanity by the UN General Assembly resolution 39/72A of 1984, Security Council resolutions 392 (19 June 1976) and 473 (13 June 1980). Including apartheid as a crime against humanity took place with the International Convention on the Suppression and Punishment of the Crime of Apartheid of 1973 and the Convention on Non-Applicability of Statutory Limitations to War Crimes and Crimes against Humanity of 1968. The following panel of important international law scholars staunchly opposed the South African amnesty process, sending a memo to the TRC: Catherine Admay, Abdullahi An-Na'im, Philip Alston, M. Cherif Bassiouni, Thomas Buergenthal, William S. Dodge, John Dugard, Richard Falk, Gregory H. Fox, Thomas M. Franch, Claudio Grossman, David J. Harris, Cynthia Crawford Lichenstein, Elliot Milstein, Steven R. Ratner, Anne-Marie Slaughter, Ronald C. Slye, Henry Steiner, Ralph G. Steinhardt, Johan D. van der Vyver and Richard J. Wilson. See 'The Mandate', *TRC Final Report*, vol. 1, pp. 94 *et seq*. Some scholars expressed doubts about the Court's interpretation; see Z. Motala. 1996. 'The Constitutional Court's Decision to International Law and its Method of Interpretation in the "Amnesty Decision": Intellectual Honesty or Political Expediency?', *South African Yearbook of International Law* 21: 29–59. M.E. Bennun, on the other, was substantially in favour of the compatibility between the South African amnesty process and international law; see M.E. Bennun. 2003. 'Amnesty and International Law', in Villa-Vicencio and Doxtader (eds), *The Provocations of Amnesty*, pp. 92–115.
13. The Court says on the matter: 'The amnesty contemplated is not a blanket amnesty against criminal prosecution for all and sundry, granted automatically as a uniform act of compulsory statutory amnesia. It is specifically authorised for the purposes of effecting a constructive transition towards a democratic order. It is available only where there is a full disclosure of all facts to the Amnesty Committee and where it is clear that the particular transgression was perpetrated during the prescribed period and with a political objective committed in the course of the conflicts of the past. That objective has to be evaluated having regard to the careful criteria listed in art. 20(3) of the Act, including the very important relationship which the act perpetrated bears in proportion to the object pursued' (§ 48).
14. As support for its interpretation seemed to be rather political, the Court argued: 'The erstwhile adversaries of such a conflict inhabit the same sovereign territory. They have to live with each other and work with each other and the state concerned is best

equipped to determine what measures may be most conducive for the facilitation of such reconciliation and reconstruction. That is a difficult exercise, which the nation within such a state has to perform by having regard to its own peculiar history, its complexities, even its contradictions and its emotional and institutional traditions. What role punishment should play in respect of erstwhile acts of criminality in such a situation is part of the complexity' (§ 42).

15. On the concept of materiality, see Gustavo Zagrebelsky's foreword to the new edition of C. Mortati. 1998. *La Costituzione in senso materiale*. Milan: Giuffrè, pp. VII–XXXVIII.
16. See *TRC Final Report*, 'Concepts and Principles', vol. 1, Chapter 5, pp. 125–28. A detailed analysis of *ubuntu* underlining its Afrocentric roots can be found in R. Wilson. 1996. 'The Siza Will Not Go Away. The Truth and Reconciliation Commission, Human Rights and Nation Building in South Africa', *African Studies* 55(2): 10–14; R. Spitz and M. Chaskalson. 2000. *The Politics of Transition. A Hidden History of South Africa's Negotiated Settlement*. Johannesburg: Witwatersrand, p. 412. On the political and philosophical aspects of this notion, see J. Derrida. 2004. 'Versöhnung, ubuntu, pardon: quel genre?', in Cassin, Cayla and Salazar (eds), *Vérité, réconciliation, réparation*, pp. 111–56.
17. The link between the Postamble and the TRC is analysed in Spitz and Chaskalson, *The Politics of Transition*, pp. 413–14.
18. Justice Mandala states '(…) the concept of ubuntu appears for the first time in the post-amble, but it is a concept that permeates the Constitution generally and more particularly Chapter III which embodies the entrenched fundamental human rights. The concepts carries in it the ideas of humaneness, social justice and fairness'; see *S. v. Makwanyane and Another* (1995) (6) BCLR 665 (CC). In addition, the other judges, such as Chief Justice Chaskalson and Justices Mahomed and Mokgoro, expressly mention the concept of *ubuntu* (for example see § 130–31 by Chaskalson). See M. Zlotnick. 1996. 'The Death Penalty and the Public Opinion', *South African Journal on Human Rights* 12(1): 70–78; P.M. Maduna. 1996. 'Death Penalty and Human Rights', *South African Journal on Human Rights* 12(2): 193–213; L. Madhuku. 1997. 'Incompatibility of the Death Penalty and the Bill of Rights: Guerra v Baptiste [1995] 3 WLR 891; [1995] 1 LRC 407', *South African Journal on Human Rights* 13: 151–54.
19. 'A culture which places an emphasis on communality and on interdependence of the members of the community. It recognises a person's status as a human being, entitled to unconditional respect, dignity, value and acceptance from the members of the community such a person happens to be part of. It also entails the converse, however. The person has a corresponding duty to give the same respect, dignity, value and acceptance to each member of the community (…). During violent conflicts and times when violent crimes are rife, distraught members of society decry the loss of ubuntu. Thus heinous crimes are the antithesis of ubuntu (…)': *Constitutional Law Report*, 1995, vol. 6, p. 754, § 224. The constitutional value and the material importance of the notion of *ubuntu* has been reconfirmed repeatedly by scholars; see N. Bohler-Muller. 2000. 'What the Equality Courts can Learn from Gilligan's Ethic of Care: A Novel Approach', *South African Journal on Human Rights* 16(4): 635; and with important consequences in terms of legal pluralism, R. English. 1996. 'Ubuntu: The Quest for an Indigenous Jurisprudence', *South African Journal on Human Rights* 12(4): 641–48.
20. See I. Routenbach and E. Malherbe. 1999. *Constitutional Law*. Durban: Butterworths, pp. 11–12; G.J. van Niekerk. 1998. 'A Common Law for Southern Africa: Roman Law or Indigenous African Law?', *Comparative and International Law Journal of Southern Africa* 31: 158–73.
21. The centrality of the practice of full disclosure is also emphasized by A. du Bois-Pedain. 2007. *Transitional Amnesty in South Africa*. Oxford: Oxford University

Press, p. 139. The author affirms that: 'the eligibility for amnesty within the legislative framework created by the TRC Act does not necessarily correlate to moral deservingness. What makes an applicant "morally deserving" of amnesty is not what he did – it is his willingness to make full disclosure.'

22. Quintilian's famous Declamation 314 states: '*Ea natura est hominis confessionis, ut possit videri demens qui confitetur de se. Hic furore impulsus est, alius ebrietate, alius errore, alius dolore, quidam questione. Nemo contra se dicit nisi aloquo cogente.*' Quoted from P. Marchetti. 1994. *Testis contra se. L'imputato come fonte di prova nel processo penale dell'età moderna.* Milan: Giuffrè, p. 266 (note 259). On the historical forms of confession, see T.N. Tentler. 1975. *Sin and Confession on the Eve of the Reformation.* Princeton: Princeton University Press; *L'Aveu. Antiquité Moyen Age.* 1986. Rome: Ecole Française de Rome; P. Fiorelli. 1961. 'La Confessione (Storia)', in *Enciclopedia del Diritto*, vol. 8. Milan: Giuffrè, p. 864; A. Prosperi. 1996. *I tribunali della coscienza. Inquisitori, confessori, missionari.* Turin: Einaudi; R. Rusconi. 2002. *L'ordine dei peccati. La confessione tra Medioevo ed età moderna.* Bologna: Il Mulino; V. Lavenia. 2004. *L'infamia e il perdono. Tributi, pene e confessione nella teologia morale della prima età moderna.* Bologna: Il Mulino.
23. See R. Dulong (ed.). 2001. *L'Aveu. Histoire, sociologie, philosophie.* Paris: Presses Universitaires de France; R. Dulong. 2000. 'Le silence comme aveu et le droit au silence', *Langage et société*, 25–44; R. Dulong. 1998. *Le témoin oculaire. Les conditions sociales de l'attestation personnelle.* Paris: Ehess; T. Reik. 1997. *Le besoin d'avouer.* Paris: Payout; P. Brooks. 1996. 'Storytelling without Fear? Confession in Law and Literature', *Journal of Legal Hermeneutics*, 277; P. Brooks. 2000. *Troubling Confessions: Speaking Guilt in Law and Literature.* Chicago: Chicago University Press; and H.C. Lea. 1911. *Storia della confessione auricolare*, vol. 1. Mendrisio: Cultura Moderna.
24. See note 41 of Chapter 3.
25. See R. Dulong and J.M. Maradin. 2001. 'Analyse des dimension constitutive de l'aveu en réponse à une accusation', in Dulong, *L'Aveu*, pp. 135–79.
26. The study of these three types of confession is in Y. Thomas. 1986. 'Confessus pro iudicato. L'aveu civil et l'aveu pénal à Rome', in *L'Aveu. Antiquité et Moyen Age.* Rome: Ecole Française de Rome, pp. 89–117; Y. Thomas. 2001. 'L'aveu de la parole au corps (Rome, V° siècle av. J.C. IV° siècle après J.C.)', in Dulong, *L'Aveu*, pp. 17-56; and Y. Thomas. 1986. 'Arracher la vérité. La Majesté et l'Inquisition (I–IV siècle ap. JC)', in R. Jacob (ed.), *Le juge et le jugement dans les traditions juridiques européennes.* Paris: Librairie Generale de Droit et de Jurisprudence, pp. 15 *et seq*; Y. Thomas. 1984. 'Se venger au forum. Solidarités traditionnelles et système pénal à Rome', in R. Verdier and Y. Thomas (eds), *Vengeance*, vol. 2. Paris: Cujas. See also N. Scapini. 1983. *La confessione nel diritto romano: il diritto giustinianeo.* Milan: Giuffrè. This reconstruction of confession is confirmed by O. Cayla. 2004. 'Aveu et fondement du droit', in Cassin, Cayla and Salazar (eds), *Vérité, réconciliation, réparation*, pp. 89–110.
27. See M. Foucault. 1975. *Surveiller et punir. Naissance de la prison.* Paris: Gallimard, pp. 45–49.
28. J. Chiffoleau. 1986. 'Sur la pratique et la conjoncture de l'aveu judiciaire en France du XIII au XV siècle', in *L'Aveu. Antiquité et Moyen Age*, pp. 341–80; J. Chiffoleau. 1990. 'Dire l'indicible. Remarques sur la catégorie du "nefandum" du XII–XV siècle', *Les Annales* 2: 289–324. Another very interesting study is P. Fiorelli. 1953. *La Tortura giudiziaria nel diritto comune*, vol. 1 and 2 (1954). Milan: Giuffrè; and I. Mereu. 2000. *Storia dell'intolleranza in Europa.* Milan: Bompiani. See also Marchetti, *Testis contra se*; Prosperi, *I tribunali della coscienza*; and I. Rosoni. 1995. *Quae singula non prosunt collecta iuvant. La teoria della prova indiziaria nell'età medioevale e moderna.* Milan: Giuffrè.

29. See Dulong and Maradin, 'Analyse des dimensions constitutives de l'aveu', pp. 135 *et seq*; O. Macchi. 2001. 'Le fait d'avouer comme récit et comme événement dans l'enquête criminelle', in Dulong, *L'Aveu*, pp. 181 *et seq*.
30. This element is analysed by Thomas, 'L'Aveu de la parole au corps', pp. 21 *et seq*; Thomas, 'Confessus pro iudicato', pp. 91 *et seq*.
31. See P.M. Gy. 1974. 'Le précepte de la confession annuelle (Latran IV, C. 21) et la détection des hérétiques Saint Bonaventure et Saint Thomas contre Raymond de Peñafort', *Revue des Sciences Philosophiques et Théologiques*, pp. 444–50; P.M. Gy. 1979. 'Le précepte de la confession annuelle et la nécessité de la confession', *Revue de Sciences Philosophiques et Théologiques*, 529 *et seq*; P. Valadier. 2001. 'Pratique catholique de la confession auriculaire: enjeux et problèmes', in Dulong, *L'Aveu*, pp. 241–56; Prosperi, *I tribunali della coscienza*; Rusconi, *L'ordine dei peccati*.
32. See Duval. 1974. 'Le concile de Trente et la confession', *Maison-Dieu* 118: 131 *et seq*; A. Amato. 1974. *Saggio di ermeneutica conciliare. I pronunciamenti tridentini sulla necessità della confessione sacramentale*. Rome: Las; and R. Pettazzoni, 1936. *La confessione dei peccati*, 2nd ed., 3 vol. Bologna: Zanichelli; J. Bossy. 1998. *Dalla Comunità all'individuo. Per una storia sociale dei sacramenti nell'Europa moderna*. Turin: Einaudi.
33. The consoling nature of the sacrament of confessing sins in psychoanalytic terms is analysed by J. Delumeau. 1983. *Le péché et la peur. La culpabilisation en Occident XIII–XVIII siècle*. Paris: Fayard; J. Delumeau. 1990. *L'aveu et le pardon. Les difficultés de la confession XIII–XVIII siècle*. Paris: Fayard; J. Bossy. 1975. 'The Social History of Confession in the Age of the Reformation', *Transactions of the Royal Historical Society* 25: 21–38; N. Berou. 1986. 'La confession dans les écrits théologiques et pastoraux du XIIIeme siècle: médication de l'âme ou démarche judiciaire?, in *L'Aveu. Antiquité et Moyen Age*, pp. 261–82. Other elements regarding the confession as *cura animarum* should be noted. Historians and theologians have analysed the manuals of confession (codified in order to aid priests during the sacrament of confession) and have demonstrated the use of medical metaphors and images associated with the sacrament of confession. The priests were 'doctors of the soul'; sin was a disease; they acted like 'obstetricians' during 'delivery', that is, during the confession. By confessing the sin, the disease is expelled. It is interesting to note the similarities with the symbolic and metaphorical language used to describe the TRC's work. Religious and medical metaphors referring to the TRC (as bearers of a redemptive approach) were mostly used by the Anglican archbishop Desmond Tutu and the leader of the Methodist Church, Alex Boraine, and depicted the Commission's works as serving the purpose of 'healing the nation'. See the official speeches made by Tutu as well as R. Botman and R. Petersen. 1996. *To Remember and to Heal. Theological and Psychological Reflections on the TRC*. Cape Town: Human and Rousseau.
34. See M. Turrini. 1991. *La coscienza e le leggi. Morale e diritto nei testi per la confessione della prima Età moderna*. Bologna: Il Mulino; P. Galtier. 1951. *Aux origines du sacrement de penitence*. Rome: Università Gregoriana; and Prosperi, *I tribunali della coscienza*.
35. See the studies of R. Rusconi. 1986. '"Ordinate confiteri": la confessione dei peccati nelle "Summae de casibus" e nei manuali per i confessor, metà XII-inizi XIV secolo', in *L'Aveu. Antiquité et Moyen Age*, pp. 297–313; Rusconi, *L'ordine dei peccati*.
36. See M. Foucault. 1988. *Technologies of the Self: A Seminar with Michel Foucault*. Amherst: University of Massachusetts Press. See also P. Prodi. 2000. *Una storia della giustizia. Dal pluralismo dei fori al moderno dualismo tra coscienza e diritto*. Bologna: Il Mulino, pp. 34 *et seq*.
37. The Puritan rite of admonition has been studied from a legal point of view by M. Vogel. 1999. 'The Social Origins of Plea Bargaining: Conflict and the Law in the Process of State Formation, 1830-1860', *Law & Society Review* 33(1): 161; M. Vogel. 2005. *Coercion to Compromise: Plea Bargaining, the Courts and the Making*

of Political Authority. New York: Oxford University Press; U. Bonanate. (ed.) 1975. *I Puritani. I soldati della Bibbia*. Turin: Einaudi. See also W.F. Kuntz. 1988. *Criminal Sentencing in Three Nineteenth Century Cities: Social History of Punishment in New York, Boston and Philadelphia*. New York: Garland Publishers; and M.H. Haller. 1979. 'Plea Bargaining: The Nineteenth Century Context', *Law & Society Review* 13: 273 *et seq*.

38. See the collection of monastic rules in E. Bianchi (ed.). 2001. *Regole monastiche d'occidente*. Turin: Einaudi.
39. The TRC's activity has been studied in relation to the legitimation and construction of the democratic post-apartheid state by R. Wilson. 2001. *The Politics of Truth and Reconciliation: Legitimizing the Post-apartheid State*, Cambridge: Cambridge University Press; and A. Boraine. 2001. *A Country Unmasked: Inside South Africa's Truth Commission*. Oxford: Oxford University Press.
40. In a legal philosophy study on the nature of the confession before the AC (Cayla, 'Aveu et fondement du droit', pp. 89–110), Olivier Cayla makes a fascinating argument in which the South African confession is an empirical and concrete version of the social contract described by Thomas Hobbes in § 13 of Chapter 17 of *The Leviathan*. Scholars of Hobbes have often claimed that the social contract is merely theoretical because it is a philosophical and logical precondition for the creation of a state. Starting with an analysis of the AC confession, Cayla instead proposes reading the social contract in concrete and empirical terms. The full disclosure represents the founding act of the post-apartheid state. Cayla disagrees that the 'pact', the foundation stone of Hobbes's contract, can be defined as a mere 'convention'. In fact, a convention requires the pre-existence in the state of a civil law (positive law) to interpret and to ensure its clauses are respected (something that is impossible in a state of nature in which no one wants the risk of being bound to obligations). The conventional form is plausible only in a later phase, in which the state and laws exist because they have already been constituted. Using Frank Lessay's interpretation of Hobbes, Cayla claims that the act of renouncing natural rights is a concrete act, as it is a real moment in which the associate effectively participates in the association (see F. Lessay. 1988. *Souveraineté et légitimé chez Hobbes*. Paris: Presses Universitaires de France). Lessay and Cayla thus reject the idea that the social contract is located in a mythical and undeterminable past moment in which the society was formed. Rather, the social contract is an act of consent that humans constantly repeat throughout the course of their lifetime. Being born in a state already in force, humans are asked to respect the authority of civil law and mechanisms of representation. Lessay claims that this act of renunciation (to one's own natural right to pursue one's own good) and hence the assent to a pact (which grants power and representation to the sovereign) is an act dictated by reason and necessity – if one does not want to succumb to the anomic violence of the state of nature. On the contrary, Cayla claims that the act of assent takes place for different reasons. Using Yan Thomas's research on confession mentioned above, Cayla argues that one does not conform with the civil law because of mere 'reason' but due to the power that the rules of a society organized in a state exerts on individuals (Cayla, 'Aveu et fondement du droit', p. 99). This form of acceptance, in Cayla's opinion, has the characteristics of the act of confession. Cayla explains that the act of assent does not have the characteristics of a promise (which underlies the concept of convention), but of confession. With a promise, a voluntary commitment is made to keep one's word (obligation or contract); a confession confirms a state of inferiority in relation to the power that pushes towards recognition (and capitulation). A promise is monologic; the speaker orders himself to obey a command; the promise relates to the gift that the promisor gives the receiver of the right to remember the word given. This exchange of words has a simplicity that is also its weakness; there always needs to be an authority that rules that the promise has been respected. A promise requires a previously-constituted 'sovereign':

a promise creates only a potential unity and does not guarantee peace. In fact, it could create a new conflict of interpretation regarding the promise made. A promise does not create a stable social bond. On the contrary, the real unity of the political body (homology) that is the basis for the social body as the first and fundamental step of the state is created, according to Cayla, through confession, which is based on capitulation, surrender and obedience. Actually, these elements are the essence of every constituent act. If all of this can be found in the full disclosure procedure before the AC, which would confirm the theory put forward here, there is nevertheless the question that confession actually intervenes at a moment subsequent to the constitution of the unity of the political body delegating sovereignty. The power that leads to a confession before the community must exist before the moment of confession. One submits to something that already exists. The confession is the act that, more so than any other act of speech, shows the existence of sovereignty and a community able to create unity.

41. The link between the AC amnesty process and the change of sovereignty is stressed by several other scholars such as du Bois-Pedain, *Transitional Amnesty in South Africa*, pp. 298–99; R.A. Wilson. 2000. 'Reconciliation and Revenge in Post-Apartheid South Africa: Rethinking Legal Pluralism and Human Rights', *Current Anthropology* 41: 79 *et seq*; R. Teitel. 2000. *Transitional Justice*. Oxford: Oxford University Press, p. 59.
42. I. Lax. 2004b. 'Le témoignage d'un commissaire. Juger les demandes d'amnistie et promouvoir la réconciliation', in Cassin, Cayla and Salazar (eds), *Vérité, réconciliation, réparation*, pp. 281–99.
43. See G. Zagrebelsky. 1974. *Amnistia, indulto e grazia. Profili costituzionali*. Milan: Giuffrè; H. Quatitsch. 1992. 'Über Bürgerkriegs- und Feind-Amnestien', *Der Staat* 31: 389–418; H. Quatitsch. 1995. *La giustizia politica. Le amnistie nella storia*. Milan: Giuffrè; O. Kirkhheimer. 1961. *Political Justice. The Use of Legal Procedure for Political Ends*. Princeton: Princeton University Press; and P. Ricoeur. 2000. *La mémoire, l'histoire, l'oubli*. Paris: Le Seuil.
44. The South African amnesty during the transition had a hybrid nature that is not to be found entirely in the institutions, for example, of the Italian constitutional order. The institutions of amnesty and pardoning, for example, underwent radical changes in Italy (constitutional law n.1/1992, which changed Art. 79 of the Constitution) and are today the subject of bitter debate, especially concerning the issue of who has the power to pardon (see M. Ainis. 2004. 'Sulla titolarità del potere di grazia', *Quaderni Costituzionali* 1: 97–109). Other constitutional orders, at times with different methods, have hybrid measures of leniency belonging to the executive or legislative branches (see M. Conan. 2001. 'Amnistie présidentielle et tradition', *Revue du droit public* 5: 1305–56).
45. See note 21 of this chapter.
46. See F. Cordero. 1988. 'La Confessione nel quadro decisorio', in L. de Cataldo Neuburger (ed.), *La giustizia penale e la fluidità del sapere: ragionamento sul metodo*. Padua: CEDAM, pp. 53–64.

Conclusion

Confession, Constituent Pact and an 'Absolutist' Communitarian Constitutionalism

In conclusion, confession before the AC integrates one of the fundamental elements of post-apartheid constitutionalism, contributing to the legitimation of the new democratic order. Through a speech act, which is free and coercive at the same time, a kind of 'communitarian democratic absolutism' seems to impose itself. Generally speaking, the act of confession not only emphasizes the power of the entity obtaining the adversary's capitulation, but also the presence of a community which the confessor is asked to be part of (with the risk of definitive exclusion by imprisonment or, in the most serious circumstances, the death penalty).

In South Africa, the constitutional order being established left no choice to those who practised political violence: capitulate by confessing or be tried in the future. This confirms that confession is a practice implying a form of subjugation; it has an unyielding and imperative nature; it is an act of sovereign power.

By limiting its own power to punish, the new state simultaneously exalts and monopolizes the power to 'pardon', which has the effect of blocking the institutionalization of 'resistance' to the new order. The adjudicative option, if executed respecting the rules of a fair trial and the right to counsel, could produce the figure of the 'martyr', that is, a person who refuses to admit, even in a criminal trial, the criminal nature of his or her own actions (which happened in trials that ended with an acquittal). On the contrary, confessing before the AC as the prerequisite for being 'pardoned' left little room for defence. It was a form of ratification by confirming an indirect accusatory paradigm. In this scheme, no prosecutor makes a formal charge, in contrast to a criminal trial; there was no need to expressly formulate an accusatory paradigm, as it was already implied.

The South African mechanism of confession became a way of authorizing the victorious constitutional order to exercise sovereignty. By making a confession, the new democratic sovereignty is recognized, instituted and legitimated; it is not without reason that the law also demands confession of members of national liberation movements. Some freedom fighters are now leading the country and in some way they legitimate themselves through the capitulation of their own fellow fighters, as well as acquiring a privileged political status. The new democratic sovereignty as a peacemaking entity had to combat the political violence of the past, and the use of confession fully satisfied this need.

It is extraordinary that the act of assent, which is the basis of confession, takes place using a constitutionalized procedure and principles: the TRC is thus a constitutional and legal device establishing the new order and law.

As in all political and legal contexts in which confession is used, the system used in South Africa proves to be of an imperative nature that demands homologation. The innovative element is that this authoritative inclusive force is in the form of a constitutional state and not a theocratic or politically ideological structure, unless attention to fundamental rights is considered to be a new form of ideology.

This hypothesis should be taken into consideration. The new democratic order, which expresses itself with a legal syntax based on the principle of equality and strong protection of fundamental rights with many bodies of judicial review, nevertheless acts in an invasive and imperative way. The ideological instruments of dogmas stated in the political arena – such as the idea of national unity, the 'Rainbow Nation', peacemaking and reconciliation by waiving primary rights like justice for apartheid victims – point to a constitutionalism that could paradoxically be defined as 'absolutist', not in an anti-democratic sense but rather in the sense of the radical imposition of the new democratic constitutional order.

The proceduralization of constituent power that broke the constituent act into segments gradually accepted by a heterogeneous group of constituent actors, the persistent strategy of inclusion and the institution of multiple bodies of judicial review limiting the state's public powers, as well as bringing the political body closer to the institutions, confirm that this constitutional project was devoted to action.

Many critics opposed to this project made their voices heard;[1] however, the ethically aggressive form of post-apartheid constitutionalism – based on the enforcement of an organized constitutional state with complex structures for implementing constitutional principles and which demanded the capitulation of perpetrators of political violence through a ceremonial representation like that used by the TRC – was justified in as much as it was a response to the dramatic social fragmentation that the new constitutional order had to confront.

The nature of the constituent pact is thus rather complex; the main objective was to stop the civil war and establish peace (or at least a break in political violence). This was the precondition for establishing a democratic sovereignty able to exercise constituent power effectively. This precondition was met by ordering those who had committed crimes for political purposes (enemies of the new democracy) to be 'brought back to their senses'. With its constitutional power, the new state in formation motivated members of the social body to unite as a community (reconciliation). From this perspective, the rhetoric of the Rainbow Nation and *ubuntu* constitutes an ideology with a strong universalistic emphasis.

All of this took place through an act of submission and obedience to the law (that imposes a sacrifice on the victims). In exchange, the black population received access to political power (at this point, they could not increase their access to economic power); whites were guaranteed the neutralization of retaliatory impulses and the economic privileges acquired in the past.

The desired result was to set into motion mechanisms of social control and the democratic procedures provided by the new Constitution that would be able to balance inequality in the future.

The history of geopolitical areas like the African continent is littered with failed constitutional experiments; the South African elite leading the transition probably strong-armed the situation in an attempt to make the liberal-democratic constitutional model long-lasting, hoping that it would produce a virtuous effect. The outcome of the operation can only be judged in the long term, pending verification that the institutional apparatus created starts functioning for the benefit of the destitute masses.

Upon further inspection, a new form of nationalism seems to be emerging; this new nationalism unites the political body and is leading South Africa inevitably to assuming a dominant economic, cultural and military role in Southern and Central Africa.

One of the merits of the post-apartheid constitutional experience was the incorporation of the delicate issue of transitional justice into its constitutional setup, which immediately became a new constitutional variable.

Transitional justice is no longer just a judicial issue for satisfying the victims' need for retribution and vengeful impulses. Transitional justice has become a fundamental part of the constitution-making process, during which important symbolic constituent elements are redrafted, such as collective memory, and a new balance is struck between the different segments of the political body.

The constitutional projects of other geopolitical areas liberated from illiberal regimes will undoubtedly have to contemplate this new interpretation of the problem of transitional justice. In many recent experiences, this issue at a constitutional level has simply remained an uncomfortable issue. However, the South African constitution-making process and new Constitution attempted for the first time a clear formalization of this issue in constitutional terms, thus acknowledging the breadth of this dynamic of justice that contributes to the form of the new political and constitutional order.

Endnote

1. Including R. Wilson. 2001. *The Politics of Truth and Reconciliation: Legitimizing the Post-apartheid State*. Cambridge: Cambridge University Press, pp. 223–30, which continues to provide important critical ideas.

Bibliography

List of Amnesty Committee Decisions

AC 020/1997
AC 025/1997
AC 045/1997
AC 026/1998
AC 032/1998
AC 027/1999
AC 172/1999
AC 230/1999
AC 345/1999
AC 350/1999
AC 036/2000
AC 055/2000
AC 059/2000
AC 082/2000
AC 084/2000
AC 120/2000
AC 121/2000
AC 122/2000
AC 142/2000
AC 149/2000
AC 209/2000
AC 215/2000
AC 224/2000
AC 034/2001
AC 048/2001
AC 068/2001

AC 128/2001
AC 161/2001
AC 232/2001
AC 248/2001
AC 270/2001

List of Constitutional Court Cases

ANC v. Minister of Local Government and Housing KwaZulu Natal, Minister of Traditional and Environmental Affairs KwaZulu Natal, Chairman of Traditional Leaders, (1998) (4) BCLR 399 (CC).

Bhe v. Magistrate, Khayelitsha and Oothers, (2004) (1) BCLR 27 (C).

Certification of the Amended Text of the Constitution of the Western Cape, (11997) (12) BCLR 1653 (CC).

Du Plessis and Others v. De Klerk and Anothers, (1996) (5) BCLR 658 (CC).

Government of the Republic of South Africa v. Grootboom, (2001) (1) SA 46 (CC).

In Re Certification of the Constitution of the Province of KwaZulu-Natal, (1996) (11) BCLR 1419 (CC).

In Re Certification of the Constitution of the Republic of South Africa, (1996) (10) BCLR 1253 (CC) .

In Re Certification of the Constitution of Western Cape, (1997) (9) BCLR 1167 (CC).

Minister of Health Care v. Treatment Action Campaign, (2002) (5) SA 721 (CC).

Premier of KwZn, Executive Council of Traditional Leaders (KwZn) v. State, (1995) (12) BCLR 1561 (CC).

President of the Republic of South Africa and Another v. Hugo (1997) (4) SA 1 (CC).

S. v. Basson (2001) (1) SACR 235(T).

S. v. Basson (2005) (1) SAa 171 (CC).

S. v. Makwanyane and Another (1995) (6) BCLR 665 (CC).

S. v. Zuma and Others, (11995) (4) BCLR 401 (CC).

Soobramoney v. Minister of Health, KwaZulu Natal, (1998) (1) SA 765 (CC).

The Azanian People Organization, (AZAPO), Nontsikelelo Margaret Biko, Churchill Mhlleli Mxenge, Chris Ribeiro v. State, (1996) (8) BCLR 1015 (CC).

Bibliography

Abel, R. 1995. *Politics by Other Means: Law in the Struggle against Apartheid*. New York: Routledge.

Accarino, B. 1999. *Rappresentanza*. Bologna: Il Mulino.

Ackerman, B. 1991. *We the People I: Foundations*. Cambridge: Harvard University Press.

______. 1997. 'The Rise of World Constitutionalism', *Virginia Law Review* 83(3): 771–97.

______. 1998. *We the People II: Transformations*. Cambridge: Harvard University Press.

Adam, H. 1994. 'Ethnic Versus Civic Nationalism: South Africa's Non-Racialism in Comparative Perspective', *South African Sociological Review* 7(1): 15–30.

Adam, H. and K. Moodley. 1992. 'Political Violence, Tribalism and Inkatha', *Journal of Modern African Studies* 30: 485–510.

______. 1993. *The Negotiated Revolution: Society and Politics in Post-apartheid South Africa*. Johannesburg: Jonathan Ball.

Adomeit, K. 1999. 'Gustav Radbruch zum 50. Todestag', *Neue Juristische Wochenschrift*, 34–65.

Ainis, M. 2004. 'Sulla titolarità del potere di grazia', *Quaderni Costituzionali* 1: 97–109.

Aldana-Pindell, R. 2003. ' In Vindication of Justiciable Victims' Rights to Truth and Justice for State-Sponsored Crimes', *Vanderbilt Journal of Transnational Law* 35: 1399–1501.

Aletta, N. 1999. 'Truth and Reconciliation: The Birth of the Present and the Reworking of History', *Journal of Southern African Studies* 25: 499–519.

Alkema, S. 1996. 'The Right to Access to Information: A Fundamental Right?', *Human Rights and Constitutional Law Journal of Southern Africa* 1(1): 32 *et seq*.

Amato, A. 1974. *Saggio di ermeneutica conciliare. I pronunciamenti tridentini sulla necessità della confessione sacramentale*. Rome: Las.

Ambos, K. and O. Mohamed (eds). 2003. *New Approaches in International Criminal Justice: Kosovo, East Timor, Sierra Leone & Cambodia*. Freiburg: Max Planck Institute for Foreign and International Criminal Law.

Amselle, J.L. and E. M'Bokolo. 1985. *Au coeur de l'ethnie*. Paris: La Découverte.

ANC. 1989. 'Constitutional Guidelines for a Democratic South Africa', *South Africa Journal on Human Rights* 5: 129.

______. 1992. *ANC Regional Policy*. Cape Town: Centre for Development Studies, University of Western Cape.

______. 1992. *Constitutional Principles and Structures for a Democratic South Africa*. Cape Town: Centre for Development Studies, University of Western Cape.

———. 1992. *Ten Proposed Regions for a United South Africa*. Cape Town: Centre for Development Studies, University of Western Cape.

———. 1993. *Draft Bill of Rights*. Cape Town: Centre for Development Studies, University of Western Cape.

———. 1995. 'Building a United Nation: Discussion Paper and Policy Proposal', Johannesburg.

Anderson, B. 1991. *Imagined Communities*. London: Verso.

Atger, F. 1906. *Essai sur l'histoire des doctrines du contrat social*. Paris: Alcan.

Atienza, M. and J.R. Manero. 1998. *A Theory of Legal Sentences*. Dordrecht: Kluwer.

Atkinson, D. 1995. 'Insuring the Future? The Bill of Rights', in S. Friedman and D. Atkinson (eds), *The Small Miracle: South Africa's Negotiated Settlement*. Johannesburg: Ravan Press, pp. 121–47.

Balibar, E. and I. Wallerstein. 1988. *Race, nation, class. Les identités ambiguës*. Paris: La Découverte.

Barbera, A. 1997. 'Le basi filosofiche del costituzionalismo', in A. Barbera (ed.), *Le basi filosofiche del costituzionalismo*. Bari: Laterza, pp. 3–42.

Barchiesi, F. 1999. *Socio-Economic Exploitation, Meaning Contestation, and the TRC Foundation for a Discourse of Social Citizenship in Post-apartheid South Africa*. Johannesburg: University of Witwatersrand.

Barile, P. 1966. 'Potere costituente', in *Novissimo digesto italiano*. Turin: Utet, pp. 443–50.

Barile, P. and U. de Siervo. 1968. 'Revisione della Costituzione', in *Novissimo digesto italiano*. Turin: Utet.

Bartole, S. 1993. *Riforme costituzionali nell'Europa centro-orientale, Da satelliti comunisti a democrazie sovrane*. Bologna: Il Mulino.

Bartole, S. and P. Grilli di Cortona (eds). 1998. *Transizioni e consolidamento democratico nell'Europa centro-orientale*. Turin: Giappichelli.

Barton, G.A. 1981. 'Standards for the Acceptance of a Plea of Guilty – A Comparative Evaluation of Section 112(1)(b) of Act 51 of 1977 (Part. I)', *South African Journal of Criminal Law and Criminology* 5: 212–23.

———. 1982a. 'Standards for the Acceptance of a Plea of Guilty – A Comparative Evaluation of Section 112(1)(b) of Act 51 of 1977 (Part. II)', *South African Journal of Criminal Law and Criminology* 6: 46–61.

———. 1982b. 'Standards for the Acceptance of a Plea of Guilty – A Comparative Evaluation of Section 112(1)(b) of Act 51 of 1977 (Part. III)', *South African Journal of Criminal Law and Criminology* 6: 158–67.

Bassiouni, C.M. (ed.). 2001. *Post-conflict Justice*. Ardsley: Transnational Publishers.

Beaud, O. 1994. *La Puissance de l'Etat*. Paris: Presses Universitaires de France.

Beaudoin, G.A. and E. Mendes. 1996. *The Canadian Charter of Rights and Freedoms*. Toronto: Carswell.

Bederida, F. 1996. *Touvier le dossier de l'accusation*. Paris: Seuil.

Beinart, W. 1992. 'Political and Collective Violence in Southern African Historiography', *Journal of Southern African Studies* 18: 455–86.

______. 1994. *Twentieth-Century South Africa*. Oxford: Oxford University Press.

Bekker, P.M. 1996. 'Plea Bargaining in the United States of America and South Africa', *The Comparative and International Journal of Southern Africa* 29(1): 168–222.

Belfiglio, V. J. 1983. 'How Will Majority Rule Come About in Azania/South Africa?', *Journal of Modern African Studies* 21(3): 509–21.

Bennun, M.E. 1993. 'Boipatong and After: Reflections on the Politics of Violence in South Africa', *International Journal of the Sociology of Law* 21: 49–72.

______. 2003. 'Amnesty and International Law', in C. Villa-Vicencio and E. Doxtader (eds), *The Provocations of Amnesty: Memory, Justice and Impunity*. Claremont: David Philip, pp. 92–115.

Benson, M. 1994. *Now Is the Time: A Personal Account of South Africa's Historic Transition from Apartheid to Democracy*. Sydney: Australian Broadcasting Corporation.

Bentivegna, R. 1996. *Operazione via Rasella. Verità e menzogna: i protagonisti del racconto*. Rome: Editori Riuniti.

Beresford, S. and A.S. Muller. 2001. 'The Special Court for Sierra Leone: An Initial Comment', *Leiden Journal of International Law* 3(14): 635–52.

Berou, N. 1986. 'La confession dans les écrits théologiques et pastoraux du XIIIeme siècle: médication de l'âme ou démarche judiciaire?', in *L'Aveu. Antiquité et Moyen Age*. Rome: Ecole Française de Rome, pp. 261–82.

Bhargava, A. 2002. 'Defining Political Crimes: A Case Study of the South African Truth and Reconciliation Commission', *Columbia Law Review*, 1304–39.

Bianchi, E. (ed.). 2001. *Regole monastiche d'occidente*. Turin: Einaudi.

Biscaretti di Ruffià, P. 1946. *La Costituzione dell'Unione del Sud-Africa*. Florence: Sansoni.

______. 1988. *Introduzione al Diritto costituzionale comparato*. Milan: Giuffrè.

Bobbio, N. 1980. *Il Contratto sociale oggi*. Naples: Guida.

Bognetti, G. 1998. *Lo spirito del costituzionalismo americano*. Turin: Giappichelli.

______. 2000. *Lo spirito del costituzionalismo americano*. Turin: Giappichelli.

Bohler-Muller, N. 2000. 'What the Equality Courts Can Learn from Gilligan's Ethic of Care: A Novel Approach', *South African Journal on Human Rights* 16(4): 623–41.

Bollyky, T.J. 2002. 'Balancing Private Rights and Public Obligations: Constitutionally Mandate Compulsory Licensing of HIV/Aids Related Treatment in South Africa', *South African Journal on Human Rights* 18: 530–69.

Bonanate, U. (ed.). 1975. *I Puritani. I soldati della Bibbia*. Turin: Einaudi.
Bonazzi, T. 1998. 'Civic Nation and Ethnic Nation', in A. Krasteva (ed.), *Communities and Identities*. Sophia: Petekston, pp. 64–85.
______. 1999. *La Dichiarazione di indipendenza degli Stati Uniti d'America*. Milan: Marsilio.
______. (ed.). 2003. *Riconoscimento ed esclusione. Forme storiche e dibattiti contemporanei*. Rome: Carocci.
Bonvecchio, C. 2000. 'Il mito dell'unità e il destino della differenza', in U. Regina (ed.), *La libertà nell'unità delle differenze*. Padua: Il poligrafico, pp. 147–60.
Boraine, A. 2001. *A Country Unmasked: Inside South Africa's Truth Commission*. Oxford: Oxford University Press.
Boraine, A. and J. Levy (eds). 1995. *The Healing of a Nation?* Cape Town: Justice in Transition.
Borer, T.A. 2003. 'A Taxonomy of Victims and Perpetrators: Human Rights and Reconciliation in South Africa', *Human Rights Quarterly* 25(4): 1088–116.
Bossy, J. 1975. 'The Social History of Confession in the Age of the Reformation', *Transactions of the Royal Historical Society* 25: 21–38.
______. 1998. *Dalla Comunità all'individuo. Per una storia sociale dei sacramenti nell'Europa moderna*. Turin: Einaudi.
Botha, C.J. 1994. 'Interpretation of the Constitution', *South African Public Law* 9: 257–63.
Botman, R. and R. Petersen. 1996. *To Remember and to Heal. Theological and Psychological Reflections on the TRC*. Cape Town: Human and Rousseau.
Boulle, L.J. 1984a. *Constitutional Reform and the Apartheid State: Legitimacy, Consociationalism, and Control in South Africa*. New York: St. Martin's Press.
______. 1984b. *South Africa and the Consociational Option. A Constitutional Analysis*. Johannesburg: Juta.
Bourgi, A. 2002. 'L'évolution du constitutionnalisme en Afrique: du formalisme à l'effectivité', *Revue françiase de droit constitutionnel* 52: 721–48.
Bramble, T. and F. Barchiesi. 2003. *Rethinking the Labour Movement in the 'New South Africa'*. Aldershot: Ashgate.
Braude, C. and D. Spitz. 1997. 'Memory and the Spectre of International Justice: A Comment on AZAPO', *South African Journal on Human Rights* 13(2): 259–69.
Brooks, P. 1996. 'Storytelling without Fear? Confession in Law and Literature', *Journal of Legal Hermeneutics/Annuario di ermeneutica giuridica*, 277–91.
______. 2000. *Troubling Confessions: Speaking Guilt in Law and Literature*. Chicago: Chicago University Press.

Buergenthal, T. 1994. 'The United Nations Truth Commission for El Salvador', *Vanderbilt Journal of Transnational Law* 27(3): 497–544.

Burdeau, G., F. Hamon and M. Troper. 1995. *Droit Constitutionnel*. Paris: Librairie Générale de Droit et de Jurisprudence.

Burger, M. and C. Gould. 2002. *Secrets and Lies: Wouter Basson and South Africa's Chemical and Biological Warfare Programme*. Cape Town: Zebra Press.

Buur, L. 1999. 'Monumental History: Visibility and Invisibility in the Work of the TRC', *TRC: Commissioning the Past Conference, Johannesburg, 11–14 June 1999*. Johannesburg: University of Witwatersrand.

Calamandrei, P. 1939. 'Il giudice e lo storico', *Rivista di diritto processuale civile* 17: 105–28.

Cameron-Dow, J. 1994. *The Miracle of a Freed Nation (South Africa 1990–1994)*. Cape Town: Don Nelson.

Campagna, L. 1998. *Gli opposti sentieri del costituzionalismo*. Bologna: Il Mulino.

Canosa, R. 1999. *Storia dell'epurazione in Italia. Le sanzioni contro il fascismo 1943–1948*. Milan: Baldini & Castoldi.

Carducci, M. 1999. *Il costituzionalismo 'parallelo' delle nuove democrazie. Africa e America Latina*. Milan: Giuffrè.

Carozza, P. 1994. 'Nazione', in *Digesto delle discipline pubblicistiche*. Turin: Utet, pp. 126–59.

Carpenter, G. 1994. 'The Republic of South Africa Constitution Act 200 of 1993: An Overview', *South African Public Law* 9: 222–32.

———. 1996. 'The South African Constitutional Court: Taking Stock of the Early Decisions', *The Human Rights and Constitutional Law Journal of Southern Africa* 1(1): 24–31.

Cassel, D. 1993. 'International Truth Commissions and Justice', *The Aspen Institute Quarterly* 5(3): 77–90.

Cassin, B. 2001. 'Politiques de la mémoire. Des traitements de la haine', *Multitudes* 3(6): 177–96. Retrieved 31 March 2008 from http://multitudes.samizdat.net/Politiques-de-la-memoire.

Cassin, B., O. Cayla and P. Salazar (eds). 2004. *Vérité, réconciliation, réparation*. Paris: Le Seuil.

Cayla, O. 1999. 'La chose et son contraire (et son contraire, etc.)', *Les Etudes philosophiques* 3: 291–310.

———. 2004. 'Aveu et fondement du droit', in B. Cassin, O. Cayla and P. Salazar (eds), *Vérité, réconciliation, réparation*. Paris: Le Seuil, pp. 89–110.

Cerri, A. 1991. 'Revisione costituzionale', in *Enciclopedia Giuridica*. Rome: Treccani.

Chapman, R.A. and P. Ball. 2001. 'The Truth of Truth Commissions: Comparative Lessons from Haiti, South Africa, and Guatemala', *Human Rights Quarterly* 23(1): 1–43.

Chaskalson, M. and D. Davis. 1997. 'Constitutionalism, the Rule of Law, and the First Certification Judgement: ex Parte Chairperson of the Constitutional Assembly in Re: Certification of the Constitution of the Republic of South Africa 1996', *South African Journal on Human Rights* 13(3): 430–45.

Chataigner, J.M. 2001. 'L'ONU et la Sierra Leone: d'une crise à l'autre (mai 1997–mai 2000)', *Afrique Contemporaine* 198: 29–50.

Cheadle, H., D.M. Davis and N.R.L. Haysom (eds). 2002. *South African Constitutional Law: The Bill of Rights*. Durban: Butterworths.

Chevallier, J. 1999. *l'État de droit*. Paris: Montchrestien.

Chiffoleau, J. 1986. 'Sur la pratique et la conjoncture de l'aveu judiciaire en France du XIII au XV siècle', in *L'Aveu. Antiquité et Moyen Age*. Rome: Ecole Française de Rome, pp. 341–80.

______. 1990. 'Dire l'indicible. Remarques sur la catégorie du "nefandum" du XII–XV siècle', *Les Annales* 2: 289–324.

Choudhry, S. 1999. 'Globalization in Search of Justification: Towards a Theory of Comparative Constitutional Interpretation', *Indiana Law Journal* 74: 819–92.

Christie, K. 2000. *The South African Truth and Reconciliation Commission*. Basingstoke: Macmillan.

Claassen, R. 1996. 'Principles of Restorative Justice', *Conciliation Quarterly* 15(3): 6.

Clarke, C.T. 1999. 'Message in a Bottle for Unknowing Defenders: Strategic Plea Negotiations Persist in South African Criminal Courts', *The Comparative and International Law Journal of Southern Africa* 32: 141–68.

Codrer, H. 1994. 'Towards a South African Constitution', *The Modern Law Review* 57(4): 491–533.

Coetzee, M. 2003. 'An Overview of the TRC Amnesty Process', in C. Villa-Vicencio and E. Doxtader (eds), *The Provocations of Amnesty: Memory, Justice and Impunity*. Claremont: David Philip, pp. 181–95.

Colvin, C.J. 2000. *We Are Still Struggling: Story-telling, Reparation and Reconciliation after the TRC*. Cape Town: Centre for the Study of Violence and Reconciliation.

Commission of Enquiry into Complaints by Former African National Congress Prisoners and Detainees Report. 1992. Cape Town: University of the Western Cape.

Conan, M. 2001. 'Amnistie présidentielle et tradition', *Revue du droit public* 5: 1305–56.

Cordero, F. 1988. 'La Confessione nel quadro decisorio', in L. de Cataldo Neuburger (ed.), *La giustizia penale e la fluidità del sapere: ragionamento sul metodo*. Padua: CEDAM, pp. 53–64.

Cunneen, C. 2002. 'Restorative Justice and the Politics of Decolonisation', in E.G.M. Weitekamp and H.J. Kerner (eds), *Restorative Justice. Theoretical Foundation*. Portland: Willan Publishing, pp. 32–49.

Cuya, E. 1996. 'Las Comisiones de la Verdad en América Latina', Ko'aga Roñe'eta 3. Retrieved 31 March 2008 from http://www.derechos.org/koaga/iii/1/cuya.html.

Daeninckx, D. and V. Staraselski. 1998. *Au nom de la loi*. Paris: Parole d'Aube.

Damaška, M.J. 1986. *The Face of Justice and State Authority*. New Haven: Yale University Press.

Darbon, D. (ed.). 1995. *Ethnicité et nation en Afrique du Sud. Imageries identitaires et enjeux sociaux*. Paris: Karthala.

______. 1995. 'Les enjeux du "droit des groupes" dans la négociation constitutionnelle en Afrique du Sud', in G. Conac, F. Dreyfus and J.O. Monteiro (eds), *L'Afrique du Sud en Transition*. Paris: Economica, pp. 133–92.

Davenport, T.R.H. 1991. *South Africa: A Modern History*. London: MacMillan.

______. 1998. *The Birth of a New South Africa*. Toronto: University of Toronto Press.

Davenport, T.R.H. and C. Saunders. 2000. *South Africa. A Modern History*. London: MacMillan.

De Grounchy, J.W. 1993. 'Guilt, Amnesty and National Reconstruction', *Journal of Theology for Southern Africa*, 3–14.

De Lange, J. 2000. 'The Historical Context, Legal Origins and Philosophical Foundation of the South African TRC', in C. Villa-Vicencio and W. Verwoerd (eds), *Looking Back Reaching Forward*. Cape Town: Cape Town University Press, pp. 14–31.

De Vergottini, G. (ed.). 1978. *Una costituzione democratica per la Spagna*. Milan: Franco Angeli.

______. 1977. *Le origini della seconda repubblica portoghese. 1974–1976*. Milan: Giuffrè.

______. (ed.). 1997. *Costituzione ed emergenza in America Latina*. Turin: Giappichelli.

______. 1998. *Le transizioni costituzionali*. Bologna: Il Mulino.

______. 2004. *Diritto costituzionale comparato*. Padua: CEDAM.

De Ville, J. 2000. *Constitutional and Statutory Interpretation*. Cape Town: Interdoc Consultants.

Degenaar, J. 1993. 'Nosizwe: the Myth of the Nation', *Indicator South Africa* 10(3): 11–16.

Delumeau, J. 1983. *Le péché et la peur. La culpabilisation en Occident XIII–XVIII siècle*. Paris: Fayard.

______. 1990. *L'aveu et le pardon. Les difficultés de la confession XIII–XVIII siècle*. Paris: Fayard.

Demandt, A. 1990. *Macht und Recht. Grosse Prozesse in der Geschichte*. Munich: Verlag C.H. Beck.

Desai, A. 2002. *We Are the Poors. Community Struggles in Post-apartheid South Africa*. New York: Monthly Review Press.

Devenish, G.E. 1999a. *A Commentary on the South African Bill of Rights*. Durban: Butterworths.

______. 1999b. 'Minority Rights and Cultural Pluralism. The Protection of Languages and Cultural Identity in the 1996 Constitution', *Tydskrif vir Hedendaagse Romains-Hollandese* 62: 201–25.

Dogliani, M. 1986. *Potere costituente: seminario di diritto costituzionale*. Turin: Giappichelli.

______. 1989. 'Costituente (potere)', in *Digesto delle discipline pubblicistiche*. Turin: Utet, pp. 281–87.

______. 1994. *Introduzione al diritto costituzionale*. Bologna: Il Mulino.

Domb, F. 1994. 'Treatment of War Crimes in Peace Settlements. Prosecution or Amnesty?', *Israel Yearbook on Human Rights* 24: 253–67.

Doxtader, E. 2003. 'Easy to Forget or Never (Again) Hard to Remember? History, Memory and the 'Publicity' of Amnesty', in C. Villa-Vicencio and E. Doxtader (eds), *The Provocations of Amnesty, Memory, Justice and Impunity*. Claremont: David Philip, pp. 121–56.

Dreyfus, F. 1994. 'La Constitution Intérimaire d'Afrique du Sud', *Revue Française de Droit Constitutionnel* 19: 465–95.

Du Bois-Pedain, A. 2004. 'Was Amnesty a Lottery? An Empirical Study of the Decision of the TRC's Committee on Amnesty', *South African Law Journal* 121(4): 785–828.

______. 2007. *Transitional Amnesty in South Africa*. Oxford: Oxford University Press.

Du Plessis, L. 1992. *An Introduction to Law*. Cape Town: Juta.

______. 1996. 'Evaluative Reflections on the Final Text of South Africa's Bill of Rights', *Stellenbosch Law Review* 7: 283–305.

______. 1998. 'Statutory Multilingualism and Textual Conflict Under the 1996 Constitution', *Tydskrif vir Hedendaagse Romains-Hollandese* 61: 276–84.

______. 1999. 'South Africa. Report on Language and Law', in E. Jaime (ed.), *Langue et Droit. XV Congrée International de Droit Comparé*. Brussels: Bruylant, pp. 44–51.

______. 2002. 'Legal and Constitutional Means Designed to Facilitate the Integration of Diverse Cultures in South Africa: a Provisional Assessment', *Stellenbosch Law Review* 3: 367–86.

Du Plessis, L. and H. Corder. 1994. *Understanding South Africa's Transitional Bill of Rights*. Cape Town: Juta.

Du Plessis, M. 2000. 'The Legitimacy of Judicial Review in South Africa's New Constitutional Dispensation: Insights from the Canadian Experience', *The Comparative and International Law Journal of Southern Africa* 33: 227–47.

Du Toit, A. 1983. 'No Chosen People: The Myth of the Calvinist Origins of Afrikaner Nationalism and Racial Ideology', *American Historical Review* 88: 920–95.

______. 1998. *Confession and Reconciliation. A Challenge to the Churches in South Africa*. Pretoria: Research Institute for Theology and Religion.

Dugard, J. 1973. *The South Africa/Namibia Dispute*. Berkeley: University of California Press.

______. 1978. *Human Rights and the South African Legal Order*. Princeton: Princeton University Press.

Dulong, R. 1998. *Le témoin oculaire. Les conditions sociales de l'attestation personnelle*. Paris: Ehess.

______. 2000. 'Le silence comme aveu et le droit au silence', *Langage et société*, 25–44.

______. (ed.). 2001. *L'Aveu. Histoire, sociologie, philosophie*. Paris: Presses Universitaires de France.

Dulong, R. and J.M. Maradin. 2001. 'Analyse des dimension constitutive de l'aveu en réponse à une accusation', in R. Dulong (ed.), *L'Aveu. Histoire, sociologie, philosophie*. Paris: Presses Universitaires de France, pp. 135–79.

Dumay, J.M. 1998. *Le procés de Maurice Papon*. Paris: Fayard.

Dunbar-Moodie, T. 1975. *The Rise of Afrikanerdom: Power, Apartheid, and the Civil Religion*. Berkeley: Berkeley University Press.

Duso, G. (ed.). 1993. *Il contratto sociale nella filosofia politica moderna*. Milan: Franco Angeli.

Duval, A. 1974. 'Le concile de Trente et la confession', *Maison-Dieu* 118: 131–80.

Dyzenhaus, D. 1998. *Truth, Reconciliation and the Apartheid Legal Order*. Cape Town: Juta.

Ebrahim, H. 1998. *The Soul of a Nation. Constitution Making in South Africa*. London: Oxford University Press.

Ellmann, S. 1994. 'The South African Constitution and Ethnic Division', *Columbia Human Rights Law Review* 5–44.

Eloff, T. 1994. 'The Process of Giving Birth', in B. de Villiers (ed.), *Birth of Constitution*. Cape Town: Juta, pp. 12–20.

Elster, J. 1996. 'Constitution Making in Eastern Europe: Rebuilding the Boat in the Open Sea', in G. Zagrebelsky, P.P. Portinaro and J. Luther (eds), *Il futuro della Costituzione*. Einaudi: Turin, pp. 209–28.

______. 2004. *Closing the Books. Transitional Justice in Historical Perspective*. Cambridge: Cambridge University Press.

Ely, J. 1980. *Democracy and Distrust: A Theory of Judicial Review*. Cambridge: Harvard University Press.

English, R. 1996. 'Ubuntu: The Quest for an Indigenous Jurisprudence', *South African Journal on Human Rights* 12(4): 641–48.

Ensalco, M. 1994. 'Truth Commissions for Chile and El Salvador: A Report and Assessment', *Human Rights Quarterly* 16: 656–75.

Erasmus, M.G. 2000. 'The Impact of the Namibian Constitution on the Nature of the State, Its Politics and Society: The Record after Ten Years', in O. Manfred et al., *The Constitution at Work. 10 Years of Namibian*

Nationhood. Windhoek: University of Namibia Press, Oxford African Book Collective, pp. 5–25.

Eusebi, L. (ed.). 1989. *La funzione della pena: il commiato da Kant e da Hegel*. Milan: Giuffrè.

Eusebi, L. and A. Acerbi (eds). 1998. *Colpa e pena? La teologia di fronte alla questione criminale*. Milan: Vita e pensiero.

Federico, V. 2003. 'La cittadinanza nell'esperienza sudafricana', *Quaderni costituzionali* 1: 113–43.

Feeley, M.M. 1979. 'Perspective on Plea Bargaining', *Law & Society Review* 13: 199–209.

______. 1982. 'Plea Bargaining and Structure of the Criminal Process', *Justice System Journal* 7: 338–55.

Fernandez, L. 1996. 'Possibilities and Limitations of Reparations for the Victims of Human Rights Violations in South Africa', in M.R. Rwelamira and G. Werle (eds), *Confronting Past Injustices. Approaches to Amnesty, Punishment, Reparation and Restitution in South Africa and Germany*. Durban: Butterworths.

Ferrajoli, L. 1989. *Diritto e ragione. Teoria del garantismo penale*. Bari: Laterza.

Finkielkraut, A. 1989. *La mémoire vaine. Du crime contre l'humanité*. Paris: Gallimard.

Fiorelli, P. 1953. *La Tortura giudiziaria nel diritto comune*. Milan: Giuffrè.

______. 1961. 'La Confessione (Storia)', in *Enciclopedia del Diritto*. Milan: Giuffrè.

Fontana, D. 2001. 'Refined Comparativism in Constitutional Law', *UCLA Law Review* 49: 539–623.

Forsthoff, E. 1964. *Rechtsstaat im Wandel*. Stuttgart: Kohlhammer.

______. 1968. *Rechtsstaatlichkeit und Sozialstaatlichkeit. Aufsätze und Essay*. Darmstadt: Wissenschaftliche Buch Gesellschaft.

Foucault, M. 1975. *Surveiller et punir. Naissance de la prison*. Paris: Gallimard.

______. 1988. *Technologies of the Self: A Seminar with Michel Foucault*. Amherst: University of Massachusetts Press.

Freeman, M. 2003. 'Lessons Learned: Practical Lessons Gleaned from Inside the Truth Commissions of Guatemala and South Africa', *Human Rights Quarterly* 25(4): 1117–49.

______. 2006. *Truth Commissions and Procedural Fairness*. Cambridge: Cambridge University Press.

Friedman, S. 1993. *The Long Journey: South Africa's Quest for a Negotiated Settlement*. Braamfontein: Ravan Press.

Friedman, S. and D. Atkinson (eds). 1994. *The Small Miracle. South Africa's Negotiated Settlement*. Johannesburg: Ravan Press.

Friedrich, C. 1968. 'Constitutions and Constitutionalism', in David L. Sills (ed.), *International Encyclopedia of the Social Sciences*. New York: Macmillan and Free Press, pp. 318–26.

Fronza, E. 1999. 'Profili penalistici del negazionismo', *Rivista italiana di diritto e procedura penale* 42(3): 1034–74.
Furet, F. 1988. *La Révolution 1770–1870*. Paris: Hachette.
Gaddes, B. 1996. 'Initiation of New Democratic Institutions in Eastern Europe and Latin America', in A. Lijphart and C.H. Waisman (eds), *Institutional Design in New Democracies. Eastern Europe and Latin America*. Boulder: Westview Press.
Galli, C. (ed.). 1986. *Carl Schmitt. Scritti su Thomas Hobbes*. Milan: Giuffrè.
______. 1996. *Genealogia della politica. Carl Schmitt e la crisi del pensiero politico moderno*. Bologna: Il Mulino.
______. 1998. 'Immagine e rappresentanza politica', in C. Galli, *Modernità. Categorie e profili critici*. Bologna: Il Mulino, pp. 53–78.
Galtier, P. 1951. *Aux origines du sacrement de penitence*. Rome: Università Gregoriana.
Gandini, J.J. 1999. *Le procès Papon. Histoire d'une ignominie au service de l'Etat*. Paris: Libro.
Garapon, A. 1997. *Bien Juger. Essai sur le rituel judiciaire*. Paris: Odile Jacob.
______. 2005. *Crimini che non si possono né punire né perdonare. L'emergere di una giustizia internazionale*. Bologna: Il Mulino.
Garkawe, S. 2003. 'The South African Truth and Reconciliation Commission: A Suitable Model to Enhance the Role and Rights of the Victims of Gross Violations of Human Rights?', *Melbourne University Law Review* 27: 334–80.
Gastrow, P. 1995. *Bargaining for Peace. South Africa and the National Peace Accord*. Washington, DC: United States Institute for Peace Press.
Gauchet, M. 1995. *La Révolution des pouvoirs. La souveraineté, le peuple et la représentation 1789–1799*. Paris: Presses Universitaires de France.
Gaudemet, P.M. 1989. 'Paul Laband et la doctrine française de droit public', *Revue de Droit Public* 4: 957.
Gentili, A.M. 1995. 'Etnia, etnicità e rappresentazioni del conflitto etnico in Africa', *Africa e Mediterraneo* 2: 4–11.
______. 2004. 'Apartheid', in N. Bobbio, N. Matteucci and N. Pasquino (eds), *Dizionario di politica*. Turin: Utet, pp. 37–40.
Gentili, A.M. and A. Lollini. 2000. 'L'esperienza delle Commissioni per la Verità e la Riconciliazione: il caso sudafricano in una prospettiva giuridico – politica', in G. Illuminati, L. Stortoni and M. Virgilio (eds), *Crimini internazionali tra diritto e giustizia: dai Tribunali internazionali alle Commissioni verità e riconciliazioni*. Turin: Giappichelli, pp. 163–216.
Giliomee, H. and L. Schlemmer. 1989. *From Apartheid to Nation Building*. Cape Town: Oxford University Press.
Ginzburg, C. 1991. *Il giudice e lo storico. Considerazioni a margine del processo Sofri*. Turin: Einaudi.
______. 2000. *Rapporti di forza: storia, retorica, prova*. Milan: Feltrinelli.

Gloppen, S. 1997. *South Africa: The Battle Over the Constitution*. Aldershot: Dartmouth.

Goldblatt, B. and S. Liebenberg. 2004. 'Giving Money to Children: the State's Constitutional Obligation to Provide Child Support Grants to Child Headed Households', *South African Journal on Human Rights* 20: 151–64.

Goldhagen, D.J. 1997. *I volenterosi carnefici di Hitler. I tedeschi comuni e l'Olocausto*. Milan: Mondadori.

Goldstone, R. 1996. 'Justice as a Tool for Peace-Making: Truth Commission and International Criminal Trials', *Journal of International Law and Politics* 28(3): 485–503.

Gonidec, P.F. 1996a. 'Constitutionnalismes Africains', *Revue juridique et politique indépendance et coopération* 50: 23–50.

———. 1996b. *Les systèmes politiques africains*. Paris: Librairie Générale de Droit et de Jurisprudence.

Gough, J.W. 1956. *The Social Contract. A Critical Study of Its Development*. Oxford: Clarendon Press.

Gozzi, G. 1999. *Democrazia e Diritti. Germania: dallo Stato di diritto alla democrazia costituzionale*. Bari: Laterza.

———. 2002. 'Stato di diritto e diritti soggettivi nella storia costituzionale tedesca', in P. Costa and D. Zolo (eds), *Lo Stato di diritto. Storia, teoria, critica*. Milan: Feltrinelli, pp. 260–83.

Grasso, P.G. 1985. 'Potere costituente', in *Enciclopedia del diritto*. Milan: Giuffrè.

Greenawalt, K. 2000. 'Amnesty's Justice', in R.I. Rotberg and D. Thompson (eds), *Truth v. Justice. The Morality of Truth Commissions*. Princeton: Princeton University Press, pp. 189–210.

Greilsamer, L. and D. Schnaidermann. 1994. *Un certain Monsieur Paul*. Paris: Fayard.

Griffin, S.M. 1996. *American Constitutionalism*. Princeton: Princeton University Press.

Gross, A.M. 2004. 'The Constitution, Reconciliation, and Transitional Justice: Lessons from South Africa and Israel', *Stanford Journal of International Law* 40: 47–99.

Gy, P.M. 1974. 'Le précepte de la confession annuelle (Latran IV, C. 21) et la détection des hérétiques Saint Bonaventure et Saint Thomas contre Raymond de Peñafort', *Revue des Sciences philosophiques et théologiques, Revue des Sciences Philosophiques et Théologiques* 444–50.

———. 1979. 'Le précepte de la confession annuelle et la nécessité de la confession', *Revue de Sciences Philosophiques et Théologiques* 529–47.

Habermas, J. 1996. *Die Eineziehung des Anderen. Studien zur politischen Theorie*. Frankfurt am Main: Suhrkamp Verlag.

Hahlo, H.R. 1960. *The Union of South Africa: The Development of Its Laws and Constitution*. London: Stevens & Sons.

Hahlo, H.R. and E. Kahne. 1991. *The South African Legal System and Its Background*. Cape Town: Juta.
Halbwachs, M. 1925. *Les cadres sociaux de la mémoire*. Paris: Albin Michel.
______. 1950. *La mémoire collective*. Paris: Albin Michel.
Haller, M.H. 1979. 'Plea Bargaining: The Nineteenth Century Context', *Law & Society Review* 13: 273–79.
Hamber, B. 1998. 'Repairing the Irreparable: Dealing with Double-Binds of Making Reparation for Crimes of the Past', *Comparisons and Transitions, 14–16 September 1998*. London: University of London.
Harding, S.K. 2003. 'Comparative Reasoning and Judicial Review', *The Yale Journal of International Law* 28(2): 409–64.
Hart, H.L.A. 1994. *The Concept of Law*. Oxford: Oxford University Press.
Hauriou, M. 1965. *Précis de droit constitutionnel*. Paris: Centre National de la Recherche Scientifique.
Hayner, P. 1994. 'Fifteen Truth Commissions – 1974 to 1994: A Comparative Study', *Human Rights Quarterly* 16(4): 597–655.
______. 1998. 'The Contribution of Truth Commissions', in B. Duner (ed.), *An End to Torture. Strategies for Its Eradication*. London: Zed Books, pp. 203–21.
Haysom, N. 1991. 'Democracy, Constitutionalism and ANC's Bill of Rights for a New South Africa', *South African Journal of Human Rights* 7: 102–09.
Heather, D. 1999. *South Africa Reborn: Building a New Democracy*. London: UCL.
Heller, H. 1971. *Gesammelte Schriften, II: Recht, Staat, Macht*. Leiden: Sijthoff.
Hexham, I. 1981. *The Irony of Apartheid: The Struggle for National Independence of Afrikaner Calvinist against British Imperialism*. New York: Edwin Mellon Press.
Hobsbawn, E. and T. Ranger. 1983. *The Invention of Tradition*. Cambridge: Cambridge University Press.
Horowitz, D.L. 1991. *A Democratic South Africa? Constitutional Engineering in a Divided Society*. Berkeley: University of California Press.
Humphries, R., T. Rapoo and S. Friedman. 1994. 'The Shape of the Country: Negotiating Regional Government', in S. Friedman and D. Atkinson (eds), *The Small Miracle. South Africa's Negotiated Settlement*. Johannesburg: Ravan Press, pp. 148–81.
Huyse, L. 1995a. 'Justice after Transitions: On the Choices Successor Elites Make in Dealing With the Past', in N. Kritz (ed.), *Transitional Justice. How Emerging Democracies Reckon With Former Regimes*. Washington, DC: United Institute of Peace Press, pp. 104–15.
______. 1995b. 'On the Choices Successor Elites Make in Dealing With the Past', in N. Kritz (ed.), *Transitional Justice. How Emerging Democracies Reckon with Former Regimes*. Washington, DC: United Institute of Peace Press, pp. 337–49.

______. 1996a. 'Justice after Transition', in J. Dugard and C. van Wyngaert (eds), *International Criminal Law and Procedure*. Aldershot: Dartmouth, pp. 495–522.

______. 1996b. 'Justice after Transition: On the Choices Successor Elites Make in Dealing with the Past', in A.J. Jongman (ed.), *Contemporary Genocides: Causes, Cases, Consequences*. Leiden: PIOOM, pp. 187–214.

Huyse, L. and E. van Dael. 2001. *Justice après des graves violations de droits de l'homme. Le choix entre l'amnistie, la commission de la vérité et les poursuites pénales*. Leuven: University of Leuven.

Igounet, V. 2000. *Histoire du négationnisme en France*. Paris: Seuil.

Jackson, V.C. 1999. 'Ambivalent Resistance and Comparative Constitutionalism: Opening up the Conversation on "Proportionality" Rights and Federalism', *University of Pennsylvania Journal of Constitutional Law* 583–639.

Jagwanth, S. 2002. 'The Constitutional Roles and Responsibilities of Lower Courts', *South African Journal on Human Rights* 18: 201–24.

Jaspers, K. 1990. *La culpabilité allemande*. Paris: Minuit.

Jaume, L. 2007 'Constituent Power in France: The Revolution and its Consequences', in M. Loughlin and N. Walker (eds), *The Paradox of Constitutionalism: Constituent Power and Constitutional Form*. Oxford: Oxford University Press, pp. 67–86.

Jeffery, A. 2000. *The Truth about the Truth Commission*. Johannesburg: Institute of Race Relations.

Jenkins, C. 2000. 'The Dilemmas of Reparation and Reconstruction in South Africa', *South African Journal on Human Rights* 16: 415–85.

Johnson, R.W. and L. Schlemmer. 1996. *Launching Democracy in South Africa. The First Open Election, April 1994*. New Haven: Yale University Press.

Jones, H., K. Östberg and N. Randeraad (eds). 2007. *Contemporary History on Trial*. Manchester: Manchester University Press.

Jung, C. and I. Shapiro. 1995. 'South Africa's Negotiated Transition Democracy, Opposition and the New Constitutional Order', *Politics and Society* 23(3): 269–308.

Kamwamgamalu, N. 1998. 'Aspects of Multilingualism in Post-Apartheid South Africa', *Journal of Cross-Cultural and Interlanguage Communication* 17(2/3): 119–328.

Kattago, S. 2001. *Ambiguous Memory. The Nazi Past and German National Identity*. London: Praeger.

Kaufmann, A. 2000. 'Gustav Radbruch und die Radbruchsche Formel. Brief an meinen Enkel FinnBaumann', *Rechtshistorisches Journal* 604–11.

Kaye, M. 1997. 'The Role of Truth Commissions in the Search for Justice, Reconciliation and Democratisation: The Salvadorian and Honduran Cases', *Journal of Latin American Studies* 29(3): 693–716.

Keightley, R. 1993. 'Political Offences and Indemnity in South Africa', *South African Journal on Human Rights* 9: 334–57.

Kirkhheimer, O. 1961. *Political Justice. The Use of Legal Procedure for Political Ends*. Princeton: Princeton University Press.

Klaaren, J. 1998. 'The Truth and Reconciliation Commission, the South African Judiciary, and Constitutionalism', *African Studies* 5: 197–208.

———. 1999. 'A Second Organisational Amnesty?', *TRC: Commissioning the Past Conference, Johannesburg, 14 June 1999*. Johannesburg: University of Witwatersrand.

Klaaren, J. and H. Varney. 2003. 'A Second Bite at the Amnesty Cherry. Constitutional and Policy Issues around Legislation for a Second Amnesty', in C. Villa-Vicencio and E. Doxtader (eds), *The Provocations of Amnesty, Memory, Justice and Impunity*. Claremont: David Philip, pp. 265–93.

Klein, C. 1996. *Théorie et pratique du pouvoir constituant*. Paris: Presses Universitaires de France.

Klug, H. 2000. *Constituting Democracy. Law, Globalism and South Africa's Political Reconstruction*. Cambridge: Cambridge University Press.

Kollapen, N. 1993. 'Accountability: the Debate in South Africa', *Journal of African Law* 37(1): 1–9.

Koppe, K. 2003. *Wiedergutmachung für die Opfer von Menschenrechtsverletzungen in Südafrika*. Berlin: Berliner Wissenschafts-Verlag.

Kritz, N.J. (ed.). 1995. *Transitional Justice: How Emerging Democracies Reckon with Former Regimes*. Washington: United States Institute of Peace Press.

Krog, A. 1998. *Country of My Skull. Guilt, Sorrow, and the Limits of Forgiveness in the New South Africa*. New York: Random House.

Kuntz, W.F. 1988. *Criminal Sentencing in Three Nineteenth Century Cities: Social History of Punishment in New York, Boston and Philadelphia*. New York: Garland Publishers.

Kutz, F. 2001. *Amnestie für politische Straftäter in Südafrika*. Berlin: Arno Spitz GmgH.

Larry, A. (ed.). 1998. *Constitutionalism. Philosophical Foundations*. Cambridge: Cambridge University Press.

Lavenia, V. 2004. *L'infamia e il perdono. Tributi, pene e confessione nella teologia morale della prima età moderna*. Bologna: Il Mulino.

L'Aveu. Antiquité et Moyen Age. 1986. Rome: Ecole Française de Rome.

Lavroff, D.M. 1976. *Les systèmes constitutionnels en Afrique noire. Les Etats Francophones*. Paris: Pedone.

Lax, I. 2004a. 'Amnesty, Reparation and the Object of Reconciliation in the Context of South Africa's TRC', in C. Villa-Vicencio and. E. Doxtader (eds), *To Repair the Irreparable: Reparation and Reconstruction in South Africa*. Cape Town: David Philip, pp. 224–41.

———. 2004b. 'Le témoignage d'un commissaire. Juger les demandes d'amnistie et promouvoir la réconciliation', in B. Cassin, O. Cayla and

J.P. Salazar (eds), *Vérité, réconciliation, réparation*. Paris: Le Seuil, pp. 281–99.

Le Vine, V.T. 1997. 'The Fall and Rise of Constitutionalism in Africa', *The Journal of Modern African Studies* 35(2): 181–206.

Lea, H.C. 1911. *Storia della confessione auricolare*. Mendrisio: Cultura Moderna.

Lessay, F. 1988. *Souveraineté et légitimé chez Hobbes*. Paris: Presses Universitaires de France.

Levinson, S. 2000. 'Trials, Commissions, and Investigating Committee: The Elusive Search for Norms of Due Process', in R.I. Rotberg and D. Thompson (eds), *Truth v. Justice. The Morality of Truth Commissions*. Princeton: Princeton University Press, pp. 211–34.

Liebenberg, I. 1996. 'The Truth and Reconciliation Commission in South Africa: Context, Future and Some Imponderables', *South African Public Law* 11(1–2): 123–60.

Lijphart, A. 1984. *Democracy. Patterns of Majoritarian and Consensus Government in Twenty-one Countries*. New Haven: Yale University Press.

______. 1985. *Power Sharing in South Africa*. Berkeley: University of California Press.

______. 1987. 'Choosing an Electoral System for Democratic Elections in South Africa, an Evaluation of the "Principal Options"', *Critical Choices for South African Society* 2: 2–13.

______. 1989. 'The Ethnic Factors and Democratic Constitution Making in South Africa', in E.J. Keller and L.A. Picard (eds), *Domestic Change and International Conflict*. Boulder: Rienner, pp. 13–24.

______. 1991. 'Constitutional Choices for a New Democracy', *Journal of Democracy* 2(1): 72–84.

______. 1992. *Parliamentary Versus Presidential Government*. Oxford: Oxford University Press.

Lijphart, A. and C.H. Waisman (eds). 1996. *Institutional Design in New Democracies. Eastern Europe and Latin America*. Boulder: Westview Press.

Linton, S. 2001. 'Cambodia, East Timor and Sierra Leone: Experiments in International Justice', *Criminal Law Forum* 12: 185–202.

Lloyd, H.A. 1997. 'Le Constitutionnalisme', in J. Burns Handerson (ed.), *Histoire de la pensée politique moderne*. Paris: Presses Universitaires de France, pp. 230–69.

Lobban, M. 1997. 'Un accord négocié: le processus constitutionnel en Afrique du Sud depuis 1991', *Revue de droit public* 1: 71–110.

Lollini, A. 1998. 'Human Rights and Past Wrongs: the Constitutional Concepts of Truth and Reconciliation Commission in South Africa', in V. Piergigli and I. Taddia (eds), *International Conference on African Constitutions*. Turin: Giappichelli, pp. 97–106.

______. 1999. 'La construction d'une mémoire collective en Afrique du Sud. La Commission vérité et réconciliation: "hypertrophie de la sentence"

ou hypertrophie de l'histoire', *Astrée. Revue de Droit Pénal et Droits de l'Homme* 8: 25–30.
———. 2002. 'Reconstructing the Past between Trials and History: the TRC Experience as "Remembrance Space"', in *Quest: An African Journal of Philosophy* 16(1–2): 61–69.
———. 2003. 'Le processus de judiciarisation de la résolution des conflits: les alternatives', in E. Fronza and S. Manacorda (eds), *La justice pénale internationale dans les décisions des TPY ad hoc*. Milan: Giuffrè, pp. 312–27.
———. 2004a. 'La "giustizia di transizione": il principio del duty to prosecute come una nuova variabile di eterodeterminazione dei processi costituenti?', in G. Gozzi and F. Martelli (eds), *Guerre e minoranze. Diritti delle minoranze, conflitti interetnici e giustizia internazionale nella transizione alla democrazia nell'Europa Centro-Orientale*. Bologna: Il Mulino, pp. 323–62.
———. 2004b. 'L'isola e l'arcipelago: la Francia ed il Sudafrica post-apartheid come modelli antitetici di tutela costituzionale di lingue minoritarie e regionali', in A. Lollini (ed.), *Pluralismo linguistico e costituzioni. Un'analisi comparata*. Bolzano: Alpha-Beta, pp. 25–84.
———. 2004c. 'L'istituzione delle giurisdizioni Gacaca: giustizia post-genocidio e processo costituente in Ruanda', *Rivista di diritto pubblico comparato ed europeo* 3: 1513–41.
———. 2005. 'Pluralismo giuridico e ordinamento costituzionale: i Traditional Leaders nella Costituzione della Repubblica del Sudafrica', in S. Baldin (ed.), *Diritti tradizionali e religiosi in alcuni ordinamenti contemporanei*. Trieste: EUT, pp. 9–26.
———. 2007a. 'La circolazione degli argomenti: metodo comparato e parametri interpretativi extra-sistemici nella giurisprudenza costituzionale sudafricana', *Rivista di diritto pubblico comparato* 479–523.
———. 2007b. 'Legal Argumentation Based on Foreign Law. An Example from Case Law of the South African Constitutional Court', *Utrecht Law Review* 3(1): 60–74.
———. 2007c. 'Revisione e manutenzione della Costituzione sudafricana', in F. Palermo (ed.), *La "manutenzione" costituzionale*. Padua: CEDAM, pp. 405–35.
Lollini, A. and F. Palermo. 2009. 'Comparative Law and the "Proceduralization" of Constitution-building Processes', in J. Raue and P. Sutter (eds), *Facets and Practices of State-building*. Leiden: Brill/Martinus Nijhoff, pp. 301–26.
Loraux, N. 1997. *La cité divisée*. Paris: Payot & Rivages.
Loughlin, M. and N. Walker (eds). 2007. *The Paradox of Constitutionalism: Constituent Power and Constitutional Form*. Oxford: Oxford University Press.
Lussana, F. 2000. 'Memoria e memorie nel dibattito storiografico', *Studi Storici* 4: 1047–81.

McAdams, J.A. 2001. *Judging the Past in Unified Germany*. Cambridge: Cambridge University Press.
Macchi, O. 2001. 'Le fait d'avouer comme récit et comme événement dans l'enquête criminelle', in R. Dulong (ed.), *L'Aveu. Histoire, sociologie, philosophie*. Paris: Presses Universitaires de France, pp. 181–221.
McCrudden, C. 2000. 'A Common Law of Human Rights?: Transnational Judicial Conversations on Constitutional Rights', *Oxford Journal of Legal Studies* 20: 499–532.
McDonald, J.M. 2000. 'Sierra Leone's Uneasy Peace: The Amnesties Granted in the Lomé Peace Agreement and the United Nation's Dilemma', *Humanitäres Völkerrecht* 13: 11–26.
Macdonald, M. 1992. 'The Siren's Song: the Political Logic of Power Sharing in South Africa', *Journal of Southern African Studies* 18(4): 709–25.
McIlwain, H.C. 1939. *Constitutionalism and the Changing World*. Cambridge: Cambridge University Press.
______. 1947. *Constitutionalism: Ancient and Modern*. New York: Cornell University Press.
Madhuku, L. 1997. 'Incompatibility of the Death Penalty and the Bill of Rights: Guerra v Baptiste [1995] 3 WLR 891; [1995] 1 LRC 407', *South African Journal on Human Rights* 13: 151–54.
Maduna, P.M. 1996. 'Death Penalty and Human Rights', *South African Journal on Human Rights* 12(2): 193–213.
Malose Motimele, M.C. and I. Mmakwena Semenya. 1993. *Constitution for a Democratic South Africa*. Johannesburg: Skotaville.
Mandela, N. 1991. 'Opening Address to the 48th National Conference of the African National Congress', Durban. Retrieved 31 March 2008 from http://www.anc.org.za/ancdocs/history/mandela/1991/sp910700-02.html.
______. 1994. *Long Walk to Freedom. The Autobiography of Nelson Mandela*. Boston: Little Brown.
Manganyi, C. and A. du Toit (eds). 1990. *Political Violence in South Africa*. London: MacMillan.
Mannozzi, G. 1996. *Razionalità e 'giustizia' nella commisurazione della pena. Il Just Desert Model e la riforma del sentencing nordamericano*. Padua: CEDAM.
______. 1999. *La mediazione penale*. Padua: CEDAM.
Mannozzi, G. and E. Paliero. 1992. 'Mediation and Reconciliation Models in Italian Legal Experience', in H. Messmer and H.U. Otto (eds), *Restorative Justice on Trial*. Dordrecht: Kluwer Academic, pp. 225–38.
Marais, D. 1991. *South Africa: Constitutional Development: A Multi-Disciplinary Approach*. Halfway House: Southern Book Publishers.
______. 1993. *South Africa: Constitutional Development. A Multi-disciplinary Approach*. Pretoria: Southern Book Publishers.
Marais, H. 1998. *South Africa: Limits to Change: the Political Economy of Transformation*. London: Zed Books.

Marchetti, P. 1994. *Testis contra se. L'imputato come fonte di prova nel processo penale dell'età moderna*. Milan: Giuffrè.

Mare, G. 1993. *Ethnicity and Politics in South Africa*. London: Zed Books.

Martin, M.L. 1999. *Les Constitutions d'Afrique francophone. Évolutions récentes*. Paris: Karthala.

Martucci, R. 2001. *L'ossessione costituente. Forma di governo e costituzione nella Rivoluzione francese (1789–1799)*. Bologna: Il Mulino.

Matela, S. 1998. 'Direct Access to Constitutional Court', *South African Journal on Human Rights* 14: 333.

Mereu, I. 2000. *Storia dell'intolleranza in Europa*. Milan: Bompiani.

Mezzetti, L. 2000. *Le democrazie incerte. Transizioni costituzionali e consolidamento della democrazia in Europa orientale, Africa, America Latina, Asia*. Turin: Giappichelli.

______. 2003. *Teoria e prassi delle transizioni costituzionali e del consolidamento democratico*. Padua: CEDAM.

Minnaar, A., I. Liebenberg and C. Schutte (eds). 1998. *The Hidden Hand: Covert Operations in South Africa*. Pretoria: HSRC.

Mirfield, P. 1985. *Confessions*. London: Sweet & Maxwell.

Moellendorf, D. 1997. 'Amnesty, Truth and Justice: AZAPO', *South African Journal on Human Rights* 13(2): 283–91.

Montalti, M. 2004. 'L'efficacia orizzontale del Bill of Rights sudafricano alla luce di alcune riflessioni comparative', *Diritto pubblico comparato ed europeo* 4: 1714–33.

Morbidelli, G. 2001. *Lezioni di diritto pubblico comparato. Costituzioni e Costituzionalismo*. Bologna: Monduzzi.

Morice, G.T. 1905. *English and Roman-Dutch Law: Being a Statement of the Differences between the Law of England as Prevailing in South Africa and Some Other of the British Colonies*. London: Butterworths.

Mortati, C. 1972. 'La Costituente (1945)', in *Raccolta di scritti*. Milan: Giuffrè, pp. 26–76.

______. 1992. 'La teoria del potere costituente', in P. Pombeni (ed.), *Potere costituente e riforme costituzionali*. Bologna: Il Mulino, pp. 183–93.

Motala, Z. 1996. 'The Constitutional Court's Decision to International Law and Its Method of Interpretation in the "Amnesty Decision": Intellectual Honesty or Political Expediency?', *South African Yearbook of International Law* 21: 29–59.

Murray, C. and R. Simeon. 1999. 'From Paper to Practice: The National Council of Provinces after its First Year', *South African Public Law* 14: 96–141.

______. 2002. 'Eight Years of Decentralisation in South Africa', *Second International Conference on Decentralization 25–27 July 2002*. Manila: Philippines.

Nadesen, S. 1997. 'Restitution, Reconstruction, Reconciliation and Redistribution: Land Reform Balancing the Interests of the Dispossessed, the Homeless and Development', *Stellenbosch Law Review* 360–77.

Naldi, G.J. 1995. *Constitutional Rights in Namibia*. Cape Town: Juta.

Nattrass, N. 1994. 'Controversies about Capitalism and Apartheid in South Africa: An Economic Perspective', *Journal of Southern African Studies* 17: 654–77.

______. 1999. 'The Truth and Reconciliation Commission on Business and Apartheid: A Critical Evaluation', *African Affairs* 98: 373–91.

Negri, A. 2002. *Il Potere costituente. Saggio sulle alternative del moderno*. Rome: Manifestolibri.

Ngwena, C. 2003. 'Access to Antiretroviral Therapy to Prevent Mother-to-Child Transmission of HIV as a Socio-economic Right, an Application of Section 27 of the Constitution', *South African Public Law* 18: 83–102.

Nicolaidis, D. (ed.). 1994. *Oublier nos crimes. L'amnésie nationale: une spécificité française?* Paris: Autrement.

Niebur Eisnaugle, C.J. 2003. 'An International "Truth Commission": Utilizing Restorative Justice as an Alternative to Retribution', *Vanderbilt Journal of Transnational Law* 36: 209–34.

Novick, P. 1985. *L'épuration française*. Paris: Ballan.

Ntsebeza, D.B. 2000. 'The Uses of Truth Commissions: Lessons for the World', in R.I. Rotberg and D. Thompson (eds), *Truth v. Justice. The Morality of Truth Commissions*. Princeton: Princeton University Press, pp. 158–69.

Nugent, R.W. 1999. 'Self-Incrimination in Perspective', *The South African Law Journal* 116: 501–22.

Olivier, P. 1995. 'Constitutionality and Society in South Africa: What Sort of Democracy', in G. Conac, F. Dreyfus and J. Montero (eds), *L'Afrique du Sud en Transition. Réconciliation et coopération en Afrique Australe*. Paris: Economica, pp. 88–109.

Oloka Onyango, J. (ed.). 2001. *Constitutionalism in Africa. Creating Opportunities, Facing Challenges*. Kampala: Fountain.

Orr, W. 2000. 'Reparation Delayed Is Healing Retarded', in C. Villa-Vicencio and W. Verwoerd (eds), *Looking Back, Reaching Forward*. Cape Town: University of Cape Town, pp. 239–49.

Orrù, R. 1998. *La Costituzione di tutti. Il Sudafrica dalla segregazione razziale alla democrazia della Rainbow Nation*. Turin: Giappichelli.

______. 1999. 'Transizione e avvio del consolidamento democratico in Sudafrica: la complessa attuazione della Costituzione del 1996', *Rivista di diritto pubblico comparato ed europeo* 3: 903–28.

Osiel, J.M. 2000. 'Why Prosecute? Critics of Punishment for Mass Atrocities', *Human Rights Quarterly* 22: 118–47.

Ottaway, M. 1993a. *Chained Together: Mandela, De Klerk, and the Struggle to Remake South Africa*. New York: Times Books.

Ottaway, Marina, 1993b. *South Africa. The Struggle for a New Order*. Washington, DC: Brookings Institution.

Pace, A. 1997. *Potere Costituente, rigidità costituzionale, autovincoli legislativi*. Padua: CEDAM.

Pactet, P. 1998. *Institutions Politiques et droit constitutionnel*. Paris: Armand Colin.
Palombella, G. 2002. *L'autorità dei diritti*. Bari: Laterza.
Parker, P. 1996. 'The Politics of Indemnities, Truth Telling and Reconciliation in South Africa. Ending Apartheid without Forgetting', *Human Rights Law Journal* 17(1–2): 1–13.
Pauw, J. 1997. *Into the Heart of Darkness: Confessions of Apartheid Assassins*. Johannesburg: Jonathan Ball.
Pegoraro, L. 1998. *Lineamenti di giustizia costituzionale comparata*. Turin: Giappichelli.
Pegoraro, L. and A. Reposo. 1986. 'Repubblica del Sudafrica', *Quaderni Costituzionali* 197–210.
Pegoraro, L. and A. Rinella. 1995. 'Repubblica del Sudafrica: il Constitution Act del 1993 tra "federalismo" e "regionalismo"', *Quaderni Costituzionali* 277–85.
______. 1997. 'La nuova Costituzione della Repubblica del Sudafrica (1996-1997)', *Rivista trimestrale di diritto pubblico* 2: 517–52.
Pennock, J.R. and J.W. Chapman (eds). 1979. *Constitutionalism*. New York: New York University Press.
Pettazzoni, R. 1936. *La confessione dei peccati*. Bologna: Zanichelli.
Philippe, X. 1996. 'La Cour constitutionnelle sud-africaine et le règlement des conflits politiques', *Revue française de droit constitutionnel* 27: 461–91.
______. 1997–98. 'Common Law et droits coutumiers dans le nouvel ordre constitutionnel sud-africain', *Annuaire des pays de l'Océan Indien* XV: 259–81.
______. 1998. 'La saisine du juge constitutionnel en Afrique Australe', in F. Delperee and P. Foucher (eds), *La saisine du juge constitutionnel aspect de droit comparé*. Brussels: Bruylant, pp. 73–93.
______. 1999. 'Droit Constitutionnel étranger: Afrique du Sud', *Revue Française de Droit Constitutionnel* 37: 159–71.
______. 2004. 'Commission Vérité et réconciliation et droit constitutionnel', in B. Cassin, O. Cayla and J.P. Salazar (eds), *Vérité, réconciliation, réparation*. Paris: Le Seuil, pp. 119–241.
Pocock, J.G.A. 1987. *The Ancient Constitution and the Feudal Law. English Historical Thought in the Seventeenth Century*. Cambridge: Cambridge University Press.
Poole, J.L. 2001. 'Post-Conflict in Sierra Leone', in C.M. Bassiouni (ed.), *Post-conflict Justice*. Ardsley: Transnational Publishers, pp. 563–92.
Pretorius, R. 1994. 'Enforcement Mechanisms in the 1993 Constitution', *South African Public Law* 9: 265–77.
Prodi, P. 2000. *Una storia della giustizia. Dal pluralismo dei fori al moderno dualismo tra coscienza e diritto*. Bologna: Il Mulino.
Prosperi, A. 1996. *I tribunali della coscienza. Inquisitori, confessori, missionari*. Turin: Einaudi.

Quatitsch, H. 1992. 'Über Bürgerkriegs- und Feind-Amnestien', *Der Staat* 31: 389–418.

______. 1995. *La giustizia politica. Le amnistie nella storia*. Milan: Giuffrè.

Radbruch, G. 1957. *Der Menche im Recht. Ausgewählte und Aufsätze über Grundfragen des Rechts*. Göttingen: Vandenhoeck & Ruprecht.

Ratner, S.R. 1995. 'Judging the Past: State Practice and the Law of Accountability', in N.J. Kritz (ed.), *Transitional Justice: How Emerging Democracies Reckon with Former Regimes*. Washington, DC: United States Institute of Peace Press.

Ratner, S.R. and J.S. Abrams 1997. *Accountability for Human Rights Atrocities in International Law. Beyond The Nuremberg Legacy*. Oxford: Clarendon Press.

Rebuffa, G. 1990. *Costituzioni e costituzionalismi*. Turin: Giappichelli.

Reik, T. 1997. *Le besoin d'avouer*. Paris: Payout.

Ricciardi, M. 1990. 'Linee storiche sul concetto di popolo', *Annali dell'Istituto storico italo-germanico in Trento* 16: 303–69.

Ricoeur, P. 2000. *La mémoire, l'histoire, l'oubli*. Paris: Le Seuil.

Rigaux, M.F. 1985. *La théorie des limites matérielles à l'exercice de la fonction constituante*. Brussels: Lancier.

Rok, A. 1992. 'Political Violence in South Africa: A Rejoinder to Morris and Hindson', *Review of African Political Economy* 55: 67–83.

Rolla, G. 2001. 'Luci ed ombre dell'esperienza delle transizioni pactdas', *Diritto pubblico comparato ed europeo* 3: 1084–96.

Romano, C., A. Nollkaemper, and J. Kleffner, (eds). 2004. *Internationalized Criminal Courts and Tribunals: Sierra Leone, East Timor, Kosovo and Cambodia*. Oxford: OUP.

Romano, S. 1950. 'L'instaurazione di fatto di un ordinamento costituzionale e la sua legittimità', *Scritti Minori*. Milan: Giuffrè, vol. 1.

Rosanvallon, P. 1998. *Le peuple introuvable*. Paris: Gallimard.

______. 2000. *La démocratie inachevée*. Paris: Gallimard.

Rosoni, I. 1995. *Quae singula non prosunt collecta iuvant. La teoria della prova indiziaria nell'età medioevale e moderna*. Milan: Giuffrè.

Rotberg, R.I. 2000. 'Truth Commissions and the Provision of Truth Justice and Reconciliation', in R.I. Rotberg and D. Thompson (eds), *Truth v. Justice. The Morality of Truth Commissions*. Princeton: Princeton University Press, pp. 3–21.

Rousso, H. 1987. *Le Syndrome de Vichy, de 1944 à nos jours*. Paris: Seuil.

______. 1994. *Un passé qui ne passe pas*. Paris: Fayard.

______. 1998. *La hantise du passé*. Paris: Textuel.

Routenbach, I. and E. Malherbe. 1999. *Constitutional Law*. Durban: Butterworths.

Rusconi, R. 1986. '"Ordinate confiteri": la confessione dei peccati nelle "Summae de casibus" e nei manuali per i confessor, metà XII-inizi XIV secolo', in *L'Aveu. Antiquité et Moyen Age*. Rome: Ecole Française de Rome, pp. 297–313.

______. 2002. *L'ordine dei peccati. La confessione tra Medioevo ed età moderna*. Bologna: Il Mulino.

Rwelamira, M.R. and G. Werle, *Confronting Past Injustices. Approaches to Amnesty, Punishment, Reparation and Restitution in South Africa and Germany*. Durban: Butterworths.

Sacco, R. 2000. 'Il costituzionalismo africano', *Rivista di diritto pubblico comparato ed europeo* 1: 3–10.

Sacco, R. et al. 1996. *Il diritto africano*. Turin: Utet.

Sacerdoti, G. 2002. *Sacrificio e sovranità. Teologia e politica nell'Europa di Shakespeare e Bruno*. Turin: Einaudi.

Sachs, A. 1989. 'Post-Apartheid South Africa a Constitutional Framework', *World Policy Journal* 6(3): 503–29.

______. 1990. *Protection of Human Rights in South Africa*. Cape Town: Oxford University Press.

______. 1992a. *Advancing Human Rights in South Africa*. Oxford: Oxford University Press.

______. 1992b. 'Affirmative Action and Good Government', in P. Hugo (ed.), *Redistribution and Affirmative Action. Working on the South African Political Economy*. Pretoria: Southern Book Publishers.

Saks, V. 1997. 'Multiculturalism, Constitutionalism and South African Constitution', *Public Law*, 672–92.

Salas, D. 1992. *Du procès penal*. Paris: Presses Universitaires de France.

Saliger, F. 1995. *Radbruchsche Formel und Rechtsstaat*. Heidelberg: Müller Juristisches Verlag.

Saltzburg, A.S. 1984. 'Self-Incrimination and Confessions', in *American Criminal Procedure. Cases and Commentary*. St. Paul: West Publishing, pp. 65–82.

Sanders, A.J.G.M. 1989. 'The Freedom Charter and Ethnicity – Towards Communitarian South African Society', *Journal of African Law* 33: 105–15.

Sarakinsky, I. 1995. 'Rehearsing Joint Rule. The Transitional Executive Council', in S. Friedman and D. Atkinson (eds), *The Small Miracle: South Africa's Negotiated Settlement*. Johannesburg: Ravan Press, pp. 60–91.

Sarkin, J. 1996. 'The Trials and Tribulations of South Africa's Truth and Reconciliation Commission', *South African Journal on Human Rights* 12: 617–41.

______. 1997. 'The Political Role of the South African Constitutional Court', *South African Law Journal* 114: 135–50.

______. 1998. 'The Effect of Constitutional Borrowings on the Drafting of South Africa's Interim Bill of Rights and the Role Played by Comparative and International Law in the Interpretation of Human Rights Provisions by the Constitutional Court', *University of Pennsylvania Journal of Constitutional Law* 1–2: 176–204.

______. 2000a. 'An Evaluation of the Role of the Independent Complaints Directorate for the Police, the Inspecting Judge for Prisons, the Legal

Aid Board, the Human Rights Commission, the Commission on Gender Equality, the Auditor General, the Public Protector and the Truth and Reconciliation Commission in Developing a Human Rights Culture in South Africa', *South African Public Law* 15: 385–425.

______. 2000b. 'L'écriture de la Constitution sud-africaine de 1996: approche formelle et matérielle', *Revue française de droit constitutionnel* 44: 747–67.

______. 2003. 'To Prosecute or Not to Prosecute? Constitutional and Legal Issues Concerning Criminal Trials', in C. Villa-Vicencio and E. Doxtader (eds), *The Provocations of Amnesty: Memory, Justice and Impunity*. Claremont: David Philip, pp. 249–61.

______. 2004. *Carrots and Sticks: The TRC and the South African Amnesty Process*. Antwerp: Intersentia.

Sartori, G. 1990. *Elementi di teoria politica*. Bologna: Il Mulino.

Scapini, N. 1983. *La confessione nel diritto romano: il diritto giustinianeo*. Milan: Giuffrè.

Schmitt, C. 1936–37. 'Der Staat als Mechanismus bei Hobbes und Descartes', *Archiv für Rechts- und Sozialphilosophie* 30.

______. 1952. 'Dreihundred Jahre Leviathan', *Universitas* 7.

______. 1965. 'Die Vollendete Reformation Bemerkungen und Hinweise zu neuen Leviathan-Interpretationen', *Der Staat* 4.

______. 1982. *Der Leviathan in der Staatlehre des Thomas Hobbes. Sinn und Fehlschlag eines politischen Symbols*. Cologne: Hohenheim Verlag.

Shea, D. 2000. *The South African Truth Commission: The Politics of Reconciliation*. Washington, DC: United States Institute of Peace Press.

Shriver, D.W. Jr. 2003. 'Truth Commissions and Judicial Trials. Complementary or Antagonistic Servants of Public Justice?', in C. Villa-Vicencio and E. Doxtader (eds), *The Provocations of Amnesty: Memory, Justice and Impunity*. Claremont: David Philip, pp. 61–91.

Siegel, R. 1998. 'Transitional Justice: A Decade of Debate and Experience', *Human Rights Quarterly* 20: 431–54.

Simeon, R. 1982. 'Criteria for Choice in Federal Systems', *Queen's Law Journal* 18: 131–57.

______. 1998. 'Considerations on the Design of Federations: the South African Constitution in Comparative Context', *South African Public Law* 13: 42–71.

Slaughter, A.M. 2003. 'A Global Community of Courts', *Harvard International Law Journal* 44: 191–219.

Slovo, J. 1992. 'Negotiations: What Room for Compromise?', *African Communist* 3/4: 36–40.

Slye, R.C. 2002. 'The Legitimacy of Amnesties under International Law and General Principles of Anglo-American Law: Is a Legitimate Amnesty Possible?', *Virginia Journal of International Law* 174–247.

Smiley, M. 2000. 'Democratic Justice in Transition', *Michigan Law Review* 99: 1332–47.

Smit, D. 1995. 'The TRC – Tentative Religious and Theological Perspectives', *Journal of Theology for Southern Africa* 3–17.

Smith, G.L. 2001. 'Immune to Truth? Latin American Truth Commissions and U.S. Support for Abusive Crimes', *Columbia Human Rights Law Review* 33(1): 241–73.

South African Law Commission. 1991. *Project 77: Constitutional Models*.

Southall, R. 1983. 'Consociationalism in South Africa: the Buthelezi Commission and Beyond', *Journal of Modern African Studies* 21(1): 77–112.

———. 1994. 'The South Africa Elections of 1994: the Remaking of a Dominant-Party State', *The Journal of Modern African Studies* 32(4): 605–29.

Sparks, A. 1994. *Tomorrow Is Another Country. The Inside Story of South Africa's Road to Change*. Chicago: University of Chicago Press.

Spitz, R. and M. Chaskalson. 2000. *The Politics of Transition. A Hidden History of South Africa's Negotiated Settlement*. Johannesburg: Witwatersrand.

Sprigman, C. and M. Osborne. 1999. 'Du Plessis Is Not Dead: South Africa's 1996 Constitution and the Application of the Bill of Rights to Private Disputes', *South African Journal on Human Rights* 15(1): 25–51.

Stacey, S. 1999. 'A New South Africa: The South Africa Truth and Reconciliation Commission's Vexed Nation-building Project', *TRC: Commissioning the Past Conference, Johannesburg, 14 June 1999*. Johannesburg: University of Witwatersrand.

Strand, P. 2000. *Decisions on Democracy. The Politics of Constitution-Making in South Africa 1990 – 1996*. Uppsala: Uppsala University Press.

Strohmeyer, H. 2000. 'Building a New Judiciary for East Timor. Challenges of a Fledgling Nation', *Criminal Law Forum* 11: 259–85.

Taguieff, P.A. 1987. *La force du préjugé*. Paris: La Découverte.

Taubner, G. 1993. *Le droit, un système autopoïétique*. Paris: Presses Universitaires de France.

Taylor, C. 1992. *The Politics of Recognition*. Princeton: Princeton University Press.

Teitel, R. 2000. *Transitional Justice*. Oxford: Oxford University Press.

Tentler, N. 1975. *Sin and Confession on the Eve of the Reformation*. Princeton: Princeton University Press.

'The Truth and Reconciliation Commission, and the Bench, Legal Practitioners and Legal Academics'. 1998. *South African Law Journal* 115: 15–106.

Thomas, Y. 1984. 'Se venger au forum. Solidarités traditionnelles et système pénal à Rome', in R. Verdier and Y. Thomas (eds), *Vengeance*. Livre III. Paris: Cujas.

———. 1986. 'Confessus pro iudicato. L'aveu civil et l'aveu pénal à Rome', in *L'Aveu. Antiquité et Moyen Age*. Rome: Ecole Française de Rome, pp. 89–117.

______. 1996. 'Arracher la vérité. La Majesté et l'Inquisition (I–IV siècle ap. JC)', in R. Jacob (ed.), *Le juge et le jugement dans les traditions juridiques européennes*. Paris: Librairie Generale de Droit et de Jurisprudence, pp. 15–41.
______. 2001. 'L'aveu de la parole au corps (Rome, Veme siècle av. J.C. IVeme siècle après J.C.)', in R. Dulong (ed.), *L'Aveu. Histoire, sociologie, philosophie*. Paris: Presses Universitaires de France, pp. 17–56.
Thompson, L. 1960. *The Unification of South Africa 1902–1910*. Oxford: Clarendon Press.
______. 1985. *The Political Mythology of Apartheid*. New Haven: Yale University Press.
______. 1990. *A History of South Africa*. New Haven: Yale University Press.
Todorov, T. 1998. *Les abus de la mémoire*. Paris: Arlèa.
______. 2000. *Mémoire du mal. Tentation du bien. Enquête sur le siècle*. Paris: Robert Laffont.
Tomuschat, C. 1999. 'Human Rights and National Truth Commissions', in P. Baehr, C. Flinterman and M. Senders (eds), *Innovation and Inspiration: Fifty Years of the Universal Declaration of Human Rights*. Amsterdam: Royal Netherlands Academy of Arts and Sciences, pp. 151–60.
Troper, M. 1992. 'Le concept d'État de droit', in *Droits* 15: 51–63.
______. 1994. 'Le concept de constitutionnalisme et la théorie moderne du droit', in *Pour une théorie juridique de l'état*. Paris: Presses Universitaires de France, pp. 203–21.
______. 1999. 'Droit et négationnisme', *Les Annales* 54(6): 1239–56.
Turrini, M. 1991. *La coscienza e le leggi. Morale e diritto nei testi per la confessione della prima Età moderna*. Bologna: Il Mulino.
Tushnet, M. 1999. 'The Possibility of Comparative Constitutional Law', *Yale Law Journal* 108: 1225–309.
Tveiten, M. 2003. 'The Right to Health Secured HIV/Aids Medicine. Socio-Economic Rights in South Africa', *Nordic Journal of International Law* 72: 41–71.
Valandier, P. 2001. 'Pratique catholique de la confession auriculaire: enjeux et problèmes', in R. Dulong (ed.), *L'Aveu. Histoire, sociologie, philosophie*. Paris: Presses Universitaires de France, pp. 241–56.
Van der Merwe, H., H. Dewhirste and B. Hamber. 1999. 'Non-Governmental Organisations and Truth and Reconciliation Commission: An Impact Assessment', *Politikon* 26(1): 55–79.
Van der Schyff, G. 2005. *Limitation of Rights: A Study of the European Convention and the South African Bill of Rights*. Nijmegen: Wolf Legal Publishers.
Van der Vyver, J.D. 1993. 'The Separation of Powers', *South African Public Law* 8: 190.
Van der Walt, J. 2003. 'Horizontal Application of Fundamental Rights and the Threshold of the Law in View of the Carmichele Saga', *South African Journal on Human Rights* 19: 517–40.

Van Huyssteen, E. 2000. 'The Constitutional Court and the Redistribution of Power in South Africa', *African Studies* 59(2): 245–65.
Van Ness, D.W. 2002. 'The Shape of Things to Come: A Framework for Thinking about a Restorative Justice System', in E.G.M. Weitekamp and H.J. Kerner (eds), *Restorative Justice. Theoretical Foundation.* Portland: Willan Publishing, pp. 1–20.
Van Niekerk, G.J. 1998. 'A Common Law for Southern Africa: Roman Law or Indigenous African Law?', *Comparative and International Law Journal of Southern Africa* 31: 158–73.
Van Wyk, D. 1991. 'The Making of Namibian Constitution: Lessons for Africa', *CILSA* 24: 341–51.
———. 1994. 'The South African Bill of Rights: An Evaluation', *South African Public Law* 9: 278–86.
Van Wyk, D. et al. 1994. *Rights and Constitutionalism: The New South Africa Legal Order*. Cape Town: Juta.
Van Zyl, P. 1999. 'Dilemma of Transitional Justice: the Case of South Africa's Truth and Reconciliation Commission', *Journal of International Affairs* 52: 647–67.
Varney, H. and J. Sarkin. 1997. 'Failing to Pierce the Hit Squad Veil: An Analysis of the Malan Trial', *South African Journal of Criminal Justice* 10: 141–61.
Vassalli, G. 2001. *La formula di Radbruch e diritto penale. Note sulla punizione dei 'delitti di Stato' nella Germania post-nazista e nella Germania post-comunista*. Milan: Giuffrè.
Vaughan, C.E. 1939. *Studies in Political Philosophy Before and After Rousseau*. Manchester: Manchester University Press.
Venter, F. 1994. 'Milestones in the Evolution of the New South African Constitution and Some of Its Salient Features', *South African Public Law* 9: 211–21.
———. 1995. 'Requirements for a New Constitutional Text: The Imperatives of the Constitutional Principles', *South African Law Journal* 112: 32–44.
———. 1997. 'Aspects of the South African Constitution of 1996: An African Democratic and Social Federal Rechtsstaat?', *Heidelberg Journal of International Law* 57: 52–82.
———. 1998. 'The Emergence of Constitutionalism in Southern Africa in the Late Twentieth Century', in V. Piergigli and I. Taddia (eds), *International Conference on African Constitutions*. Turin: Giappichelli, pp. 11–24.
———. 2000. *Constitutional Comparison. Japan, Germany, Canada and South Africa*. Cape Town: Juta-Kluwer Law Int.
Verges, J. 1988. *Je défends Barbie*. Paris: Jean Picollec.
Villa-Vicencio, C. and E. Doxtader. 2003. *The Provocations of Amnesty, Memory, Justice and Impunity*. Claremont: David Philip.
Visser, P.J. 1997. 'Public Schools Based on a Common Language, Culture or Religion not Constitutionally Sanctioned', *Tydskrif vir Hedendaagse Romains-Hollandese* 60: 341–48.

Viviani Schlein, M.P. 1997. *Rigidità costituzionale. Limiti e graduazioni.* Turin: Giappichelli.

Vogel, M. 1999. 'The Social Origins of Plea Bargaining: Conflict and the Law in the Process of State Formation, 1830–1860', *Law & Society Review* 33(1): 161–246.

______. 2005. *Coercion to Compromise: Plea Bargaining, the Courts and the Making of Political Authority.* New York: Oxford University Press.

Volpe, G. 2000. *Il Costituzionalismo del novecento.* Bari: Laterza.

Voster, M.P., M. Wiechers and D.J. van Vuuren. 1985. *The Constitution of Transkei, Bophuthatswana, Venda, and Ciskei.* Durban: Butterworths.

Walgrave, L. 2002. *Restorative Justice and the Law.* Portland: Willan Publishing.

Webb, H. 1998. 'The Constitutional Court of South Africa: Rights Interpretation and Comparative Constitutional Law', *University of Pennsylvania Journal of Constitutional Law* 205–83.

Weitekamp, E.G.M. and H.J. Kerner (eds). 2002. *Restorative Justice. Theoretical Foundation.* Portland: Willan Publishing.

Wesson, M. 2004. 'Grootboom and Beyond. Reassessing the Socio-Economic Jurisprudence of the South African Constitutional Court', *South African Journal on Human Rights* 20: 284–308.

Wiechers, M. 2000. 'Namibia: the 1982 Constitutional Principles and Their Legal Significance', in O. Manfred et al., *The Constitution at Work. 10 years of Namibian Nationhood.* Windhoek: University of Namibia Press, Oxford African Book Collective, pp. 1–21.

Wiesnet, E. 1980. *Die Verratene Versöhnung: zum Verhältnis von Christentum und Strafe.* Düsseldorf: Atmos Verlag.

Wieviorka, A. 1998. 'Justice, histoire et mémoire. De Nuremberg à Jérusalem', *Droit et Société* 38: 59–67.

Wilson, R. 1996. 'The Siza Will Not Go Away. The Truth and Reconciliation Commission, Human Rights and Nation Building in South Africa', *African Studies* 55(2): 1–20.

______. 1998. 'Human Rights, Globalisation and Culture. The Experience of the TRC in South Africa', *Transnational Conference, Manchester 16–18 May 1998.* Manchester.

______. 2000. 'Reconciliation and Revenge in Post-Apartheid South Africa: Rethinking Legal Pluralism and Human Rights', *Current Anthropology* 41: 75–98.

______. 2001. *The Politics of Truth and Reconciliation: Legitimizing the Post-apartheid State.* Cambridge: Cambridge University Press.

Woller, H. 1991. *Politische Säuberung in Europa. Die Abrechnung mit Faschismus und Kollaboration nach dem zweitem Weltkrieg.* Munich: Oldenbourg.

______. 1997. *Conti con il fascismo. L'epurazione in Italia 1943–1948.* Bologna: Il Mulino.

Yacoob, Z. 1996. 'The Constitution Making Process: An Overview', *The Human Rights and Constitutional Law Journal of Southern Africa* 1(1): 18–24.

Yerushalmi, Y.H. 1982. *Zakhor. Jewish History and Jewish Memory*. Seattle: University of Washington Press.

Yerushalmi, Y.H. et al. 1988. *Les usages de l'oubli*. Paris, Seuil.

Zagrebelsky, G. 1974. *Amnistia, indulto e grazia. Profili costituzionali*. Milan: Giuffrè.

———. 1984. *Il sistema costituzionale delle fonti del diritto*. Turin: Eges.

Zalaquett, J. 1992. 'Balancing Ethical Imperatives and Political Constraints: the Dilemma of New Democracies Confronting Past Human Rights Violations', *Hastings Law Journal* 43(6): 1425–38.

Zlotnick, M. 1996. 'The Death Penalty and the Public Opinion', *South African Journal on Human Rights* 12(1): 70–78.

Index

Subject Index

Author Index